CONTEMPORARY GERMAN WRITERS

UWE TIMM

Series Editor

Rhys W. Williams has been Professor of German and Head of the German Department at University of Wales Swansea since 1984. He has published extensively on the literature of German Expressionism and on the post-war novel. He is Director of the Centre for Contemporary German Literature at University of Wales Swansea.

CONTEMPORARY GERMAN WRITERS
Series Editor: Rhys W. Williams

UWE TIMM

edited by

David Basker

CARDIFF
UNIVERSITY OF WALES PRESS
1999

© The Contributors, 1999

British Library Cataloguing-in-Publication Data
A catalogue record for this book is available from the British Library.

ISBN 0-7083-1447-3

All rights reserved. No part of this book may be reproduced, stored in a retrieval system, or transmitted, in any form or by any means, electronic, mechanical, photocopying, recording or otherwise, without clearance from the University of Wales Press, 6 Gwennyth Street, Cardiff, CF2 4YD.

Cover design by Olwen Fowler.
Printed in Great Britain by Dinefwr Press, Llandybïe.

Contents

	page
List of contributors	vi
Preface	vii
Abbreviations	xi
1 Das Nahe, das Ferne: Schreiben über fremde Welten *Uwe Timm*	1
2 Uwe Timm: Literary Career *David Basker*	17
3 'Eine Deklaration gegen Gewalt und Tod': Gespräch mit Uwe Timm *Colin Riordan*	26
4 The Writer as Anthropologist: The Works of Uwe Timm *Keith Bullivant*	38
5 'Uwe Timm oder unsicher in die 70er Jahre': *Heißer Sommer* and *Kerbels Flucht* *Rhys W. Williams*	47
6 'Der Weg in die Zukunft': Uwe Timm and the Problem of Political Ecology *Colin Riordan*	66
7 'Die Wandlung des Alltags in Bedeutung': Social History and 'die Ästhetik des Alltags' *David Basker*	82
8 Bibliography *David Basker*	111
Index	146

List of Contributors

David Basker is Lecturer in German at University of Wales Swansea. His study *Chaos, Control and Consistency: The Narrative Vision of Wolfgang Koeppen* was published in 1993. He has published on all aspects of Koeppen's literary career and is co-editor of the *Sarah Kirsch* volume in the Contemporary German Writers series.

Keith Bullivant is Professor of German and Chair of the Department of Germanic and Slavic Studies at the University of Florida. He has published extensively on German literature of the nineteenth and twentieth centuries, with particular emphasis on the Weimar Republic and the Federal Republic. His *Realism Today* (1987) and *The Future of German Literature* (1994) both contain lengthy analyses of the work of Uwe Timm.

Colin Riordan is Professor of German at the University of Newcastle. He is the author of a book and several articles on Uwe Johnson. He has published extensively on post-war German literature and has edited a book on the history of Green issues in Germany. He is editor of the *Peter Schneider* and *Jurek Becker* volumes in the Contemporary German Writers series.

Rhys W. Williams is Professor of German at the University of Wales Swansea and Director of the Centre for Contemporary German Literature. He has published extensively on German Expressionism (Sternheim, Benn, Carl Einstein and Toller) and on contemporary literature (Andersch, Böll, Siegfried Lenz, Martin Walser and Peter Schneider).

Preface

Contemporary German Writers

Each volume of the Contemporary German Writers series is devoted to an author who has spent a period as Visiting Writer at the Centre for Contemporary German Literature in the Department of German at the University of Wales Swansea. The first chapter in each volume contains an original, previously unpublished piece by the writer concerned; the second consists of a biographical sketch, outlining the main events of the author's life and setting the works in context, particularly for the non-specialist or general reader. A third chapter will, in each case, contain an interview with the author, normally conducted during the writer's stay in Swansea. Subsequent chapters will contain contributions by invited British and German academics and critics on aspects of the writer's œuvre. While each volume will seek to provide both an overview of the author and some detailed analysis of individual works, the nature of that critical engagement will inevitably depend on the relative importance of the author concerned and on the amount of critical material which his or her work has previously inspired. Each volume includes an extensive bibliography designed to fill any gaps or remedy deficiencies in existing bibliographies. The intention is to produce in each case a book which will serve both as an introduction to the writer concerned and as a resource for specialists in contemporary German literature.

Uwe Timm

The current volume opens with an essay by Uwe Timm that charts his early interest in far-away countries, an interest that, as Timm describes through the perspective of his experiences on Easter Island, has stimulated much of his writing. David Basker then provides an overview of Timm's literary career. The interview in Chapter Three covers, among other topics, Timm's experience of the student movement and his attitude towards politically committed writing in post-unification Germany. Keith Bullivant's essay connects with Chapter One, in that he traces in detail the influence of anthropological approaches throughout Timm's work, but with particular reference to *Morenga, Der Schlangenbaum,* and *Kopfjäger.* Rhys W. Williams re-examines the student novels, *Heißer Sommer* and *Kerbels Flucht,* with particular reference to Timm's essay on Peter Handke. The essay argues that the interference of personal concerns with political convictions means that the texts are much closer to the 'Innerlichkeit' of West German literature in the 1970s than has hitherto been recognized. Colin Riordan analyses Timm's ecological views, not only in *Der Schlangenbaum,* but also in *Morenga,* a text that is not generally viewed from the green perspective. His conclusion is that Timm's view of the chances for effective political change in an ecological direction is a particularly bleak one. David Basker then applies the theoretical views expressed in *Erzählen und kein Ende* to some of Timm's most recent prose works, *der Mann auf dem Hochrad, Die Entdeckung der Currywurst,* and *Johannisnacht.* As in previous volumes of the series, the book concludes with an exhaustive bibliography.

Abbreviations

Full bibliographical details appear in Chapter Eight.

The following abbreviations refer to the editions stated in brackets after the titles and are valid for each of the chapters in this volume unless otherwise stated.

HS	*Heißer Sommer* (1985)
M	*Morenga* (1982)
KF	*Kerbels Flucht* (1991)
MH	*Der Mann auf dem Hochrad* (1986)
S	*Der Schlangenbaum* (1989)
K	*Kopfjäger. Bericht aus dem Inneren des Landes* (1993)
EC	*Die Entdeckung der Currywurst* (1995)
J	*Johannisnacht* (1996)

1

Das Nahe, das Ferne:
Schreiben über fremde Welten

UWE TIMM

Ein Reklamezettel hat mich bewogen, den Anfang umzuschreiben. Ich habe ihn zufällig gefunden, einen Prospekt des Rimbaud Verlags aus Aachen, und auf diesem Faltblatt abgedruckt ist die ausführliche Besprechung eines Langgedichts des Mexikaners José Gorostiza: 'Endloser Tod / Muerte sin fin' aus der NZZ. Geschrieben hat die Besprechung Klaus Meyer-Minnemann.

Mit eben diesem Klaus Meyer bin ich als Kind an die Elbe gefahren, wo wir im Weidengestrüpp die Quellen des Orinoco gesucht haben, ausgerüstet mit einer Eisernen Ration, die man damals für 30 Pfennige aus alten amerikanischen Armeebeständen kaufen konnte. Wir haben Sümpfe durchwatet, mit Krokodilen gekämpft, und aus dem Weidengebüsch war immer wieder das Gebrüll des Jaguars zu hören. Heute leitet Meyer-Minnemann das iberoamerikanische Institut in Hamburg, und Sie wissen vielleicht, ich habe einen Roman geschrieben, der in Lateinamerika spielt, der *Schlangenbaum*, einen Roman, der nicht geschrieben worden wäre, hätte ich nicht eine Frau kennengelernt und geheiratet, die aus Argentinien kommt. Natürlich ist es nicht so, daß aus den kindlichen Spielen zwangsläufig folgt, daß man Lateinamerikanerinnen heiratet oder Hispanist wird. Aber je älter man wird, desto weniger sieht man bloße Zufälle für die eigene Biografie als bestimmend an. Etwas von diesen fernen kindlichen Wünschen, diesen Tagträumen, hat eine eigentümliche Kraft, die unser Verhalten in späteren Jahren steuert, das heißt, uns wählen läßt, auch unbewußt und dennoch zielsicher, wenn sich alternative Möglichkeiten anbieten. Ich vermute, die kindlichen Träume und Alpträume ziehen in späteren Jahren die Gegenstände unserer Interessen an wie die Magneten die Eisenspäne.

Die Frage, warum Meyer-Minnemann und ich damals ausgerechnet die Orinocoquellen gesucht haben, kann heute weder er noch ich beantworten, aber wahrscheinlich war es die Folge von Lektüre, und die war sicher nicht von der feinen Art, also kein Alexander von Humboldt, sondern eher ein Heftchenroman, kolportagehaft die Handlung und der Held ganz fraglos eurozentristisch.

Die Treibsätze unserer Wünsche werden zuweilen durch Vorstellungen und Beispiele gezündet, die weder politisch korrekt noch vom Geist der Aufklärung bestimmt sind. Mein zweites Beispiel macht das noch deutlicher. Mein mich durchs Leben begleitendes Interesse für Afrika, speziell für Südwestfrika – das heutige Namibia – hat, vermute ich, seinen Grund in den abendlichen Erzählungen jener älteren Kameraden meines Vaters, die als Offiziere in Südwest gedient hatten. Sie erzählten Geschichten über die 'Eingeborenen', die nicht pünktlich waren, nicht arbeiten wollten, kräftig logen, und ihre Kinder auch nicht ordentlich erzogen, also nicht prügelten. Paradiesische Zustände für mich, ein Kind, das nach preußischen Tugendmustern erzogen wurde, und ein guter Grund, sich fortan für Afrika und die Afrikaner zu interessieren, ein Interesse, das mich begleitet hat, durch die Schule, durch die Universität, wobei sich das Bild ausdifferenzierte, das Interesse kritischer und vor allem selbstkritischer wurde, eine entschieden politische Richtung in der Studentenbewegung nahm, und schließlich zum Engagement in der Antiapartheidbewegung führte.

In der Studentenbewegung wurde intensiv Franz Fanon und Che Guevara gelesen und in zahlreichen Arbeitsgruppen wurde die kulturelle und ökonomische Situation in der dritten Welt untersucht und die Ausbeutungsstrategien der westlichen Metropolen diskutiert. Zugleich kam es zu symbolischen Protestaktionen. In Hamburg haben protestierende Studenten das vor der Universität stehende Denkmal von Wissmann, einem Afrikareisenden, der auch eine zeitlang Gouverneur von Deutsch Ostafrika gewesen war, vom Sockel gerissen. Diese Szene, die ich im Roman *Heißer Sommer* beschrieben habe, brachte mich wiederum darauf, wie sehr in meinem Bewußtsein noch Relikte aus der deutschen Kolonialgeschichte eingelagert waren. Das war die Motivation für Recherchen, Reisen und für die Arbeit an dem Roman *Morenga*. Eine Reise in die deutsche Geschichte, in eine zeitliche und räumliche Ferne, die zugleich aber auch Selbsterkundung war.

Das Nahe, das Ferne

Wie Edward Said ausführlich in *Culture and Imperialism* untersucht hat, werden die positiven Wertungen der eigenen Kultur durch die Erniedrigung anderer gewonnen. Als Beispiel für die deutsch-afrikanischen Beziehungen wäre das despektierliche Schlagwort von der Hottentottenwirtschaft zu nennen, das dann Legitimation war, mit gutem erzieherischen Gewissen in Afrika 'aufzuräumen'. Und wir wissen aus der deutschen Kolonialgeschichte mit welch mörderischer Konsequenz das geschah. Die Niederschlagung des Hereroaufstands 1904 in Deutsch-Südwest kam einem versuchten Genozid gleich.

Und jetzt das dritte und letzte biografische Beispiel für die Begegnung mit der Fremde: Anfang der Fünfziger Jahre habe ich mich an einem Vorlesewettbewerb in der Schule beteiligt, der mir dann, vierzig Jahre später, eine von der Zeitschrift *Merian* bezahlte Reise in den Pazifik beschert hat: zum Nabel der Erde, zum Ende des Himmelslichts, zur Milch, zur großen Erde – so nannten früher die Einwohner die Insel. Wahrscheinlich waren damit nur Teile und bestimmte Gebiete der Insel gemeint, sie als Ganzes hatte vermutlich keinen Namen, da sie für ihre Einwohner alles war, einfach die Welt. Jahrhunderte ohne jeden Kontakt nach außen, umgeben vom Pazifik, 3700 Kilometer vom südamerikanischen Festland entfernt. Wir kennen die Insel unter dem Namen Osterinsel, Easter Island, Isla de Pascua. Der Name stammt – bezeichnenderweise – von dem ersten europäischen Entdecker.

Am Ostermontag des Jahres 1722 sichtete der Holländer Jacob Roggeveen die Insel. Gleich bei der ersten Begegnung der Einwohner mit den Europäern kommt es zu einem Konflikt zwischen den beiden Kulturen, es ist ein Konflikt, dessen Grundmuster auch alle späteren Begegnungen bestimmen wird.

Ein Mann schwimmt zu dem ankernden Schiff, kommt an Bord, zeigt sich freundlich, neugierig, insbesondere für die Takelage interessiert er sich, und mit Hilfe eines Seils vermißt er das Schiff. Nachmittags gehen die Holländer an Land. Wenig später kommt es zu einem Handgemenge, die Holländer feuern eine Salve ab. Nachdem der Pulverdampf sich verzogen hatte, so heißt es in dem Bericht, lagen mehrere Eingeborene röchelnd auf dem Boden, darunter auch der lustige Geselle, der morgens an Bord gekommen war.

Wie es dazu kam?

Die Holländer waren nicht direkt angegriffen worden. Wahrscheinlich war irgendeinem Matrosen der Hut gestohlen worden, das löste dieses Blutbad aus.

Unblutig verlief der Besuch eines spanischen Schiffs unter Filipe González y Haedo im Jahr 1770. Aber auch aus dem spanischen Bericht wird die kulturelle Differenz deutlich. Die Spanier waren überrascht, als ein Häuptling, von dem man drei Kreuze unter einem Vertrag erwatete, diesen regelrecht unterschrieb. Es waren eigentümliche, nie gesehene Zeichen. So wurden die Spanier gewahr, daß die 'nackten Wilden' eine eigene Schrift hatten. Auch die Spanier wurden bestohlen. Es kam jedoch zu keiner Gewalt. Der Bericht empört sich aber über den Zynismus der 'eingeborenen' Männer, die duldeten, daß sich ihre Frauen den Spaniern anboten, dies geradezu förderten, um sodann die derart abgelenkten Matrosen leichter bestehlen zu können.

Das Verhalten der Insulaner wird selbstverständlich nie zu dem eigenen in Beziehung gesetzt, bzw. als Reaktion darauf verstanden. So bleiben die eigenen Werte unbefragt. Zwei Spezifika der abendländischen Kultur sind mit besonders strikten Tabus belegt: Eigentum und Monogamie. Wobei gerade aus katholisch-spanischer Sicht von den Frauen Treue und ein ausgeprägtes Schamgefühl verlangt wird. Für die damalige Zeit wäre aber auch der Gedanke nicht so abwegig gewesen, das Verhalten der Matrosen als zynisch einzustufen. So wie es vier Jahre später der deutsche Georg Forster tat, der ähnliche Szenen beobachtet hatte.

Forster kam im März 1774 unter dem Kommando von James Cook auf die Osterinsel. In seiner *Reise um die Welt* 1784 hat er sie und ihre Bewohner beschrieben. 'Am 13ten, früh Morgens, liefen wir dicht unter die südliche Spitze der Insel. Die Küste ragte in dieser Gegend senkrecht aus dem Meer empor, und bestand aus gebrochenen Felsen, deren schwammige und schwarze eisenfarbige Masse volcanischen Ursprungs zu seyn schien. Zwey einzelne Felsen, lagen ohngefähr eine Viertelmeile vor dieser Spitze in See.'

Und dann heißt es weiter: 'Die Leute ließen uns ruhig ans Land steigen und machten überhaupt nicht die mindeste unfreundliche Bewegung; sondern fürchteten sich vielmehr vor unserem Feuergewehr, dessen tödtliche Würkung ihnen bekannt zu seyn schien.'

Jetzt, von oben, bei Nacht, erkenne ich nach einem stundenlangen Flug über den Pazifik die Lichter einiger Häuser, dann die Leuchtschnüre am Rand der Landebahn. Die Maschine rollt aus und hält vor einem kleinen flachen Gebäude. Die meisten Passagiere fliegen weiter nach Tahiti, mit uns steigt nur eine kleine italienische Reisegruppe aus, die meisten sind Padres. Sie werden mit Blumenkränzen begrüßt, nicht wir, die Einzelreisenden. Ein stämmiger junger Mann greift sich die Koffer, will mir die Reisetasche abnehmen, die ich nicht hergebe, all diese Berichte im Kopf von den Einwohnern, die so hemmungslos klauen. Es ist mir durchaus bewußt und zugleich peinlich, wie ich die Tasche und mit ihr an einem Klischee festhalte. Aber man weiß ja nicht. Später, das soll hier gleich gesagt werden, wurde uns die Tasche, die wir in einem kleinen Restaurant vergessen hatten, von einer Frau samt Schecks und Bargeld nachgetragen.

Das Hotel ist ein einfacher langgestreckter Flachbau. Vor der Terrasse, deren Zementboden von der salzhaltigen Luft angefressen ist, steht eine kleine struppige Palme, ein Stück Wiese, dann die Abbruchkante zum zerklüfteten Ufer, dunkles vulkanisches Gestein. Das Rauschen des Meeres, hin und wieder hört man ein lautes Dröhnen. Das ist dann jedesmal eine besonders hohe Welle, die sich in einer nahen Caverne bricht, ein leises Beben und für einen Moment liegt dann der intensive Geruch von Algen und Seewasser in der Luft.

Hanga Roa ist der einzige Ort auf der Insel, und um dieses Dorf zu sehen, müßte man wahrlich nicht um die halbe Welt fliegen. Eine Hauptstraße mit einstöckigen Gebäuden, Wellblech gedeckt. Eine Kirche, schmucklos, nein, von einer brutalen Häßlichkeit. Davor zwei Zelte, Spruchbänder, die auf Spanisch Unabhängigkeit verlangen, weiße Laken sind in einer uns unverständlichen Sprache beschriftet, aber man erkennt, groß geschrieben, Rapa Nui, so nennen die Einwohner sich und die Insel heute. Neben dem einen Zelt weht eine Fahne, die ein stilisiertes Schiff mit zwei Köpfen zeigt. Abbild eines dieser wunderbaren Schnitzwerke aus früheren Jahrhunderten, das man heute im Museum von Paris bewundern kann. An der Straße einige kleine Läden, Cafes, Andenkengeschäfte. Ungewöhnlich sind nur die Reiter, die über die Straßen galoppieren. Sie mustern den Fremden ziemlich finster. Grüßt man dann aber unbeirrt, winken sie plötzlich freundlich zurück. Die Verhältnisse sind einfach und klar. Das Interesse der Bewohner der Insel ist, an den Touristen Geld zu verdienen, und das der Touristen geht normalerweise an den Bewohnern vorbei und richtet sich auf die kolossalen Steinstatuen, die Moais.

Wer diese gewaltigen Statuen gemeisselt hat und warum, darüber gibt es die unterschiedlichsten wissenschaftlichen Theorien, die aber stets mit der Frage nach der Besiedlung der Insel zusammenhängen. Woher kamen die Bewohner der Osterinsel? Brachten sie die Steinmetzkunst mit, oder hat sich diese erst hier auf der Insel herausgebildet, und zwar, wie man heute genauer datieren kann, in den Jahren zwischen 800 bis 1600 n.Chr? Wie wurden diese tonnenschweren Statuen transportiert? Und wer waren die Schöpfer dieser Kultur, die sogar eine eigene noch immer nicht ganz entschlüsselte Schrift entwickelt hat? Waren es die Vorgänger der Inkas, oder Polynesier, oder Inder? Hobby-Anthropologen glaubten, Wikinger seien auf der Insel gewesen und Herr v. Däniken hat sogar 'Ankömmlinge aus dem Kosmos' hierher bemüht.

Die Wissenschaftler deuten die Kolosse als Ahnenbilder, Halb-Mensch, Halb-Gott, beinlose, massige Gestalten, die man sehen muß, um die Wucht ihrer Ausdruckskraft zu ermessen. 12 stehen nebeneinander auf einem Altar und blicken in düsterer Monumentalität auf das Meer hinaus.

Wobei bis heute noch nicht geklärt ist, wie diese riesigen Statuen transportiert worden sind.

Ganz anders ist der Eindruck am Hang des Vulkans Rano-Roraku, in dem Steinbruch, aus dem diese Standbilder herausgemeisselt wurden. Fast 100 Statuen gibt es hier, von denen 28-30 aufrecht stehen, säuberlich gearbeitet, erkennt man die langen Ohren, ihre Hände, die feingliedrige Finger, und die langen Fingernägel, die auf ihre gehobene soziale Stellung deuten. Die Gesichter der Statuen zeigen, bei aller Ähnlichkeit der Grundstruktur, feine unterschiedliche Züge, etliche blicken machtvoll-überlegen mit einer verächtlich vorgeschobenen Unterlippe ins Tal, andere zeigen ein feines Lächeln, wieder andere sind maskenhaft ausdruckslos.

Das Unerklärliche, ja Beunruhigende ist die Unordnung, in der sie am Hang des Vulkans stehen, es sei denn, diese Unordnung wäre die Ordnung. Sie stehen da wie in einer Versammlung, kleine Figuren von 2 Metern und große, 10 bis 12 Meter hoch, einige starren nach vorn geneigt, regelrecht grüblerisch vor sich hin, andere, nach hinten geneigt, blicken in den Himmel, als wollten sie sich nach einem Moment des Nachdenkens und Beratens wieder auf den Weg zum Meer machen. Wer diese Ansammlung sieht, versteht den Mythos, der berichtet, die steinernen Giganten seien dem weichen Tuffgestein des Vulkans entstiegen und selbst zum Meer hinuntergegangen.

Die Monumentalität der Statuen und die schon von Georg Forster bestaunte exakte Verfügung der Steinaltäre, hat unter anderem Heyerdahl auf die These gebracht, die Insel sei von Südamerika aus besiedelt worden. Das war denn auch der Anlaß seiner Reise mit dem Holzfloß Kon Tiki. Er wollte den Beweis erbringen, daß man von dem peruanischen Festland allein durch die Strömung und den Wind getrieben, die pazifischen Inseln erreichen konnte. Dahinter verbirgt sich implizit die Annahme, daß diese ungewöhnliche megalithische Kultur importiert und nicht von der ansässigen Bevölkerung, die höchstens 7000 Menschen betragen haben kann, geschaffen worden sei. Sprachanalysen zufolge kamen die Osterinsulaner jedoch aus Ostpolynesien. Heyerdahls These von der Besiedlung aus Südamerika gilt nach dem augenblicklichen Forschungsstand als falsch.

Es wäre interessant zu erfahren, welche Wünsche Heyerdahl zu seinen Unternehmungen, die ja viel Kraft und Energie gekostet haben und durchaus nicht ungefährlich waren, getrieben haben. Und um auf den Grund zurückzukommen, der mich zu dieser Insel geführt hat: Ich habe bei jenem Lesewettbewerb in der Volksschule einen Abschnitt aus Kon Tiki von Thor Heyerdahl vorgelesen, eine Episode, in der der Papagei von einer Welle über Bord gewaschen wird. Ein Lehrer mit pädagogischem Eros hatte mir die Stelle ausgesucht. Ich war wohl elf Jahre alt. Bis dahin hatte ich, las ich im Unterricht, immer wieder nur für Gelächter gesorgt. Ich verlas mich oft und meist sinnentstellend, sonderbarerweise hatte ich mehr Schwierigkeiten mit den Substantiven, weniger mit den Verben. Es war am Anfang nicht nur dieses Zusammenlesen der einzelnen Zeichen, der Buchstaben, was mir nicht von der Zunge ging, sondern die Wörter suchten noch immer die Dinge, die zu bezeichnen sie vorgaben. Es war eine mühsam überwindbare Kluft. Und die Abstrakta schwebten sowieso nur schwer greifbar in der Luft. Aber jetzt las ich flüssig, und der Junge, der dort oben auf dem kleinen Podium saß, war für die, die ihn sonst lesend kannten, nicht wiederzuerkennen, er las, ohne sich auch nur einmal zu verlesen, ohne zu stottern, gut betont, und so leicht und locker, wie mir später die Direktorin, als ich schon studierte, immer wieder erzählte. Genaue Beobachter hätten sehen können, wie der Junge die Zehen in die Sandalen verkrallt hatte. So saß ich auch innerlich verkrallt und löste mich erst langsam – während des

Lesens. Aber es war schon in den vorhergehenden Tagen etwas Merkwürdiges passiert. Bei dem Üben, dem Mehrmalslesen, machte ich, da es ja zum ersten mal laut und intensiv geschah, diese Entdeckung, wie die bisher feindseligen Zeichen sich mir anverwandelten, durch Betonung, durch Rhythmisierung, sinnlich erfahrbar wurden, wobei gesagt sein muß, daß es sich ja nicht um Dichtung, sondern um ein Sachbuch handelte, wenn auch, darf ich heute vermuten, um ein gut übersetztes. Die Wörter bekamen ihren Körper, kamen durch den Resonanzboden im Kopf zum Klingen. Zugleich wurde auch die Situation deutlicher, wie Heyerdahl mit seinen Leuten auf dem Floß trieb, wie sie das Holz untersuchten, wie sie entsetzt feststellten, daß es inzwischen derart vollgesogen war, daß ein einzelner Span davon unterging. Und dann diese Situation, als bei heftigem Sturm der Papagei über Bord gespült wurde. Innen und außen wurde aufgehoben, für mich, wie auch für die Zuhörer, denn die Schüler und die Lehrer saßen und hörten zu, still.

Es ist wahrscheinlich eine Entwicklung, die jeder aus seiner Biografie kennt, daß aus dem mühseligen Lesen, plötzlich das lustvolle Lesen wird, weil die Wörter nicht umständlich ihre Bedeutungen hinter sich herziehen und erst nochmal rückgekoppelt werden müssen. Auf einmal begleitet die Bedeutung das Lesen, treibt es sogar voran, selbst dann, wenn wir einmal innehalten oder nachlesen müssen. In meinem Fall war das unter dem Druck, vorlesen zu müssen, so spät wie plötzlich gekommen. Es war etwas Befreiendes für mich, und als Prämie bekam ich auch noch das Buch Kon Tiki geschenkt.

Ich habe es damals nicht nur, was gar nicht verlangt war, ganz gelesen, sondern gleich mehrmals und fortan war mein Interesse geweckt. Ich las Reise- und Forschungsberichte über die Osterinsel und suchte in den Völkerkundemuseen die Abteilungen, in denen Kunstwerke der Osterinsel ausgestellt waren, eigentümlich anthropomorphe Figuren, wunderbar geschnitzt aus dem glatten, harten, hellen, zuweilen weißen Toromiro-Holz. Nicht verwunderlich, das gerade die Surrealisten sich neben der afrikanischen Kunst auch für die Kultur der Osterinsel interessierten, daß Picasso von Abbildungen der Steinfiguren beeinflußt, den Kubismus schon vorwegnehmend, Portrait-Zeichnungen machte.

So hat diese Insel, ihre Bevölkerung, ihre Kultur, für mich auf eine zunächst zufällige, aber dann doch prägende Weise, eine biographische Bedeutung. Nicht nur lese ich seitdem gern, ich lese

Das Nahe, das Ferne

auch gern vor. Hinzu kommt dieser Wunsch andere Kulturen zu 'lesen', also zu verstehen. In einem meiner Romane, dem *Kopfjäger*, schreibt der Held, ein Wirtschaftsbetrüger und Schwindler, an einem Buch über diese Insel, die das Ziel seiner Kindheitsträume war. Und dieser Roman *Kopfjäger* war dann wiederum der Anlaß, daß ich von der *Merian* Redaktion gefragt wurde, ob ich nicht zur Osterinsel fahren und einen Bericht schreiben wolle. Ja, selbstverständlich. So war da auch etwas durchaus Eigennütziges an meinem Interesse an der Osterinsel, die von ihren Bewohnern Rapa Nui genannt wird. Etwas, was sich der Fremde bedient hat, so wie Edward Said es beschrieben hat: daß die Erzählung, gemeint ist die europäische, eine Struktur der Einstellung und Referenz hat, die das europäische Subjekt ermächtigt, sich in überseeische Territorien einzunisten, Nutzen daraus zu ziehen, um ihnen letztlich aber Autonomie oder Unabhängigkeit zu verweigern. Ich sage das durchaus selbstkritisch und denke, eben das muß der Schriftsteller, der aus Europa oder den USA und Canada kommt und die Länder der Dritten Welt bereist, um über sie zu schreiben, mitreflektieren, um sich ihrer nicht nur parasitär ästhetisch zu bedienen.

Allein die Neugier auf das Fremde reicht nicht aus. Die Gier Neues zu sehen und zu hören, garantiert noch keineswegs eine Sichtweise, die Verstehen ermöglicht. Das setzt etwas Anderes, Grundsätzlicheres voraus: das Staunen. Ein Staunen darüber, wie die Menschen, wie die Dinge beschaffen sind, das heißt, anders sein können als man selbst ist. Die Wahrnehmung dieser Differenz erst läßt eine Reflexion der eigenen Wahrnehmung zu und damit die Möglichkeit der eigenen emanzipatorischen Veränderung im Verstehen.

Ein Verstehen, das sich bemüht, die eigene Wahrnehmung als vorläufig und geschichtlich bedingt anzunehmen, also auch sich selbst als fremd und abhängig zu erfahren, um so den anderen, Fremden in seiner Würde wahrzunehmen.

Das ist, bezogen auf jene Völker, die von Europa kolonisiert wurden, heute, in postkolonialer Zeit, kein Gnadenakt, sondern das wird von der Realität eingefordert, sei es durch die einfache Problempräsenz dieser Länder: Armutsmigration, Bürgerkriege, Epidemien, die wiederum die westlichen Länder bedrohen, aber durchaus auch positiv, durch kulturelle Gegenentwürfe, die verstärkt aus den Ländern Lateinamerikas, Afrikas und Asiens kommen.

Die Geschichte literarischer Einflüsse ist nicht nur die Geschichte kultureller Machtpositionen und kultureller Kolonisation, sondern auch eine Geschichte literarischer Bedürfnisse und Bedürftigkeiten. Wenn im letzten und vorletzten Jahrhundert die Kultur des antiken Griechenlands einen so prägenden Einfluß auf die deutsche Literatur und Kunst gehabt hat, dann auch deshalb, weil mit diesen ästhetischen Modellen emanzipatorische Gegenentwürfe zu der feudalen Gesellschaftsform geliefert wurden. Ich denke da an Winckelmann und Johann Heinrich Voß und dessen Übersetzung von Homer, insbesondere der Odyssee 1781 und der folgenden, umgearbeiteten Fassung von 1793 oder, um ein Beispiel aus der bildenden Kunst zu nehmen, die Ikonografie der phrygischen Mütze.

Für die neuere Zeit ist der Einfluß der amerikanischen Literatur auf die deutsche Nachkriegsliteratur eingehend untersucht worden. Der Einfluß entsprach der historischen Situation: Eine dominierende Macht konnte in einem besiegten Land ihre kulturellen Vorstellungen entfalten; sie traf dabei zugleich, zumindest in den intellektuellen Kreisen, auf ein Bedürfnis (und eine Bedürftigkeit) nach demokratisch geprägten Lebens- und Schreibhaltungen.

Wenn seit zwei Jahrzehnten auch die lateinamerikanische Literatur in der europäischen Literatur an Einfluß gewonnen hat, so weist das einmal auf die gewachsene kulturelle Bedeutung dieser Länder und das heißt auch Qualität dieser Literatur hin, zugleich aber auch auf literarischen Bedürfnisse, auf bestimmte Leseerwartungen.

Ich wage einmal die These, daß die breite Rezeption von Autoren wie García Márquez, Vargas Llosa, Alejo Carpentier, Carlos Fuentes, Julio Cortázar in der deutschen Leserschaft möglicherweise mit dem Mangel an Welthaltigkeit der eigenen, deutschen Literatur zusammenhängt. Die Komplexität der modernen Welt, die Schwierigkeit adäquate Formen für ihre Darstellung zu finden, führte zu einem Rückzug in die Selbstreferenzialität. Was aber nichts wesentlich Neues brachte, meist sogar hinter den Erkenntnissen der Avantgarde der klassischen Moderne zurückblieb. Gefördert wurde diese Literatur-Literatur von Kritikern, die sich ironischerweise dann gerade für die erzählende lateinamerikanische Literatur begeistern konnten. Aus einer ganz unreflektierten eurozentristischen Sicht ließ diese Literaturkritik, so muß man wohl folgern, die sozusagen 'naivere' Darstellungsform bei den Ländern gelten, die nicht so kompliziert entfaltet waren wie die der Ersten Welt.

Wer als Schriftsteller der Fremde naherückt, wird oft mit einer anderen Art von Kritik konfrontiert: Er sei nicht lange genug dort gewesen. Wie lange muß man da gewesen sein? Zehn Jahre, zwei Jahre, einen Monat oder ein Leben lang? Ich gebe zu bedenken, daß die Frage nur über die Methode der Beschreibung beantwortet werden kann. Kafkas Roman *Amerika* würde nach solchem schnittmusterhaften Denken sofort als mangelhaft ausscheiden. Kafka war bekanntlich nie in Amerika, sondern hat Reiseprospekte studiert. Es ist also eine Frage der literarischen Methode, ob sie Authentizität vorspiegelt, und sprachliche Wertungen ungefragt weiterschreibt.

Mit der Frage nach der Authentizität ist oft der Vorwurf verbunden, die fremde Welt sei falsch oder sehr einseitig und nicht objektiv genug dargestellt. Meine Vorstellung von Literatur ist nicht, daß sie objektiv sein sollte, im Gegenteil, ich wünsche mir den sehr subjektiven Blick. Das Nächste ist oft das Fernste, nämlich man selbst. Und dieses Selbst, kann es denn staunen, hält es sich offen, die Wahrnehmung auszukorrigieren, erfährt sich in der Fremde als fremd. Das interessiert mich an einem literarischen Text, die besondere Brechung, die diese Wirklichkeit im Bewußtsein des Schreibers erfährt. So wird sie im Schreiben neu bedeutet. Darum auch der Versuch, ersteinmal die subjektiven Gründe zu prüfen, warum und wie man zu bestimmten Themen kommt, welche Wünsche, welche Ängste sich dahinter verbergen. Die Beschreibung der fremden Welt ist eben auch eine Selbstprüfung, eine Selbstbeschreibung, Selbstanalyse.

Zurück zur Osterinsel. Die Attraktion dieser Insel ist, daß auf einem so überschaubaren Raum – die Insel hat die Größe von der Ostseeinsel Fehmarn, an der weiter nichts Besonderes ist, einmal abgesehen davon, daß viele Bewohner Timm heißen – daß also auf einem so überschaubaren Raum derart eigenartige Kunstwerke entstanden sind, die zugleich rätselhaft sind, ungeklärt in ihrer Bedeutung, auf eine nicht lösbare Weise fremd bleiben. Man weiß nicht, warum diese hohe Kunst der Steinstatuen im 16. Jahrhundert plötzlich abbricht, und zwar so, daß einige dieser Steinfiguren beim Transport auf dem Weg liegenblieben, andere – darunter eine 22 Meter große Statue – liegen fast fertig wie schlafend im

Vulkangestein, daneben die Obsidianäxte, mit denen sie herausgemeißelt wurden, so als hätten die Handwerker sie eben mal beiseite gelegt.

Es gibt dafür viele Theorien, Theorien, die Katastrophen verantwortlich machen, gesellschaftliche oder natürliche. Wahrscheinlich kam es aufgrund der Überbevölkerung zu bürgerkriegsähnlichen Auseinandersetzungen, die auch das Ende dieser megalithischen Kunst bedeuteten. Die Kultur der Bewohner, ihre Schrift, ihre Religion, ihre gesellschaftliche Organisation wurde dann später von Fremden zerstört.

Nach den ersten Entdeckungsreisenden, die noch der Aufklärung verpflichtet waren wie Cook, Georg Forster und der Franzose La Perouse, kamen andere, die in den dort lebenden Menschen nur die Wilden sahen, auf die, wie auf Wild, geschossen werden durfte. 1862 läuft ein peruanisches Geschwader die Insel an und bringt mehr als 2000 Bewohner als Sklaven nach Peru. Nur 15 von ihnen kamen zurück und schleppten die Pocken ein. Die Inselbevölkerung sank auf nur 200 Menschen. 1868 ließ sich der Franzose Dutroux-Bornier auf der Insel nieder, errichtete eine Schafzucht und ein Terrorregime. Nachdem er ermordet worden war, ging die Schafzucht an eine englische Gesellschaft über, später an eine chilenische. Die Schafe konnten sich frei auf der Insel bewegen, die Einwohner lebten in einem eingezäunten Pferch. Französische und belgische Missionare kamen und verbrannten die heiligen Tafeln, die für die Entschlüsselung der Schrift so unersetzlich waren, die Missionare scheren dem letzten König und Priester, einem Kind, das zu berühren absolut tabu war, die Haare. 1888 annektiert Chile die Insel. Im Kleinen geschieht, was in anderen Ländern im Großen passiert. Die Einwohner sind rechtlos, dürfen die Insel nicht verlassen, man will sie erst zivilisieren, d. h. das Fremde, Unverstandene soll ausgelöscht werden. Auch in Chile denkt man eurozentristisch. In diesem Jahrhundert werden die Bewohner chilenisiert: Sie müssen Spanisch lernen und werden von der katholischen Kirche in Chile betreut. Ein deutsche Pater Engler kommt und wirkt über vierzig Jahre auf der Insel. Er sammelt die letzten Reste dieser ausgelöschten Kultur, die Mythen, Erzählungen, Berichte. Wobei die Ironie der christlichen Missionsarbeit einmal mehr daran deutlich wird, daß sie, nachdem sie die autochtone religiöse Tradition und damit die Identität der jeweiligen Gesellschaft zerstört hat, in einer zweiten Phase die letzten Zeugnisse der zerfallenen Kultur zu sammeln und zu retten sucht.

Das Nahe, das Ferne

In der Bevölkerung halten sich bis heute Erzählungen, daß bis in die fünfziger Jahre dieses Jahrhunderts hinein unliebsame, widerständige Einheimische von den chilenischen Behörden in die Leprastation gebracht worden seien, ein kleines Sanatorium, in einem von mächtigen Eukalyptusbäumen eingeschatteten Hain, in Hanga Roa. Wer sich der Logik der herrschenden Macht, das heißt der chilenisch-westlichen 'Zivilisierung' widersetzte, wer auf Selbstbestimmung insistierte, der konnte nicht normal sein, der war immer noch der Wilde, also krank.

Hier soll nun der andere deutsche Dichter, selbst Fremder, und Exilant, erwähnt werden, der die Osterinsel besucht, aber nicht betreten hat: Adalbert von Chamisso. Chamisso machte als Naturwissenschaftler auf der russischen Bark 'Rurik' unter dem Kommando Otto v. Kotzebues, Sohn des Dramatikers August v. Kotzebue, eine Weltreise mit. Im Jahr 1816 traf das Schiff bei der Osterinsel ein, die Expedition konnte damals aber nicht an Land gehen, weil die Einwohner sich feindlich verhielten. 1808 war der amerikanischer Schoner 'Nancy' gelandet, der Kapitän hatte 12 Männer und 10 Frauen verschleppt, wobei es zu einem Blutbad unter den Einwohnern gekommen war. Chamisso berichtet von dieser furchtbaren Episode und hat mit dem Blick auf die Osterinsel, die er nicht betreten konnte, einen schönen, von der Aufklärung bestimmten Satz geschrieben:

'Ich ergreife diese Gelegenheit, auch hier gegen die Benennung "Wilde" in ihrer Anwendung auf die Südseeinsulaner feierlichen Protest einzulegen. ... Ein Wilder ist für mich der Mensch, der, ohne festen Wohnsitz, Feldbau und gezähmte Tiere, keinen anderen Besitz kennt, als seine Waffen, mit denen er sich von der Jagd ernährt. Wo den Südsee-Insulanern Verderbtheit der Sitten schuld gegeben werden kann, scheint mir solche nicht von der Wildheit, sondern vielmehr von der Übergesittung zu zeugen. Die verschiedenen Erfindungen, die Münze, die Schrift u.s.w., welche die verschiedenen Stufen der Gesittung abzumessen geeignet sind, auf denen Völker unseres Kontinents sich befinden, hören unter so veränderten Bedingungen auf, einen Maßstab abzugeben für diese insularisch abgesonderten Menschenfamilien, die unter diesem wonnigen Himmel ohne gestern und morgen dem Momente Leben und dem Genusse.' (*Reise um die Welt*, s. 81)

Noch ist der Himmel blau, am Horizont schiebt sich eine Wolkenbank hoch, schnell treibt sie vom Wind getrieben, auf die Insel zu, plötzlich ist dieser Regen in der Luft, aber so fein wie aus einem Wasserzerstäuber. Es ist das Eigentümliche, man spürt, daß die Wolken von weither kommen und weithin gehen, so tief treiben sie über dem Meer. Dann nach wenigen Minuten scheint wieder das Blau durch, erst zart, dann strahlend und der Blick geht über das sanft gewellte Land auf dem das kniehohe Gras steht. Bewegt silbern, eingeschattet von einer nachschwebenden Wolke.

Dieses Land gehört noch immer dem chilenischen Staat. Das ist einer der Gründe, warum eine Gruppe von Rapa Nuis den Kirchplatz besetzt halten. Eine Frau erzählt uns auf Spanisch, daß das Rapa Nui, diese nur von 1600 Menschen gesprochene Sprache, in Gefahr sei, verloren zu gehen. In der Schule sei Spanisch obligatorisch. Spanisch ist alleinige Amts- und Gerichtssprache. Mit der Sprache Rapa Nui würde man seine eigene Geschichte verlieren. Es sei wie mit diesen Baum, dem Taromiro, dieser auf der Welt einmaligen Baumart, die ausgestorben ist, von der Heyerdahl noch ein paar Samen gefunden hat, die in Göteborg und Bonn nachgezüchtet werden konnten. Am Hang des Vulkans Rano Kao versucht man, den Taromiro wieder heimisch zu machen. Aber die kleinen Pflanzen wüchsen einfach nicht. Die chilenischen Biologen bewässern sie, sagt die Frau, aber ohne Liebe. Diese nur auf dieser Insel existierende Baum braucht die Pflege der Rapa Nui, eine besondere Liebe. Erst dann würde er gedeihen. Die Forderung der Besetzer, der politischen Aktivisten, ginge nicht nach politischer, sondern nach kultureller Unabhängigkeit der Insel.

Wenn man das Inselmuseum betritt, hat man vor Augen, was diesen Menschen, was dieser einmaligen Kultur, angetan worden ist. Sie, die all das hervorgebracht haben: bewundernswerte Schnitzwerke, eine eigentümliche Zeichenschrift, die auf einigen der Rongorongo-Tafeln überliefert ist, all das ist über die ganze Welt verstreut, in allen größeren Völkerkundemuseen zu finden und zu bewundern, aber die Rapa Nui haben in ihrem Museum lediglich zwei Originale.

Die Frage nach den Dieben stellt sich so ganz neu. Die lächerlichen Diebereien der Insulaner, die den europäischen Eindringlingen Hüte und Taschentücher stahlen, waren nichts gegen die systematische kulturelle Ausplünderung der Insel.

Es wäre von europäischer und amerikanischer Seite eine bescheidene Wiedergutmachung für das, was diesem kleinen Volk angetan wurde, wenn man wenigstens einen Teil seiner Kunstwerke, die teilweise unzugänglich in Magazinen lagern, zurückgäbe, vor allem einige dieser einmaligen Schrifttafeln. Und es müßten die Voraussetzungen dafür geschaffen werden, daß die Sprache der Rapa Nui in der Schule unterrichtet wird, daß Gottesdienste, da die Christanisierung ja so erfolgreich war, auf Rapa Nui gehalten werden, – vielleicht kann dann einmal jenes Buch in Rapa Nui geschrieben werden, das von dieser Geschichte erzählt: von den mörderischen Bürgerkriegen, von den ersten europäischen Eindringlingen, von Moais die zum Meer hinunterwanderten, von den Missionaren, die dem letzten Königskind und Priester vor allen Augen die Haare abschnitten, von der Zeit, als die Insel den Schafen gehörte, während die Insulaner eingepfercht lebten, von dem Franzosen mit seinem kleinen mörderischen Terrorsystem, wie er getötet wurde, Sklavenhändler, die Menschen entführten, die Chilenen, die diese Insel in Besitz nahmen, die Amerikaner, die hier aus strategischen Gründen einen Flughafen anlegten, (der nicht Chile, und schon gar nicht den Rapa Nuis gehört), auf dem nun die Touristen landen, zu denen auch ich gehöre.

Die Bucht von Anakena: Ein geschwungener weißer Sandstrand. Hier stehen Palmen, die erst vor gut zwanzig Jahren gepflanzt wurden, als man die Insel für Touristen erschloß. Der Strand ist leer, kein Mensch zu sehen. Das Wasser ist tatsächlich grün und so durchsichtig wie es immer beschrieben wird. Dem Schwimmenden geht beim Anblick der Bucht natürlich dieses Wort durch den Kopf: Klischee. Aber es stört ihn nicht weiter. Er macht in der sanften Dünung den toten Mann. Wird er von einer Welle gehoben, hat er die massigen Moais, die am Ufer stehen, gut im Blick. Er denkt daran, wie er vorgelesen hat, die Zehen in die Sandalen verkrallt. Jetzt wird er getragen. Gern würde er jetzt laut jauchzen. Aber dann würde seine Frau womöglich einen Schreck bekommen. Es soll ja Haifische geben. Also freut er sich im Stillen und so, wie es Chamisso beim Anblick dieser Insel für sich beschrieben hatte: 'da freute ich mich wie ein Kind; alt nur darin, daß ich zugleich mich auch darüber freute, mich noch freuen zu können.'

Am Strand, mit den Blick auf die Bucht, also auch auf den Schwimmenden, stehen auf einem Altar die sieben Moais und etwas seitlich auf einem kleinen Hügel ein einzelner, wuchtiger, runder, archaischer Moai, alle blicken sie über das Meer zum Horizont, von dorther sollen die Ahnen gekommen sein und mit ihnen begann die Geschichte der Insel. Diese Figuren in ihrem wuchtigen dunklen Ernst sind selbst das Symbol des Fremden. Sie stellen, dem heutigen Betrachter, wenn er denn nicht in einer fraglosen

Gläubigkeit eingebunden ist, eine Frage, die den ethonolgischen, kulturkritischen und politischen Fragen vorangeht und sie transzendiert: Woher wir kommen, wohin wir gehen.

2

Uwe Timm:
Literary Career

DAVID BASKER

In his essay 'Ein Autor der mittleren Generation' Manfred Durzak locates Uwe Timm in the second generation of West German authors, among the likes of Sten Nadolny, F. C. Delius, and Peter Schneider, writers whose work has to some extent existed under the shadow of illustrious predecessors, at least as far as perceptions among the literary establishment are concerned.[1] Durzak goes on to differentiate between Timm and his peers, however, in that his family background is not that of the relative privilege of middle-class life in the West Germany of the 1950s.[2] Timm was born in Hamburg on 30 March 1940, the son of a furrier who ran a small family business that just about maintained financial solvency. Timm was evacuated with his mother to stay with relatives in Coburg in 1943 during the heaviest period of Allied bombing, but the end of the Second World War saw his return to the city. From this point on, his childhood experience was of working-class life in inner-city Hamburg, a tightly knit community in which the young Timm absorbed many of the stories of daily life, of which he was to make professional use in later life.[3] Having attended *Grundschule* in Hamburg Timm went directly into an apprenticeship in his father's trade, and thence into the family business, which he ran himself for four years. He only returned to formal education after this experience of working life. Not until 1963 did he complete his *Abitur* at the Braunschweig-Kolleg, a college for mature-age students. Thus it was through the second half of the 1960s – the period, of course, of unrest at universities in a number of cities throughout the world – that Timm was a student of philosophy and literature at the Ludwig-Maximilians-Universität in Munich and at the Sorbonne in Paris. He was directly involved in student protest, specifically with the anti-authoritarian movement in the Sozialistischer Deutscher

Studentenbund (SDS). In retrospect, Timm is clear about the significance of this stage of his life for his literary career:

> Aber mit der Studentenbewegung und durch die Studentenbewegung habe ich eine für mich und mein Schreiben wichtige Erfahrung gemacht, die ich mit vielen aus meiner Generation, die in der Studentenbewegung oder in deren Umkreis engagiert waren, teile. Die Erfahrung: daß man aus seiner Isolation herauskam, aus einer Isolation der eigenen Sichtweise, aus einem bedrängenden und beengenden Subjektivismus, aus Ängsten und Schuldgefühlen.[4]

At the same time, Timm now recognizes in his earlier self a certain ironic distance from the events of the student movement, which he ascribes to the fact that he had had wider practical experience of working life than the majority of his peers. He was subsequently able to use this awareness of the movement's 'Merkwürdigkeiten' to good literary effect.[5]

Timm's involvement in student protest clearly did not hinder his academic progress. In 1971 he was awarded a doctorate for his dissertation *Das Problem der Absurdität bei Albert Camus*. Alongside further academic study, this time in the fields of sociology and economics, he began his career as a free-lance writer in the same year, with the publication of the volume *Widersprüche*, a collection of twenty-three poems of an explicitly political nature. The influence of his experience of the student movement of the late 1960s is obvious both in the criticisms of West German society that the poems express and in the volume's *Nachwort*, in which he sets out his own view of the role of the political poet. The politically committed writer, Timm contends, faces the problem of overcoming a linguistic barrier in order to bring any message to the working people whom such writing is supposed to help. According to this conception, language is a political tool used by the ruling classes to manipulate a particular view of reality, a view that is propagated through the mass media. In order to expose and alter this view, the political poet must develop not only a different ideological standpoint, but also a new form of linguistic expression. Language is thus not simply the medium for political debate, but should also be its subject.[6]

Timm's views on the relationship between politics and literature were developed further in this period in a number of essays and articles. In 'Zwischen Unterhaltung und Aufklärung', for example, he takes issue both with established bourgeois literature, for its exclusivity and avoidance of contemporary social issues, and with the type of popular literature which, although accessible and topical, tends to affirm the capitalist *status quo*. Effective political literature should be accessible but should take a critical stance towards capitalism and thus reveal the system's abuses. Such literature might communicate a utopian vision, but should stimulate the reader to act in a practical way to improve society. A form of *Entwicklungsroman*, showing the development of a protagonist from individualism towards an awareness of collective responsibility is the genre Timm regards here as the most appropriate to achieve this end. Critics have drawn obvious parallels between the literature that this theoretical position advocates and the novels of East German Socialist Realism.

Perhaps surprisingly, Timm's theoretical position found very practical support in the capitalist circumstances of the Federal Republic, through his activities as an editor and promoter of literature in the course of the early 1970s. Most notable of these activities was his role as co-founder of the AutorenEdition in Munich in 1972, an undertaking designed to promote precisely the kind of politically committed writing Timm envisaged. With the backing of the C. Bertelsmann publishing company, the Federal Republic's largest media enterprise, Timm joined forces with his fellow-writers Uwe Friesel, Richard Hey and Hannelies Taschau to form a press in which editorial and publication decisions were taken collectively; an independent editorial committee consisting of the four founders, an agent from Bertelsmann (the *Lektor* Andreas Hopf, whose editorial views were close to Timm's) and a representative of the author whose work was to appear in the series was constituted to give writers greater control over the publication process. Economic and ideological pressures took their toll on the AutorenEdition in the course of the 1970s, however. Hopf was removed in 1976, amid reassurances from Bertelsmann that the series would continue, but on condition that its programme become more commercially viable; and following the 'Deutscher Herbst' of 1977, the AutorenEdition was accused of supporting terrorism. When Timm and his colleagues attempted to include Peter O. Chotjewitz's *Die Herren des Morgengrauens* in their programme, Bertelsmann withdrew its support. The AutorenEdition then came under the patronage of the Verlagsgruppe Athenäum, Hain, Scriptor und Hanstein. This publishing group in turn ran into financial difficulties in the early 1980s and by 1982 the AutorenEdition was no longer in existence.

Of Timm's own work which appeared with the AutorenEdition imprint, it is his first novel *Heißer Sommer* (1974) that comes closest to putting into practice the author's theoretical views of the early 1970s. In setting and atmosphere the novel clearly leans heavily on Timm's own experience of life as a student in the Munich of the late 1960s. It is an *Entwicklungsroman* of the sort Timm sought to promote, in that his protagonist Ullrich Krause undergoes a personal journey from selfish individualism to an awareness of social responsibility, albeit in a way that some critics have found barely credible. Ullrich's transformation comes through initial commitment to the student movement, membership of the SDS, and participation in the anti-Springer demonstrations in Hamburg following the attack on Rudi Dutschke. Growing disillusionment with the inflexibility of the SDS leads Ullrich into more direct contact with ordinary working people. Through these relationships with the people whom the social revolution is intended to help, Ullrich reaches a new understanding of the practical contribution he can make to a fairer society.

By contrast, although Timm's third novel in the AutorenEdition series, *Kerbels Flucht* (1980), returns to life in and around Munich University, the potential for social – or even personal – development has disappeared, a reflection perhaps of the disillusionment surrounding the collapse of the protest movement by the late 1970s. Timm himself recognizes his own sense of political frustration over this period. Having abandoned the increasingly fruitless debates of the anarchist anti-authoritarian wing of the SDS, he joined the DKP (Deutsche Kommunistische Partei) in 1973, 'weil ich glaubte, sie könne eine politische Alternative bilden und auch diejenigen erreichen, die man in der Studentenbewegung immer erreichen wollte, aber nie erreicht hat, die Arbeiter, Angestellten und sozial Deklassierten'.[7] By the mid-1970s Timm had become disillusioned with the DKP's subservience to the East German SED (Sozialistische Einheitspartei Deutschlands), particularly over the expulsion of Wolf Biermann in 1976. This waning enthusiasm for the effectiveness of organized politics feeds into the sombre tone of *Kerbels Flucht*. Kerbel is a student, a former political activist who, following an agonizing break-up with his girlfriend, can no longer find points of orientation for his life in politics, study or personal relationships. Under increasing mental pressure he turns to alcohol, which only results in his losing his job as a taxi driver. The bleak conclusion to the novel – Kerbel is shot by the police for failing to stop at a checkpoint and hardly anyone comes to his funeral – is a long way from the positive ending of *Heißer Sommer*.

Between *Heißer Sommer* and *Kerbels Flucht* in Timm's series of novels for the AutorenEdition came *Morenga* (1978). Its subject matter, too, owes something to the concerns of the student movement, of which Timm had had such direct experience, for it is to the issue of the exploitation of the Third World that he turns his attention here. This is not an abstract concern for American involvement in Vietnam, however, but a practical demonstration of how very recent German history connects the society of the Federal Republic to the worst abuses of colonialism. The German army vet Gottschalk, a figure whose background locates him firmly in the strict tradition of Prussian authoritarianism, gradually sees his inherited attitudes challenged by his direct contact with the cultures of the Hereros and the Nama in South-West Africa. Through a combination of documentary material drawn from a range of sources, and the experiences of fictional characters Timm explores in detail the background to Germany's colonial involvement in the area and makes implicit connections with subsequent German history. The research for *Morenga* also gave rise to a work of documentary photographs edited by Timm, entitled *Deutsche Kolonien* (1981).

In setting, theme and theoretical inspiration all three of the AutorenEdition volumes are rooted in Timm's experience of student politics in the turbulent years of the late 1960s. It is perhaps worth noting, however, that Timm did not follow a number of his peers in taking the conclusions of the political debate of 1968–9 to an aesthetic extreme. While others assembled works of *Dokumentarliteratur* as the most effective literary form of political commitment, or even declared the death of literature, Timm continued to work his political stance into a narrative form. His own list of writers who influenced him suggests the way in which he locates his books of this period; the list includes the critical theories of Marcuse, Horkheimer, and Adorno, but also Brecht and the novels of Andersch, Koeppen and Böll.[8]

Timm's work following the collapse of the AutorenEdition has moved away from open political commitment towards a literary approach that uses the detail of everyday life as a stimulus for narration. Characteristic of a number of Timm's later texts is his recourse to family memories and to recollections of life in Hamburg in the immediate post-war period for literary inspiration. The first work to draw heavily on family connections was *Der Mann auf dem Hochrad* (1984). Subtitled *Legende*, the text re-creates a series of events from the life of the narrator's Great-Uncle Franz, the first man to ride a penny-farthing bicycle in the provincial town of Coburg in the second half of the nineteenth century. The immediate stimulus for the story is a silver toothpick which the narrator inherited from his uncle. The object unlocks the narrator's personal memories, encourages him to research further into his uncle's life, and provokes the creative act of recounting episodes from that life. Uncle Franz's story is more than just personal memory, however; his experiences – and the narrator's memory of them – intersect with fundamental changes in the social and political fabric of Germany, most notably with the impact of technology.

Timm's next novel, *Der Schlangenbaum* (1986), develops a number of issues found in his earlier work. The theme of the impact of technology is familiar from *Der Mann auf dem Hochrad*; and the novel has much in common with *Morenga* in its representation of the First World's exploitation of the Third World. Timm himself connects *Der Schlangenbaum* most closely with *Kerbels Flucht*, in that both novels express a sobering lack of faith in the capacity of organized politics to improve people's lives.[9] In *Der Schlangenbaum*, the German engineer Wagner escapes his disastrous personal life by attempting to set up a paper factory on behalf of a German company in the middle of the South American jungle. Culturally at sea and in an environment in every way hostile to the technology of late twentieth-century Europe, Wagner is confronted with the erosion of all the beliefs which hitherto had structured his life. His enterprise cannot succeed. If the factory is built successfully, the rain-forest will be destroyed; if the rain-forest is saved, the local population will remain the victims of terrible poverty. Despite his personal crisis it is almost with a feeling of relief that Wagner sees nature swallow up all trace of the factory at the end of the novel.

Timm's fascination with the problems of existence in another place, with sociological comparisons, is one that finds expression in subsequent works, too. Indeed, Timm himself was drawn to leave Munich in the early 1980s and live for a period in Rome, an account of which experience appears in literary form as *Vogel, friß die Feige nicht. Römische Aufzeichnungen* (1989). His stay in Rome offers many points of comparison between Italian and West German society, from attitudes to driving, through bureaucracy, to different reactions to physical contact. The classical cultural heritage and details of Italian history, evidence of which the narrator/Timm finds all around, are subjects for further reflection; in particular, it is the discovery of the grave of Antonio Gramsci in the Protestant cemetery in Rome that brings the narrator to assess the effectiveness of his own political commitment. The text ends with a moving tribute to Timm's friend and fellow-author Heinar Kipphardt.

In some respects, Timm's next novel, *Kopfjäger. Bericht aus dem Inneren des Landes* offers an ironic counterpoint to those works which rely heavily on the author's biography. The protagonist Peter Walter has embezzled huge sums of money through his financial investment business in Hamburg and, having staged a jail break during the subsequent court case, he is on the run from the authorities, firstly in Spain, then in South America, and finally on Easter Island. Walter commits his experiences to the memory of his laptop computer, including episodes from his childhood in the Hamburg of the immediate post-war years. These frequently concern an uncle only slightly older than Walter who, following a period as a student in Munich around 1968, has become a writer. Walter is contemptuous of the uncle's profession as an adult, just as he was of his sensitive nature as a child; Timm's background, personality and literary achievements are thrown into ironic relief by a character who can criticize from the benefit of close personal experience. The fact that that character is guilty of cheating people out of huge sums of money hardly impinges on those criticisms. The first-person account shows Walter almost to be a romantic figure, someone who has succeeded because of his ability to tell stories, as his 'Bericht' proves. In some respects, he, too, is a victim of a society which encourages greed and financial exploitation. His fascination with the society of Easter Island – where the authorities finally catch up with him – stands in stark contrast to his observations on life in the Federal Republic.

In his two most recent works of fiction, Timm returns to a literary approach very similar to the one he adopted in *Der Mann auf dem Hochrad*: a first-person narrator uses family history and apparently ordinary objects as a stimulus for very unusual stories which in turn connect with wider historical and social issues. *Die Entdeckung der Currywurst* (1993) is set in Timm's native Hamburg and plays with the genre of the *Novelle* in focusing on the experiences of Lena Brücker, the woman whom, the narrator single-mindedly contends, 'discovered' the definitive recipe for curried sausage in the early post-war period; and *Johannisnacht* (1996) sees a narrator in search of an article on the potato embark on a series of picaresque adventures in post-unification Berlin. Just like his counterpart in *Der Mann auf dem Hochrad*, the narrator of *Johannisnacht* is encouraged to begin his literary quest because of an uncle, this time Uncle Heinz, who possessed the remarkable talent of being able to identify types of potato simply by tasting them. Readers familiar with all of Timm's work will note that the three stories overlap, especially as far as family connections are concerned, and in that the narrators are, for all practical purposes, the same person, someone with a biography very close to Uwe Timm's own.

Along with *Die Entdeckung der Currywurst*, the year 1993 also saw the publication of a collection of essays, *Erzählung und kein Ende* in which Timm sets out his theory of literature. The essays were first given in the course of his tenure of the 'Paderborner Gastdozentur für Schriftsteller' in the winter semester 1991–2. Subtitled *Versuche zu einer Ästhetik des Alltags*, the collection deals entertainingly with Timm's conception of 'sprechende Situationen' and 'gezeichnete Dinge', the triggers for narration that populate everyday life. He acknowledges in the essays that he has left behind the didactic approach of his early literary career: 'Heute denke ich, daß ein wesentliches Kennzeichen von Literatur darin liegt, *überflüssig* zu sein' (*EkE*, 111).

Timm might describe his relationship with his own family as a 'sprechende Situation', since it has given rise to a number of texts alongside the main stream of his career. *Die Zugmaus* (1981), *Die Piratenamsel* (1983), *Rennschwein Rudi Rüssel* (1989), and *Der Schatz auf Pagensand* (1995) are children's stories which emerged from Timm's capacity to invent stories to entertain his own children. *Rennschwein Rudi Rüssel* won the Deutsche Jugendbuch-Preis in 1990.

Indeed, this is not the only prize that Timm's work has won, despite Manfred Durzak's identification of the shadow cast over his generation – in the eyes of the literary establishment, at least – by older figures. Recognition of his work includes the Bremer Förderpreis für Literatur in 1979, the New York-Stipendium des Deutschen Literaturfonds in 1989, and the Münchner Literaturpreis in 1990 for his work as a whole. Now resident in Munich, Uwe Timm continues his literary career and is currently engaged in working on a film script.

Notes

[1] Manfred Durzak, 'Ein Autor der mittleren Generation', in Keith Bullivant, M. Durzak and Hartmut Steinecke (eds.), *Die Archäologie der Wünsche. Studien zum Werk von Uwe Timm* (Cologne, Kiepenheuer & Witsch, 1995), 13–25 (13).

[2] 'Ein Autor der mittleren Generation', 19.

[3] See, for example, the episodes drawn from life in the block of flats where the narrator's grandmother/aunt lives in Hamburg in *Kopfjäger* (K, 52) and *Die Entdeckung der Currywurst* (EC, 127).

[4] Manfred Durzak, 'Die Position des Autors. Ein Werkstattgespräch mit Uwe Timm', in *Die Archäologie der Wünsche*, 311–54 (312).

[5] 'Die Position des Autors', 315.

[6] Of course, Timm is not the only left-wing critic of linguistic manipulation in the mass media at the time. See, for example, Hans Magnus Enzensberger's essays on what he calls 'Die Bewußtseins-Industrie'.

[7] 'Die Position des Autors', 329–30.

[8] See 'Die Position des Autors', 319. South-American narrative literature, made popular in Germany not least by Timm's wife, who is of German-Argentinian background and works as a translator, also features in his list of literary influences ('Die Position des Autors', 326).

[9] Timm refers to the novels as 'die beiden finsteren Bücher', 'Die Position des Autors', 336.

3

»Eine Deklaration gegen Gewalt und Tod«: Gespräch mit Uwe Timm

COLIN RIORDAN

CR: Wie bist Du eigentlich Schriftsteller geworden? Wie kam das zustande?

UT: Ich denke, daß das aus einer Störung herauskam, die ich mit dem Schreiben hatte. Ich habe große Schwierigkeiten gehabt, richtig zu schreiben, weil ich eine sehr starke bildhafte Einbildung hatte, die in Wörter und Zeilen umzusetzen mir Schwierigkeiten bereitete. Dieser Umsetzungsprozeß, etwas Gedankliches in Zeichen zu bringen, hat bei mir dazu geführt, daß ich immer wieder ins Erzählen ausgewichen bin. Auch Situationen, die vorgegeben waren, in der Kindheit und in der Schulzeit, habe ich immer wieder versucht, durch Beschreibung von Bildern aufzulösen. Dabei kam es eben auch zu fürchterlichen Fehlern, die immer wieder moniert wurden. Ich habe sehr unter dem Deutschunterricht gelitten, aber zugleich auch inbrünstig geschrieben. Das ist das Merkwürdige gewesen, es war also ein sehr zwiespältiges Verhältnis, das ich zum Deutschunterricht hatte. Auf der einen Seite hat es mir Spaß gemacht, etwas zu erzählen, auf der anderen Seite war da wie ein spanischer Schuh immer diese Einengung, daß ich das jetzt irgendwie in Zeichen bringen mußte, und das verformte sich. Ich hatte mit der Orthographie meine Probleme, was dann immer wieder dazu führte, daß ich von den Lehrern gemaßregelt wurde, besonders von einem, dem Herrn Blumenthal, wurde ich in einer unangenehmen Weise, man würde heute sagen unpädagogisch, behandelt. Er versuchte immer wieder, mich lächerlich zu machen. Ich beobachte das immer noch bei mir: Wenn ich spontan etwas schreibe, deformiert sich die Orthographie völlig, und ich muß es dann erst später im zweiten Gang zurechtrücken.

Bei mir ist das Schreiben schon in der Schulzeit ein Resultat davon gewesen, mir Gedanken zu machen über meine Probleme, die ich damals hatte. Ich hatte auch keine sehr glückliche Kindheit in der Zeit, hatte einen sehr autoritären Vater, mit dem ich mich auseinandersetzen mußte. Schreibend habe ich versucht, mir darüber klarzuwerden, wobei eben dieses Schreiben, wie gesagt, mit großen Schwierigkeiten verbunden war. Es war eine merkwürdige Situation – man sollte annehmen, es hätte mich abgeschreckt – aber es hat dazu geführt, es dennoch immer wieder zu versuchen, und erst langsam hat sich das dann ausgeglichen.

CR: Wann hast Du genau angefangen zu schreiben?

UT: Ich habe mit zwölf Jahren angefangen, einen Roman zu schreiben, in der Schule, wo ich mich gräßlich gelangweilt habe. Es war eine Geschichte über einen Mann, der in Hamburg in einer napoleonischen Zeit aus der Stadt rausgeworfen wurde. Dieser Roman hat genau sechsundsiebzig Seiten erreicht, und dann hat der Lehrer, Herr Blumenthal, das entdeckt und hat das unterbunden. Das waren die ersten Versuche, aber ich habe konstant immer geschrieben; immer wieder in Zeiten, in denen ich Probleme hatte, habe ich mit dem Schreiben von Gedichten und Prosa darauf reagiert, zunächst natürlich nicht veröffentlicht. Zuerst in der Studentenzeit habe ich angefangen, das dann auch zu veröffentlichen, und die ersten Veröffentlichungen waren Gedichte in Zeitungen, in der *FAZ*, in der *Welt* dann, in den größeren Tageszeitungen.

CR: Es war ein konstanter Prozeß, die Veröffentlichungen waren nur eine Phase in der Entwicklung.

UT: Ja, aber am Anfang war gar nicht mal so die Absicht da, ein Buch zu schreiben. Ich denke, es ist bei vielen Schriftstellern der Fall, daß sie das immer vor Augen haben, dieses sichtbare Zeichen der Bildung in dem Bücherschrank zu haben. Das war es wirklich nicht, sondern es war einfach Notwehr, Notwehr darauf, daß ich damals sehr unglücklich war und weder mit der Schule noch zuhause mit meinem Vater zurechtkam. Gottseidank hatte ich ein sehr gutes Verhältnis zu meiner Mutter, die das abfedern konnte. Die Disziplinierung, die in der Schule stattfand, habe ich immer als extrem empfunden. Nicht nur, daß man stundenweise sitzen-bleiben mußte, sondern eben auch der ganze Vorgang der Erlernung der Schrift beispielsweise. Das habe ich als einen Würgegriff in Erinnerung. Ich denke, das geht vielen so. Sie verdrängen das dann bloß, oder passen sich langsam an, daß man das nachher einfach gar nicht mehr bemerkt.

CR: Wann kam die Zeit, wo Du Dich von diesem Würgegriff befreien konntest, nach der Schule, oder erst später?

UT: Ja, das ist eine gute Frage. Ich denke, daß das erst viel später einsetzte, eigentlich genau mit der Studentenbewegung. Ich war ein guter Student und hatte keine Schwierigkeiten, ich bekam ein Stipendium, aber es war immer ein ungeheurer Druck. Das Versagen war zugleich ein grundsätzlich empfundenes Selbstversagen. Und diesen Leistungsdruck, der auch durch die Erziehung internalisiert ist, in Frage zu stellen und zu erfahren, daß es nicht nur Eigenverschulden ist, sondern daß das ein gesellschaftliches Phänomen ist, worunter viele leiden, das ist erst in der antiautoritären Bewegung möglich geworden. Erst um 1967 lernte ich, Dinge aufzugeben, die mir keinen Spaß machten, zum Beispiel Bücher nicht zu Ende zu lesen, sondern einfach wegzulegen. Aber diese Lockerheit mußte ich erst lernen. Daß Lernen auch Spaß bringen muß, das war eine Forderung. Der Lustgewinn war ein Begriff, mit dem man gegen das Establish-ment, gegen die vorherrschende Wissenschaftsordnung vorging. Man sagte, wo ist eigentlich der Lustgewinn? Das kippte dann später wieder um, wo das ausschließlich eingeklagt wurde, nur noch Lust, das ist auch nicht der richtige Weg gewesen. Das zu relativieren war für mich nur in der Studentenbewegung richtig möglich.

CR: Wie stehst Du denn heute zu dieser Bewegung? Wir hatten letztes Jahr Peter Schneider hier in Swansea, und es ist ganz offensichtlich – das hat er auch geschrieben – daß er jetzt sehr kritisch dazu steht, vor allem was das Antifaschistische daran betrifft. Er hat diese Theorie vom Unschuldswahn, nämlich daß man die Verbrechen der Eltern zurückgewiesen, aber für sich selbst eine große Unschuld in Anspruch genommen hat.

UT: Ich sehe das nicht so kritisch wie er, aber das hängt damit zusammen, daß er damals dezidiert Maoist war. Da hatte ich eher ein kritisches Verhältnis, und meine Entwicklung ist sicherlich ganz anders als seine. Ich war nie Wortführer in der Studentenbewegung, sondern habe mich da engagiert und mitgemacht in der SDS. Erst später bin ich dann in die DKP gegangen, aber auch da mit einem linken kritischen Vorbehalt, und bin dann auch wieder ausgetreten, nachdem sich die Schwierigkeiten und die Konflikte verstärkten. Aber ich bin reingegangen aus der Erfahrung, daß gesellschaftliche Veränderungen allein im universitären Bereich nicht oder nur begrenzt möglich sind. Ich dachte, man muß in die Betriebe gehen, beziehungsweise insbesondere auf die Leute zugehen, die unmittelbar davon betroffen sind, also Arbeiter, Angestellte, Rentner und dergleichen mehr. Das habe ich dann auch versucht umzusetzen. Mich hat der friedliche Flügel des Anarchismus sehr interessiert, insbesondere Kropotkin. Dadurch habe ich ein etwas entspannteres Verhältnis, weil ich mich nicht mit bestimmten Modellen identifiziert habe, wie z. B. dem chinesischen Modell. Es schien mir absurd, das auf bundesrepublikanische oder mitteleuropäische Verhältnisse zu übertragen.

CR: Also keine unbedingt negative Einstellung zur Studentenbewegung heute.

UT: Ich sehe die Studentenbewegung sehr positiv. Ich denke, das ist die einzige wirkliche radikaldemokratische Bewegung gewesen nach 1945, die sehr viel verändert hat, im Bereich der Pädagogik zum Beispiel. Geradezu entscheidende Arbeiten sind damals nicht nur akademisch verfaßt, sondern auch in die Praxis umgesetzt worden. Daß es da auch gleichzeitig Übertreibungen gab, antiautoritäre Kindergärten beispielsweise, das ist wohl wahr. Aber wichtig ist, daß man Autoritäten in Frage stellte, daß die Pädagogik sich änderte, daß die Beziehung Mann/Frau im Sinne einer Emanzipation sich änderte, insbesondere auch das Problem der dritten Welt. Da war nicht nur der Protest gegen die Eltern. Man setzte sich massiv mit dem Faschismus auseinander. Der Faschismus ist in der deutschen Literatur immer kritisiert worden, und das finde ich ganz wichtig. Alle wesentlichen Autoren haben sich mit dem Faschismus in ihren Büchern auseinandergesetzt, ob es Böll ist, oder Koeppen, oder Walser, oder auch Grass, oder Arno Schmidt oder Schnurre, man findet das überall. Aber in den ganzen Institutionen war der Faschismus verankert. Im Bereich der Justiz, des Militärs, der Wirtschaft saßen überall Nazis. Er hatte sich richtig festgesetzt, und da kam aus der Studentenbewegung massiv im universitären Bereich zum ersten Mal in der deutschen Geschichte eine linke Bewegung, die das Gesellschaftssystem, und vor allem die Vergangenheit, kritisch betrachtete. Ich finde, das ist wirklich ein Einschnitt gewesen. Es hat auch bestimmte Reformen zur Folge gehabt, im universitären Bereich, im Schulbereich, Mitbestimmung. All das sind Folgen von '68, wo eine verstärkte Basisdemokratie eingeklagt wurde. Darauf könnte und müßte man sich viel mehr besinnen, zumal auch im Zusammenhang mit dem Problem der dritten Welt. Das einzige, was man damals nicht gesehen hat, war das Problem der Ökologie. Man war sehr, ich auch, sehr fortschrittsgläubig. Man sah nicht die verheerenden Probleme, die schon vor der Haustür abzulesen waren. Das ist erst später in der ökologischen Bewegung wiederaufgenommen worden.

CR: Aber das ist auch zum Teil daraus erwachsen.

UT: Ja, natürlich. Da sind auch personelle Verbindungen, viele Leute aus der grünen Bewegung kamen aus der Studentenbewegung oder aus der APO-Bewegung heraus. Das ist wirklich ein Einschnitt in jeder Beziehung, auch im Wissenschaftsbetrieb. Heute werden die Studentenbewegung und die APO-Zeit, die damit verbundene Demokratisierungsbewegung von Konservativen in Frage gestellt, bis hin zu Botho Strauß, wo Erscheinungen wie die Skinheads in Rostock der Studentenbewegung und der antiautoritären Erziehung in die Schuhe geschoben werden, was Irrsinn ist und jede Kausalität auseinanderhebelt. Aber da ist einfach ein Interesse der Bourgeoisie, der Herrschenden in der Bundesrepublik, eine Verbindung herzustellen, die gar nicht da war. Was Peter Schneider macht, das ist einmal seine Position zu kritisieren, was ganz legitim und richtig ist. Aber er ist einer, der damals mit Gesellschaftsmodellen herumhantierte, die von anderen Ländern übernommen wurden, beispielsweise von China. »Laßt hundert Blumen blühen« und »die Literatur abschaffen« hat er ja propagiert, und das muß er in irgendeiner Weise auch biographisch erklären. Ich habe es nicht getan, ich fand Literatur immer wichtig und habe in der Zeit der Studentenbewegung Literatur geschrieben, allerdings Agitprop. Wir haben Straßentheater gemacht und geschrieben ...

CR: Und auch die ersten Gedichte?

UT: Ja, ich habe wie gesagt Gedichte geschrieben, aber sie waren unpolitisch. Ich habe dann sehr stark politisiert, also Agitprop-Literatur geschrieben und auch publiziert. Beispielsweise wurde im Hamburger Audimax Lyrik gelesen. Es waren über zweitausend Leute da, es war eine tolle Stimmung. Derzeit paßte das, es waren kritische Gedichte, aber drei, vier Jahre später waren diese Gedichte eben nicht mehr passend, einfach weil sie bestimmte Einsichten formulierten, die inzwischen verbreitet waren. Sie hatten ihre Berechtigung eine bestimmte Zeit lang und dann nicht mehr. Dann sah man auch, daß die Agitprop-Literatur, oder überhaupt die Literatur, die auf bestimmte Zielgruppen bezogen war, ihre Zielgruppen überhaupt nicht fand, die Arbeiter beispielsweise. Ich kann mich entsinnen, wir haben vor Fabriken Gedichte gelesen, wo zwei Leute zuhörten, die auch schnell nach Hause gingen, weil es regnete. Diese Form paßte einfach nicht, während andere Dinge ihre Berechtigung hatten. Es gab Filme, es gab Dokumentation, da ist ein breites Spektrum entwickelt worden. Fassbinder ist aus Straßentheateraktionen zur Notstandsgesetzgebung entstanden, er hat mit seiner Truppe draußen auf der Straße gespielt. Es ist sehr viel an neuen Formen entdeckt worden. Wenn man erklärt hat »keine Literatur«, dann muß man sich in irgendeiner Weise dazu verhalten. So wie ich meinen Versuch kritisieren muß, mit der Literatur andere Leserkreise zu erreichen – da habe ich Illusionen gehabt.

CR: Sind die Illusionen jetzt aufgelöst? Wie siehst Du die Möglichkeiten im neuen Deutschland?

UT: Ich sehe das jetzt nicht mehr so blauäugig und hoffnungsfroh wie damals. Das hängt einfach damit zusammen, daß ich natürlich jemand bin, für den Literatur eine große Rolle gespielt hat. Für mich war Literatur wirklich bewußtseinsbildend. Weil ich Lehrling war, habe ich eine andere Sozialisation als diejenigen, die vom Gymnasium kamen, wo zu Hause fleißig gelesen wurde, die dann an die Uni gingen. Für mich ist das eben etwas anderes gewesen. Lesen in der Schule und später in der Lehre war etwas, was für mich wie ein Rettungsring wirkte. Es war unerhört wichtig. Ich habe immer an die bewußtseinsbildende Funktion der Literatur geglaubt, und ich glaube heute noch daran. Aber: eingeschränkt, und zwar korrigiert von der Wirklichkeit. Die Vorstellung von der Literatur, die wir in der Studentenbewegung hatten, einer Literatur, die nicht vereinfacht und trivial sein sollte, die sich aber bestimmter Mittel bedient, um auch Menschen zu erreichen, die nicht unbedingt Zugang zur Literatur haben, das ist, glaube ich, so nicht möglich. Aber was Literatur immer noch leisten kann, und davon bin ich überzeugt, ist, daß sie auf eine sehr langsame Weise Sehweisen, Sprachverhalten, Emotionen ändern kann. Ich würde heute sagen, ich habe überhaupt kein resigniertes Verhältnis, sondern nur ein differenziertes. Literatur geht viel langsamer vor in ihrem Erkenntnisprozeß, als man sich das gewünscht hat. Ich würde heute sagen, Literatur muß man aus der politischen Aktion herausnehmen, und sie müßte ihre Funktion darin haben, in jeder Beziehung widerborstig zu sein: Sich gerade nicht auf Ideologien einlassen, sondern radikal subjektive Bedürfnisse formulieren und artikulieren, und das möglichst genau. Man soll sich keinen Illusionen hingeben, der Kapitalismus ist nicht hübscher geworden, sondern nur verkleideter und alternativloser – man sieht, wo Bedürfnisse manipuliert werden und wo andere Bedürfnisse denen entgegenstehen. Mich interessieren Leute, die Widerstand leisten, die eigenwillig sind, ohne daß sie deshalb gleich in einen politischen Rahmen einzuordnen wären.

CR: Heißt das, die Studentenbewegung hatte und hat einen allgemeinen oder umfassenden Einfluß auf Dein Werk?

UT: Ich denke, ein Roman wie *Morenga* ist aus dem Umkreis der Studentenbewegung zu verstehen, obwohl man das zunächst gar nicht glaubt. Er hat einmal diesen sehr subjektiven Bezug, weil ich aus einem Haus komme, in dem immer wieder von Kolonien erzählt wurde, wo Kameraden meines Vaters sich trafen, die in Kolonien gekämpft hatten. Sie erzählten von diesen »Negern«, die nicht ordentlich sind, nicht pünktlich sind, die Kinder *nicht* prügeln, und das war für mich das Paradies, eine tolle Situation als Kind. Wir vom SDS haben damals in Hamburg ein Denkmal umgerissen, einen deutschen Kolonisator. Da kam ich auf dieses Morenga-Thema. Dieser Bezug zur dritten Welt bleibt bis heute bestimmend: In den nächsten Jahrzehnten wird das Verhältnis der ersten Welt zur dritten Welt das brennende, sogar hochgefährliche Problem sein. Das ist eines der ganz wichtigen Dinge, die in der Studentenbewegung geleistet wurden, die ganzen Arbeitsgruppen

Salvador, Namibia und Südafrika usf. Das ist jetzt wieder alles abgeschnitten worden. Das muß neu aufgebaut werden, aber es kommt, einfach weil die Probleme nicht vom Tisch sind. Die Frage ist, wie verhält man sich; gibt man denen Almosen, oder baut man Armeen auf, um diese Armutswanderung zu stoppen, was jetzt schon der Fall ist, das Problem aber nie löst. Das ist ein Produkt der Studentenbewegung, daß ich über kulturelle Implikationen nachgedacht habe, die ich internalisiert hatte: Ordnungsvorstellungen, Leistungen, den Zeitbegriff, habe ich in *Morenga* vier Jahre lange aufgegriffen.

CR: Warum hast Du Dich in diesem Buch so schwer auf Dokumentation gestützt? Zum Teil grenzt es an einen Roman. Ich denke da natürlich an Heinar Kipphardt.

UT: Ja, das ist auch wichtig gewesen, ich war mit Heinar Kipphardt befreundet und es war für mich eine sehr wichtige Freundschaft, auch weil ich literarisch sehr viel gelernt habe. Er hat *Morenga* ja lektoriert. Das ist ein Roman, der zwar fiktional erzählt, z. B. diese ganzen Rindergeschichten sind natürlich reine Fiktion, aber es gibt auch ganz harte Dokumentation. Beides gehört in einer für mich wichtigen Weise zusammen: Es ist einmal der Versuch, das Ungeheuerliche, nämlich den Vorweggriff auf Auschwitz zu dokumentieren. Das Phänomen Auschwitz ist sicherlich einmal aus der spezifisch deutschen Geschichte zu erklären, aber es ist auch gleichzeitig europäische Geschichte. Der Eurozentrismus hat überall in der dritten Welt dazu geführt, daß die Leute kurzerhand erschossen, niedergeknüppelt oder auch ausgepeitscht und geprügelt wurden. In allen Kolonien wurde geprügelt, nicht um die Schuld von den Deutschen wegzunehmen; in den englischen und den französischen, in den belgischen, aber nur in den deutschen wurde darüber Buch geführt. Die Deutschen haben das akribisch festgehalten. Es wurde geschrieben wieviel, wann, warum, das kann man alles aus den Akten entnehmen. Und es ist sicherlich nur in der deutschen Tradition denkbar, daß eine lange Diskussion über den Sinn der Prügelstrafe stattfindet: Ob man mit dem Ochsenziemer oder mit dem Stockprügel schlagen sollte, darüber gibt es medizinische Gutachten. So was kann man sich gar nicht ausdenken, das kann man nur dokumentieren, und es ist dokumentiert, das habe ich als Dokument in den Roman aufgenommen. Aber andere Sachen, die sind da nicht dokumentarisch, vor allen Dingen dieser Veterinär Gottschalk, das ist alles Fiktion.

CR: Wo liegt denn da die Grenze zwischen Dokumentation und Fiktion?

UT: Einmal kann man das ablesen; immer da wo ein Zitat angegeben wird, da handelt es sich um reine Dokumentation, das sind aber nicht mal 5% des Romans. Aber die andere Grenze ist schwer zu sagen, da gibt es eben Teile, die authentisch sind. Z.B. hat es den Morenga gegeben, und das ist eine ganz faszinierende Figur, die in der Geschichte praktisch vergessen wurde. Er hat mit 300 Guerilleros 16000 Mann deutsche Elitetruppe geschlagen. Um sich das zu erklären, haben die Deutschen, die preußischen Offiziere, gesagt, er müsse irgendwann Clausewitz gelesen haben, was theoretisch möglich war, weil er sehr gut Deutsch konnte. Er konnte Englisch, Deutsch, Afrikaans und seine eigene Sprache, die Nama-Sprache. Es gibt wunderbare Interviews von ihm in der *Cape Times*, die ich gefunden habe. Das ist eine historische Figur, aber ich habe immer gedacht, ich könnte ihn nie richtig beschreiben, er tritt ja nie auf, obwohl er dem ganzen Roman den Namen gegeben hat, weil das ganze Vorgehen der Deutschen von ihm bestimmt wird.

CR: Es wäre zu heikel gewesen, aus seiner Sicht zu erzählen?

UT: Genau das ist es, das ist einfach zu heikel. Ich habe es mir überlegt, aber es wäre einfach unmöglich gewesen. Sich in die Sicht des Opfers, dann noch eines Afrikaners zu versetzen, das wäre für mich irgendwie unlauter gewesen. Aber der historische Raum stimmt sehr genau.

CR: Und es stimmt wirklich, daß das ein großer Beitrag ist zu dieser Geschichte. Ich meine nicht nur ein Beitrag, sondern das wird zur Geschichte, indem es als Roman veröffentlicht und vom Publikum gelesen wird. Das wäre sonst vielleicht gar nicht der Fall gewesen, wenn es nur eine Dokumentation gewesen wäre.

UT: Ja, genau, das finde ich sehr richtig gesehen. Es wird zur Geschichte, was man so in der Dokumentation nicht gehabt hätte, es ist plötzlich ein Teil der eigenen Geschichte. Das Buch ist zwar nicht leicht zu lesen, man muß schon ein gewisses Leseengagement mitbringen. Aber wenn man sich reinbegibt, begibt man sich auf eine Reise in eine andere Welt, in ein anderes Land, aber auch zugleich auf eine Reise in sich selbst, weil wir natürlich alle diese Sichtweise in uns tragen, oder zumindest Reste davon, die der Gottschalk hat.

CR: Was für ein Verhältnis hast Du zu Deinen Hauptfiguren wie Gottschalk in *Morenga* oder Wagner im *Schlangenbaum*?

UT: Es sind fast immer Figuren, von denen aus sich das Ganze leitet und bildet. Wagner zum Beispiel habe ich getroffen. Ich war in Argentinien – ich bin mit einer Deutsch-Argentinierin verheiratet, und war zehn oder elf Mal in Argentinien – und habe an einer Busstation, wo ich wartete, einen Mann getroffen, der betrunken war, aber einen eleganten, wenn auch schlabberigen und dreckigen Anzug trug. Er war Deutscher, er war Bauingenieur, hatte einen Bau übertragen bekommen im Norden Argentiniens. Der Bau, ein Neubau, versank im Morast. Er war in eine Spanierin verliebt, die verschwunden war, und die er gesucht hatte. Das ist die Geschichte, dann kam mein Bus und ich fuhr weiter. Ich hatte nie gedacht, einmal einen Roman zu schreiben, der in Argentinien spielt. Aber dieser Mann und sein Schicksal, das hat sich so im Kopf festgesetzt, daß ich über ihn schreiben mußte. Man hat dann keine Wahl mehr. Das beschäftigte mich so sehr, daß dann dieser Roman entstanden ist.

CR: Aber haben diese Personen dann sozusagen ein eigenes Leben?

UT: Am Anfang ist man Herr darüber und hat alle Freiheiten. Je weiter man schreibt, desto stärker wird auch die Logik der Figur. Es gibt eine Logik des Textes, gegen die man nicht verstoßen kann. Das Geheimnis des Schreibens liegt nicht am Anfang, das wirkliche Geheimnis ist der Schluß, denn diese Logik wird immer zwingender.

CR: Es gibt Autoren, die ihre Figuren wie lebende Personen behandeln, Grass oder Johnson zum Beispiel.

UT: Das verstehe ich. Man geht mit ihnen so lange um im Kopf. An dem *Schlangenbaum* habe ich drei Jahre geschrieben und an *Morenga* vier Jahre. Man ist nachher so vertraut mit diesen Figuren, sie führen dann wirklich ein Eigenleben. Sie sondern sich sprachlich ab. Eigentlich sind sie Vampire. Aber sie bekommen dann natürlich auch ein eigenes Gesicht durch den Leser. Ihre Plausibilität kann so stark werden, daß sie in die Wirklichkeit hineinreichen, ja sogar die Wirklichkeit mitbestimmen. Und darum würde ich heute darin das Moment des Kognitiven in der Literatur sehen, nämlich daß sie so widerständig ist und daß sie eine eigene Wirklichkeit schafft, die nicht genormt ist, sondern die Wirklichkeit *per se* in Frage stellt.

CR: Hat die Literatur auch eine moralische Aufgabe? Ich meine nicht sexuelle Moral, sondern eine humanitäre Aufgabe, oder kann sie eine haben?

UT: Ich denke nicht sehr an Moral. Moral ist immer etwas Vorgegebenes, ein Konsens, den die Gesellschaft hat. Das dürfte die Literatur in dem Sinn nicht haben, sondern sie müßte auch herrschende Moral in Frage stellen. Du sagst, nicht im Sinne der Sexualität, aber das gehört doch auch dazu. Sexualität, Verhaltensformen, die sind ja immer moralisch kodifiziert. Im Kopf zumindest, manchmal auch schriftlich. Und wenn sie dazu beiträgt, finde ich das problematisch. Moral im Sinne von human, da würde ich schon festhalten, daß Literatur immer ein grundsätzliches Recht auf Unversehrtheit des Lebens einklagt. Das heißt, sie schreibt gegen den Tod und gegen Verletzungen an. Es hängt damit zusammen, daß Literatur aus dieser Einmaligkeit heraus entsteht, die im menschlichen Leben liegt, und die durch den Tod erst gegeben wird. Wenn wir ewig leben, können wir alles wiederholen und könnten keine Fehler machen. Diese Einmaligkeit ist ganz wesentlich in der Zeitstruktur, die die Literatur aufnimmt. Insofern ist für mich gute Literatur etwas, das sich dagegen richtet, daß Menschen in irgendeiner Weise dehumanisiert oder gegängelt werden – etwas, das sich auch dagegen richtet, daß das Individuum so präpotent wird, daß es andere unterdrückt. Es ist immer dieses Moment der Freiheit drin, ein Anspruch auf Freiheit, und ein Anspruch, daß das Individuum nicht zerstört wird. Und wenn man das so versteht, dann ist Literatur eine Deklaration gegen Gewalt und Tod, eine Deklaration gegen Ideologien, die das

Individuum einschränken. Insofern hat es auch noch eine politische Funktion.

CR: Wie stehst Du in dem Fall dann zu Literatur, die das Gegenteil darstellt? Ich denke da an Bret Easton Ellis, oder Süskinds Grenouille in *Das Parfum* ...

UT: ... oder diesen Film *Natural Born Killers*. Das ist eine fatale Sache. Man muß so was natürlich auch schreiben dürfen, das darf man nicht eingrenzen. Aber das wäre wirklich nicht meine Literatur, denn die Täter – da müßte man wieder auf Kipphardt kommen – die Täter müssen immer auch als Opfer gezeigt werden, das heißt, daß Gesellschaft immer irgendwo auftauchen muß, die so etwas produziert. Also wenn man Eichmann, wie der Kipphardt das gemacht hat, für alle Massenmörder nimmt, dann muß man fragen, was die gesellschaftlichen Verhältnisse sind, die so was erst ermöglichen? Und das bedeutet immer auch, daß sie änderbar sind. Das ist das Humane daran, daß jemand nicht genetisch festgelegt ist, von Geburt an Killer zu sein, sondern daß es ein Umfeld gibt, das solche Menschen produziert. Diese Dialektik der Opfer und Täter interessiert mich. Ich erkenne noch die gesellschaftliche Relevanz der Literatur.

4

The Writer as Anthropologist: The Works of Uwe Timm

KEITH BULLIVANT

The great voyages of discovery of the last six hundred years, with but few exceptions, were colonial undertakings. The major aim was exploitation of the resources of new territories or, as in the slave trade, the exploitation of the natives themselves. The presence of the military, administrators, engineers and tradesmen led to an enforced and speedy Europeanization of the settled territories, with only the missionaries concerned in any way with the well-being of the natives, but even their position was but a more humane form of colonial re-education, as we might term it. Through this the representatives of the so-called civilized world hoped to liberate primitive people from the allegedly barbaric nature of their traditional mode of existence.

It was not until our present century that anthropologists began to study indigenous cultures threatened by the spread of the Eurocentric cultural attitudes and lifestyle of colonists throughout the great empires of Britain, France and the Netherlands, in particular. The last great voyages into the unknown on this planet were undertaken by ethnographers like Bronislaw Malinowski, Edward Evans-Pritchard, Margaret Mead and Ruth Benedict, who were concerned to document foreign cultures threatened with extinction and to preserve information about them for later generations. But even these pioneers were colonialists, in that their work and their attitude towards the various foreign cultures proceeded from a conviction as to the superiority of the cultural values of modern Western civilization and a belief in its inevitable triumph over these exotic primitive cultures. Only in the more recent post-colonial era has this basic attitude of anthropologists changed: in the last twenty years there have been very vigorous debates about the theoretical basis, the methodology and the writing style of

The Writer as Anthropologist

ethnological studies, in the context of which many of the very same texts were cited as those that figure in the theoretical debates about postmodernism and literature. That is one aspect of a recent congruence between the approach of anthropologists on the one hand and writers and theorists of literary practice on the other. The other aspect is a move by literature in the direction of the working methods and the stuff of anthropology. The first author who could be cited in this context would be the late Bruce Chatwin; in the context of contemporary German literature it would undoubtedly be Hubert Fichte, whose ethnographic treatment of his experiences in the Caribbean, South and Central America in *Xango* (1976) and *Petersilie* (1980) was followed in 1987 by the commencement of the posthumous publication of his enormous cycle *Die Geschichte der Empfindlichkeit*. The perspective of this enormous enterprise was widened even further by his incorporating into the cycle further observations on the gay cultural scene of Hamburg's St Pauli district that he had first addressed in his novel *Die Palette* (1968). Less well known is the anthropological bent in the work of Uwe Timm, and this is no doubt in part due to the fact that, unlike Hubert Fichte, he did not set out consciously to write about anthropology, despite the fact that he attended lectures by Claude Lévi-Strauss while a graduate student at the Sorbonne. This aspect of his work was entirely unconscious until Ted Norris, a friend and professor of anthropology at the University of Münster, drew his attention to it. Norris was, in fact, the first scholar to address this element in Timm's work[1], which Timm himself was to write about at length in his Paderborn Lectures, published in 1993 as *Erzählen und kein Ende*.

Uwe Timm's second novel *Morenga* was regarded at the time of its publication in 1978, and by no means incorrectly, as a significant example of the renewal of the historical novel that characterizes West German literature of that time; it was at the same time read – equally correctly – as having been consciously written against the tradition of the German colonial novel. The portrayal of the suppression of the natives and of the unscrupulous collaboration between German and English troops in the extermination of the rebellious Herero tribesmen under the leadership of Morenga was seen as continuing the anti-imperialist attitudes central to the student movement of the late sixties, and also as an act of solidarity with Swapo in Namibia, the former German South-West Africa in particular, and with all freedom fighters in the Third World in general. The novel was also championed by the protagonists of the avantgarde in literature because of its use of the montage-technique. No one seemed to notice the similarities between the narrative perspective and writings in modern ethnology. Unlike the traditional colonial novel and conventional anthropological reports, this novel is multi-perspectival: there are reports and observations from the military at home and in Africa, from members of the German Colonial Office, from the missionaries, from those with commercial interests in the new colony, as well as personal statements from the diaries of the veterinary surgeon Gottschalk and of Morenga himself. The Germans in Berlin and Windhoek are equally concerned only with the economic exploitation of the country, with people disagreeing only as to whether the extermination of the Hereros was inevitable if the country was to be successfully colonized, or whether it would make better economic sense to exploit them as useful working animals. The missionaries consider themselves to be the 'Träger der Kultur und Zivilisation', having a duty to replace the indigenous culture with that of Christian Western Europe. Gottschalk, the main protagonist of the novel, begins his tour of duty with the typical attitude of the would-be colonist on the look-out for a suitable farmstead, but rapidly finds himself questioning the entire colonial venture; he is unable to comprehend how a country can envisage colonializing another country 'wenn man sich nicht einmal die Mühe macht, die Eingeborenen zu verstehen' (*M*, 98). Under the influence of Kropotkin's *Mutual Help in Development* and the notes on it made by his former colleague Wenstrup, whose attitude has meanwhile forced him to desert, Gottschalk begins to observe what is going on around him very carefully and also starts to familiarize himself with the history of the beginnings of German colonialization in the region, not from official accounts, but from local oral historians. His observations amount to a deconstruction of his initial utopian dreams of life in the colony. He becomes increasingly alienated from his colleagues, who are in turn struck by his growing 'Verkafferung'; he eventually resigns and returns to Germany. The affinity with postmodern ethnology lies not only in the changed attitude of Gottschalk to the indigenous people, the rape of their culture and the whole colonial venture, but also in the combination of open ending and polyphonic style. Timm is not an omniscient narrator representing the values of Western Europe, but is a mediator for the voices of others, some of whom were condemned to silence in the time of empire. The style also involves the reader in the process of rediscovery.

After *Morenga* Timm published a sort of companion volume, *Deutsche Kolonien* (1981), an alternative photographic history of German colonial life, before turning in 1986 in *Der Schlangenbaum* from the ashes of the colonial dream to its modern-day equivalent, aid to developing countries, which also proceeds from the notion of the absolute supremacy of Western technology. Wagner, an engineer well known for rescuing troublesome projects, agrees to take over responsibility for finishing the building of a factory in a South American country. His life upon arrival has superficial similarities with the colonial one of earlier days, in that he is quartered with other foreign technical experts in a luxurious part of the city separated from the rest of town by a high wall. But he soon discovers that the similarities end there: the exclusive neighbourhood is a stronghold designed to defend the foreigners from the violent consequences of internal political unrest. He and the others are mercenaries in the pay of a corrupt regime. On the building site everything that Wagner attempts in his efforts to complete the project is condemned to failure. Then his Spanish teacher and sometime lover, through whom he had hoped to establish better contacts with workers and state administrators, disappears without trace. Finally, the incomplete factory building literally sinks in the mud, having been built, as the perplexed Wagner discovers, without adequate foundations. In the multi-faceted confrontation with the other, he is also confronted with himself, with his mind-set and his value-system as another, just as it happens, according to James Clifford, to contemporary ethnologists.[2] Wagner's inability to ward off disaster suggests that the premises on which developed countries offer aid are untenable. The obsession with modern technology takes account neither of the attitude of the local population nor of the terrain; no one asks what the real needs of the country are, but the Europeans unquestioningly assume they are identical with those of their own country. Wagner is confronted with an amazing symbol of such thinking when he rides over the high-tech bridge built years ago in the middle of the jungle and never connected to the highway network. The attitude of developed nations also takes no account of other forces at work in Third World countries. The rational mind can, of course, explain that the failure of the project was due to faulty design and corruption amongst senior local workers, but the local legend embodied in the title offers another interpretation. An unfathomable force makes Wagner drive over and kill the snake, an act that ruins any possibility of a good relationship with his superstitious workers. Local Indians had always said 'daß derjenige, der die Schlange tötet, ertrinken wird' (S, 127), and it can be argued that the man who Wagner had hitherto been and all he embodied drowns in the mud of the jungle along with the factory.

A particular feature of the work of postmodern ethnologists is that they not only examine foreign, primitive cultures for their otherness, but scrutinize their own in the same way. This started understandably enough here in the USA with the examination of Native American culture and later of immigrant culture. Such ethnologists operate without any sense of a set of normative cultural values; 'We need', states Paul Rabinow, 'to anthropologize the West: show how exotic its constitution of reality has been; emphasize those domains most taken for granted as universal [. . .]; make them seem as historically peculiar as possible'.[3] Recent years have correspondingly seen the emergence of the 'indigenous ethnologist'.[4] If we now look back at Uwe Timm's career we can see, in his first and third novels, *Heißer Sommer* (1974) and *Kerbels Flucht* (1980), to what extent the narrative consists in such voyages of discovery within his own country. The former examines the APO scene of 1968, the latter the existential problems of the 68ers after the 'Tendenzwende' of 1973. Even in *Heißer Sommer* there are signs of the multi-perspectival narration we noted in *Morenga* and this is continued in *Kerbels Flucht,* in which novel the diary of the protagonist again forms one of the major narrative strands. In these early works Timm anticipates one of the postulates of postmodern ethnology, according to which, so we are told by Michael M. J. Fischer, fictional autobiographies are particularly well suited to the examination of modern pluralist society.[5]

Another important source of information for the modern ethnologist is collective memory. In his fourth novel, *Der Mann auf dem Hochrad* (1984) Timm turns for the first time to the oral history of his own family, here used as a major source of a fictional account of life at a time of incipient change, the late nineteenth century, in Coburg, the residence of the Herzog von Sachsen-Coburg und Gotha. Through the work of Onkel Franz, the gifted taxidermist, we are confronted with the unchanged life of the local aristocracy, while his introduction of the bicycle or the 'Cyclisation' of Coburg, first by the penny-farthing, quickly to be superseded by the modern form we know that his business rivals introduce, mobilizes the citizens in more than the literal sense, destabilizes the still essentially feudal social structure and leads to the abdication of the local nobility in 1918. Timm's generation of a consciously exaggerated literary model that graphically illustrates the rapid social change that Germany underwent around the turn of the century has, according to Ted Norris, many similarities with ethnological examinations of the effects of aid to developing countries.

In the nineties the focus of Timm's publications turns to the Federal Republic and this is also a time when he formulates in *Erzählen und kein Ende* his notion of 'everyday aesthetics', which he sees as being essentially ethnographic in nature. Writers, he says – using the plural form, although he is clearly talking personally – are concerned:

> das Alltägliche mit dem Blick des Fremden zu sehen, [...] mit dem genauen, forschenden Blick des engagierten Ethnographen. Diese wundersame Reise führt mit der Sprache in das eigene Bewußtsein. Die gewöhnlichen Dinge als ungewöhnlich sehen, der vertrauten Sprache unvertraut begegnen, nahe Menschen – also auch sich selbst – von fern betrachten und darüber erzählen [...] (*EkE*, 144)

This ethnographic perspective characterizes both Timm's novella *Die Entdeckung der Currywurst* (1993), set in the working-class world of Hamburg towards the end of the Second World War, and his latest novel *Johannisnacht* (1996), set in a changing Berlin Mitte, but is most clearly observable in *Kopfjäger* (1991), on which I shall here briefly focus, a novel the ambiguous title of which immediately suggests such a perspective: cannibalism is, after all, one of the favourite topics of anthropologists.

The story of the massive embezzlement of stockbroker Peter Walter, his arrest, escape from prison and flight to various allegedly safe foreign havens, culminating in his arrest on Easter Island, represents, according to the sub-title of the novel, a 'Bericht aus dem Inneren des Landes'. Its topic is, one could argue, everyday cannibalism in the Federal Republic, cannibalism in the sense of the striving for maximum profit at the expense of others. Walter promises his customers huge potential profits in the futures market but siphons off most of the funds into his own Luxemburg bank account. Most investors have more money than they know what to do with, they crave excitement and therefore accept the unwritten rules of the game, accepting the risk of huge losses in the hope of the big pay-day. Walter is clearly one of the 'Desperados', who, according to Timm, 'auf einer kritischen Distanz zum Zeitgeist bleibt und das Gewöhnliche ungewöhnlich zeigt [...]. Diese Haltung ist jenem kritischen, subversiven Erzählen im Alltag vergleichbar, das sich mit dem Lauf der Dinge nicht einverstanden erklärt' (EkE, 110). But Walter is also a lay anthropologist with a particular interest in Easter Island. One of the narrative strands of the novel, which is written in narrative blocks on Walter's laptop while he is on the run, consists of his notes on the mysterious island. A number of similarities between the indigenous culture of the island and that of the Federal Republic are striking, such as the search for ways of coping with boredom, but it is concern with the concept of exploitation in the context of Easter Island that offers a sort of parallel text to the main story. He is particularly interested in the local concept of theft at the time of the discovery of the island by the Europeans, which he views 'als eine Art Geschenk [...], das den Beschenkten und den Schenkenden verbindet, man ist zu Gegengeschenken verpflichtet. Auch der Fremde kann sich ja etwas nehmen' (K, 32). Thus the islanders shamelessly stole things off the Europeans under the assumption that they would in turn take what they wanted, in this case their pleasure with the local women. But the Europeans, who felt that they could take the women in primitive countries as and when they liked without any form of payment, and who also did not understand the local rules governing exchanges, viewed theft and petty deceptions by the islanders as theft in the European sense, reacted with force and soon imposed rigid control on the natives. Such a way of interpreting the ground rules on Easter Island, which in turn explains the swift outbreak of violence after the discovery of the island as having been caused by 'Spielverderber', spoilsports, i.e. the Europeans, can then be applied very easily and appositely to the relationship between Walter and his clients. They have money enough for a comfortable life, but are bored and therefore very ready to enter into a highly risky speculative venture that might pay off, but which is above all exhilarating. Apart from the excitement he brings to their lives, Walter also diverts them with his amazing stories, offering as his counter-trade his role as storyteller, as would have happened in less advanced societies with a reliance on oral literature. Significantly, Walter's activities are only blown when a small-time speculator, who needs to get at least his initial capital back and who is therefore playing by a different set of rules than the other clients, who is in effect a 'spoilsport', reports Walter to the police.

What then, let us now ask, does Uwe Timm seek to achieve with this sort of writing? *Morenga*, an important example of the post-colonial novel in Germany, had tremendous impact in Africa, drawing the attention of Swapo to one of its then unknown and unsung heroes. Since then it has been the focus of much attention by South African Germanists.[6] In Germany it had particular impact through the TV film version of the novel, the premiere of which in 1985 was preceded by scenes of incredible police violence in a South African township. *Der Schlangenbaum*, which received a mixed and rather muted reception in Germany, met with a far greater and essentially very positive response in the United States, a country that has (effectively) far more post-colonial experience in South America than Germany; *Kerbels Flucht* is a deeply insightful treatment of the post-68 world of the protagonists of the student movement that goes so much further than Peter Schneider's much better known *Lenz*, and this again achieved heightened impact through a TV film version. The fictional world of *Der Mann auf dem Hochrad*, of Walter's stories and those from the 'Wohnküche' of the narrator's aunt in *Kopfjäger,* as well as those of Frau Brücker in *Currywurst*, perhaps the best examples of Timm's indigenous ethnology, are vibrant in a way that contrasts with and is at times subversive of normal bourgeois existence, particularly in the modern day. The passion of Onkel Franz's campaign on behalf of the aesthetic advantages of the inherently impractical penny-farthing is in stark contrast to the purposive rationality of the technological age that was then dawning and in which we live. The evocation of life in the Kiez of Hamburg in both *Kopfjäger* and *Currywurst* brings back to life an almost forgotten world based on community and mutual support, rather than exploitation and profit, a world of individuality, rather than the uniformly chic. Both too bring out the vitality of oral culture in a pre-TV era. In these works our modern world is, as Paul Rabinow demanded, anthropologized as a historically peculiar value system based on exploitation and confronted with alternative values. By doing this Timm hopes to go some way towards breaking the 'momentan allgemeine[n] und zugleich lähmende[n] Konsens' as to the profit motive and to generate a 'kritische, eine radikal subjektive Wahrnehmung des Alltäglichen' (*EkE*, 110) in the mind of his reader that might possibly lead to a quizzical attitude towards the given and seemingly self-evident.

Notes

[1] Cf. his 'Literatur und Ethnologie des 20. Jahrhunderts: Hubert Fichte, Bruce Chatwin und Uwe Timm', in K. Bullivant, Manfred Durzak and Hartmut Steinecke (eds.), *Die Archäologie der Wünsche. Studien zum Werk von Uwe Timm* (Cologne, Kiepenheuer & Witsch, 1995), 267-90.

[2] In his introduction to J. Clifford and G. E. Marcus (eds.), *Writing Culture: The Poetics and Politics of Ethnography* (Los Angeles, London, University of California Press, 1986), 23. The later reference to James Clifford is also taken from this introduction.

[3] Rabinow, 'Representations are Social Facts', in Clifford and Marcus, 241.

[4] James Clifford, 9.

[5] Fischer, 'Ethnicity and the Post-Modern Arts of Memory', in Clifford and Marcus, 195.

[6] Cf. in particular Gunther Pakendorf, 'Morenga oder Geschichte als Fiktion', *Acta Germanica*, 19 (1988), 144–58, Peter Horn, 'Fremdsprache und Fremderlebnis. Dr. Johannis Gottschalks Lernprozeß in Uwe Timms 'Morenga'', *Jahrbuch Deutsch als Fremdsprache*, 14 (1988), 75–91, and Peter Horn, 'Über die Schwierigkeit, einen Standpunkt einzunehmen. Zu Uwe Timms *Morenga*', in *Die Archäologie der Wünsche*, 93–118.

5

'Uwe Timm oder unsicher in die 70er Jahre':
Heißer Sommer and *Kerbels Flucht*

RHYS W. WILLIAMS

The idyll with which Uwe Timm's *Heißer Sommer* ends is one which sustains its hero, Ullrich Krause, throughout the sentimental and political education to which he is exposed in the novel. Reconciled with his politically active friend Petersen, he recalls a childhood experience:

> Ich bin früher gern rausgefahren, gleich nach Schulschluß. Ich habe an einem Waldrand im Gras gelegen und stundenlang in den Himmel gesehen. Ich habe dann an nichts gedacht. Nur manchmal, wenn in der Luft ein Bussard schwebte und plötzlich zur Erde herunterkippte, war das wie ein Stich. Fressen und Gefressenwerden. Ich hab versucht, mir vorzustellen, wie das wäre, eine Welt, in der niemand gequält würde. Ein ruhiges, anhaltendes Glück wie in einem heißen Sommer, wenn man in einer tiefen Wiese liegt und über sich die Wolken ziehen sieht. Als ich älter wurde, habe ich nicht mehr daran denken mögen. Da war dann dieses Wort Kitsch dazwischen. (*HS*, 309–10)

The components of Ullrich's habitual responses to experience are all present here: a naïve delight in sensuous experience, a desire to escape the burden of consciousness, the tendency to interpret all experience as implicitly ideological, as symptomatic of power relationships, and an awareness that a sensitivity to nature can all so easily be dismissed as kitsch. But what is perhaps more striking is that Timm here employs a motif which Peter Handke had employed to quite different effect in *Die Angst des Tormanns beim Elfmeter* (1970). Through Bloch, the eponymous goalkeeper, Handke is more concerned to register the semiotic or epistemological implications of a similar perception:

> Über einem Feld sah er einen Habicht kreisen. Als der Habicht dann auf der Stelle flatterte und herabstieß, fiel Bloch auf, daß er nicht das Flattern und Herabstoßen des Vogels beobachtet hatte, sondern die Stelle im Feld, auf die der Vogel wohl herabstoßen würde; der Habicht hatte sich im Sturzflug gefangen und war wieder aufgestiegen.[1]

While Handke confronts the dissociation of sensibility in which habitual expectations and anticipations are confounded, but which is wholly free of political implications in the widest sense, Timm insists on the ideological dimension. Small wonder that Timm should have attacked Handke roundly for his 'Manier [...], stets neue Methoden, neue Modelle zu finden, ohne deren Inhalt zu berücksichtigen'.[2] For Timm, Handke's refusal to confront the socio-political implications of language, represents the antithesis of his own literary project: 'Daß Handke nach einer solchen freiwilligen Beschränkung auf Sprachstrukturen auch keine Möglichkeit sieht, daß Literatur Alternativen zu bestehenden gesellschaftlichen Zuständen leisten könnte, daß sie also nicht diese historische Situation zu transzendieren vermag, ist nur konsequent'.[3] Yet, for all Timm's irritation at Handke's steadfast refusal to confront political realities, he is drawn to certain features of Handke's writing. Timm's central characters share the sensitivity to language and to perception displayed by Handke's; his figures, too, react unexpectedly to external stimulus and display a hypersensitivity to apparently trivial experiences, to the consternation of those around them. What is different, of course, is that Timm's characters, for all their 'Innerlichkeit', for all their obsession with ways in which their consciousness is structured, are ultimately driven by political imperatives, even if their openness to experience suggests that they are as concerned with their own psychological adaptability as with revolutionary action.

In his essay 'Zwischen Unterhaltung und Aufklärung'[4] Timm approaches the issue of Peter Handke, clearly a major irritant for him at this time, from a slightly different perspective. Defining a 'systemkonforme Unterhaltungsliteratur' ranging from Simmel at one extreme to Handke at the other, Timm concedes that, while the former offers 'die heile Romanwelt als Ersatzbefriedigung für die kaputte Freie Welt', the latter does seek 'mit seinen literarischen Innovationen bestimmte Erkenntnisse zu vermitteln'.[5] Nevertheless, Handke's failure lies in his theoretical intention 'die Irritation nur im sprachlichen Bereich, in der literarischen Methode aufzuzeigen, ohne daß dabei deren soziale Bedingtheit erkennbar würde'.⁶ It is not too fanciful to define Timm's own literary aspiration as that of seeking to extend into the socio-political that irritation which Handke had confined to language. Indeed, later in the same essay he offers the alternative model of an 'Unterhaltungsliteratur' which is subversive:

> Aufgabe der Literatur wäre es, darzustellen, was der Entfaltung des Menschen zur Betätigung der menschlichen Wirklichkeit entgegensteht, das wäre die aufklärerische Funktion der Literatur, die sie mit der Theorie teilt, zugleich aber könnte sie unmittelbar Phantasie und Emotionen ansprechen – was die Theorie kaum kann; sie könnte zeigen, wie sich die menschlichen Fähigkeiten frei entfalten können, indem sie Sehen, Hören, Riechen, Schmecken, Fühlen, Denken, Anschauen, Empfinden, Wollen, Tätigsein, Lieben in ihrer Darstellung aufnimmt und sie der deformierten Wirklichkeit entgegenstellt. Literatur wird damit eine Utopie artikulieren [. . .]⁷

Timm defines his potential novel as 'sowohl aufklärerisch als auch unterhaltend', as a 'negative Bildungsroman', which would depict 'den Weg eines Individuums, das aus seiner borniert Vereinzelung zu einem kollektiven Bewußtsein gelangt, in einem Kollektiv lebt und arbeitet'.⁸ Here we have as precise a description as possible of Timm's own reflections on the novel form as he was embarking on *Heißer Sommer*. He clearly acknowledges Handke's success in exploring ways of registering the stream of information which presses itself upon the consciousness, and he is also drawn towards an appreciation of the ways in which popular culture, television, the cinema, advertising and pop-music, inform contemporary experience; what he refuses to accept is Handke's exclusion of a utopian vision. His alternative project is unambiguously political: 'Literatur, die versucht, die gesellschaftlichen Widersprüche darzustellen an Menschen, die solche Widersprüche erfahren, muß selbstverständlich die Isolation zeigen, aber auch die Möglichkeit der Solidarität'.⁹ Timm's *Heißer Sommer*, then, is conceived as an exemplar. It is constructed with the express purpose of demonstrating a political possibility. Whether it succeeds in this aim is more questionable, for in many ways Timm is a child of his time. He succeeds far more convincingly in conveying the isolation, the subjectivity, of his central character, than in awakening much enthusiasm for the collective.

The outward action of *Heißer Sommer* is unproblematic: the central character, Ullrich Krause, from whose perspective the narrative unfolds, experiences three key political events: the shooting of Benno Ohnesorg on 2 June 1967 and the resulting political demonstrations in Munich; the growing politicization of the Hamburg SDS, and the Springer blockade, culminating in the assassination attempt on Rudi Dutschke on 11 April 1968; and the campaign against the Emergency Legislation in 1968, which prompts Ullrich to seek work in a factory, to join a union and to return to Munich to become a trainee teacher. Ullrich embarks, at the end of the novel, on 'the long march through the institutions' advocated by Dutschke.[10] While these political events form the framework, each phase in Ullrich's development is accompanied by private and intensely personal experiences. As if in response to Marcuse's dictum that 'the personal is the political', Ullrich breaks off a relationship with Ingeborg (whose abortion requires him to work as a labourer), seduces with cynical ease 'die Blondine' Gaby, and falls in love with the North German Christa, a factor which (we assume) helps to shape his desire to study in Hamburg. On his arrival in Hamburg, the personal begins to take second place to the political, and Ullrich, after a disastrous visit to Christa's parents, seeks his pleasure with Alice, before beginning a relationship with Renate, whose unconventional style attracts him during his hippy phase but alienates him when he begins to involve himself in the world of work. His return to Munich finds him on good terms with Ingeborg, Christa and Renate, but involved with none of them. Solidarity, it seems, does not yet encompass relations with the opposite sex.

Heißer Sommer has frequently been located within the peculiarly German tradition of the 'Bildungsroman'.[1] While Timm's book deals merely with a small phase in the education of its hero, it certainly leaves the hero on the threshold of social integration. Yet the 'Bildung' in this case is extraordinarily truncated. Nothing in Ullrich's early life prepares him for the changes which will occur in society. It is social and ideological change which the novel foregrounds, rather than merely the adjustments of the central character. Moreover, the process of education is anything but organic; Ullrich rebels against all the values with which he is confronted. His political and emotional development, his 'éducation sentimentale', actually presupposes less the accommodation of the central character to the world, than the perception that the central character cannot accommodate himself to such a world and wishes to change it. The 'Bildungsroman' model proves to be an irritant, even an affront. Yet there is progress in the novel. Ullrich begins his studies of German literature in Munich with an unstated conviction that his academic work will lead him to an understanding of the world in which he lives. He swiftly realizes that the 'Ordinarienuniversität' is predicated on privilege and power: a whole section (Chapter 5, Part One) is devoted to the ritual of a seminar; another section (Chapter 9, Part One) to the tyranny exercised by Professor Betz, whose name is pronounced with a long vowel, over his students; yet another section (Chapter 11, Part One) to Ullrich's desperate efforts to gain an extension for his essay on the various versions of two Hölderlin odes from Professor Ziegler. The self-abasement and embarrassment which Ullrich experiences is given a delightful twist by its juxtaposition with another set of reactions: viewing the vapour trail of a jet plane, Ullrich is asked by Christa whether it is a Starfighter. His response covers both the notoriously fallible aeroplane and the complacent Professor: 'Genau wissen wir es erst dann, wenn das Ding abstürzt' (HS, 88).

Ullrich experiences annoyance, even alienation, from his studies in Munich; at this time the world of work is significant (it occupies by far the longest section of Part One), but it is merely casual labour, unregulated, non-unionized, and pure exploitation. Ullrich undertakes it solely to pay off the debts which he has incurred for Ingeborg's abortion. In Part Two his self-absorption is diminished. While he is still engaged in academic activity, public events play an increasingly important part in his life. Ullrich's involvement in public protest in Hamburg offers the first inkling of acceptance: 'Jetzt war er angekommen' (HS, 199). This insight is a prelude to a more profound self-understanding; he suddenly recognizes

> den Grund für seinen Haß, für seine Einsamkeit, seine Ziellosigkeit, seine Angst, seine Lügen, seine Gehässigkeit, für sein Aufschneiden, seinen Neid und immer wieder für die Lügen.
> Das war veränderbar. (HS, 202)

The final section of the novel takes Ullrich through a process of self-discovery. His initial inclination is self-indulgence, a drug-induced alternative reality: 'Jetzt seh ich alles ganz neu, sagte er. Endlich kann man das machen, was Spaß macht' (HS, 219). Throughout this section Petersen operates as a kind of socialist conscience. While Ullrich places all the emphasis on changing his perception of things, Petersen retains a conviction that social change is possible. Ullrich's question: 'Wenn wir uns nicht selbst ändern, was soll sich dann ändern?' *(HS,* 227), suggests that he is still immersed in his own personal journey of self-discovery. Initially, Ullrich confines his quest for social integration to a private sphere; he seeks 'mit anderen zusammenzuwohnen' *(HS,* 228); but gradually he regains a sense of his social roots, partly because he encounters in Renate's family a set of social values which he finds uncongenial. Ullrich becomes increasingly obsessed with the industrial proletariat as a social force: initially he seeks to bring an 'Agit-prop' theatre to the workers, but gradually the realization dawns that he must involve himself in the practice of work, not least because he earns the right to condemn capitalism only when he turns himself into its victim. Ullrich's involvement, however superficial and temporary, gives him the confidence to speak with first-hand experience about exploitation: '[es] war ihm, als sei er nach einem langen Marsch ans Ziel gekommen' *(HS,* 276). On this basis alone can he make the decision to embark on a career as a teacher, though, given Ullrich's extreme volatility, the reader is entitled to wonder whether this resolve will be anything but a passing fancy.

One of the key factors in Ullrich's development is his relationship with his father. While *Heißer Sommer* is not normally subsumed under the category of 'Vaterliteratur', it prefigures that literary fashion. If Ullrich has the tendency to dismiss all forms of authoritarian behaviour as 'fascist', this may be understandable in the light of his father's obsessive preoccupation with his war on the Russian front *(HS,* 14, 44), his early membership of the SA *(HS,* 92), the volumes of Simmel and Dwinger which rub shoulders with Goethe and Schiller in the family bookcase. The episode when Ullrich returns home with Christa serves as a reminder of the parental values from which he seeks escape. His father's war memories *(HS,* 101) and stereotypical judgements on foreigners trigger in Ullrich reflections on an alternative German past, on Albrecht and his resistance to National Socialism. Ullrich's Chistmas visit from Hamburg prompts a radical break with his father *(HS,* 152) and memories of the petty tyrannies which he had to endure as a child. What prompts the quarrel, as Ullrich reports to his friends, is his father's sentimentality about the war:

> Sein Vater habe gesagt, damals habe man noch Weihnachten feiern
> können oder so ähnlich. Er habe ihn daraufhin gefragt, wann das ge-
> wesen sei. Unvergeßlich, habe sein Vater gesagt und dabei zum
> Weihnachtsbaum hinübergesehen, unvergeßlich sei ihm die letzte
> Kriegsweihnacht geblieben, vierundvierzig, damals.
> Da hab ich ihn angeschrien. Ich hab gesagt, er solle doch nach Vietnam
> fahren, da hätte er seine Kriegsweihnacht. (HS, 158)

The father makes an attempt at reconciliation when he visits Ullrich the following summer, but despite Ullrich's pleasure at the visit, his uncompromising reactions to his father's questions, particularly the comments about money, prompt what seems to be a final rupture of their relationship. The question of his family background continues to preoccupy him; during a visit to Renate's parents, their relative wealth triggers in Ullrich a sense of his own family's social failure. He recounts his father's ambitions, the disastrous deal with the kidney-shaped tables, his father's unshaken belief in the bourgeois virtues of self-reliance and thrift. The embarrassment of Renate's parents at Ullrich's bitterness signals the beginning of the end for his relationship with Renate: what distinguishes Renate's family from his own is not ideology, so much as success; the exemplary failure of his own father enables Ullrich to link the National Socialist past and its values with the ideals and goals of the West German consumer society in the early 1970s. Ullrich's rage against his father is born out of a sense that his father is the dupe of a social system through which he, Ullrich, can see so clearly.

Although *Heißer Sommer* has been criticized[12] as a programmatic propagation of the author's own political convictions, there is a subtlety in the writing which critics have been slower to appreciate. Timm exploits the literary possibilities of Ullrich's seminar paper on Hölderlin to excellent effect. Ullrich first cites Hölderlin's 'Der blinde Sänger' immediately after Ingeborg's sudden departure:

> Das Herz ist wach, doch bannt und hält in
> Heiligem Zauber die Nacht mich immer. (HS, 9)

But the text continues: 'Hemmt die erstaunende Nacht mich immer, sagte Ullrich. Wieso erstaunt die Nacht?' (HS, 9). What Ullrich asks refers, not to the lines cited in the text, but to a later reference in the poem:

Das Herz ist wieder wach, doch bannt und
Hemmt die unendliche Nacht mich immer.[13]

Ullrich is remembering imperfectly, recalling the second not the first quotation and transposing 'erstaunende' for 'unendliche'. Small wonder that he is finding his seminar paper difficult to complete. Yet the poem, curiously enough, evokes nature as experienced by the blind singer in his youth ('da ich ein Jüngling war'); and it is an image of nature perceived when he was young which represents the recurrent idyll for Ullrich himself, as the first and last lines of the novel indicate: 'In einer Wiese liegen, stellte sich Ullrich vor. In der hereinbrechenden Dämmerung die aufsteigende feuchte Kühle spüren' *(HS, 7)*. It is the 'Professorengequatsche über Hölderlin' *(HS, 11)* which alienates Ullrich; the poetry itself finds its way into his consciousness and begins to shape his perceptions. As he wanders through Munich past the illuminated windows of the wealthy, the lines from Hölderlin's 'An die Hoffnung' are interpolated into the text: 'Und über mir die immerfrohen Blumen, die blühenden Sterne, glänzen' *(HS, 19)*, appropriate for the hour, though less relevant to his relationship with Ingeborg, for which all hope seems lost. In the episode with Walter, Ullrich recounts that he had initially wanted to interpret Hölderlin's 'Die Liebe', and manages to recall a verse more or less accurately (though 'Volks' appears in Timm's text as 'Volkes'). The irony that Ullrich should be so drawn to Hölderlin's poem, even as he is embarking on a series of casual affairs, is not lost on the reader. This particular verse is repeated on the occasion of a later seminar, as Ullrich listens to the interpretation of the poem by another student. That it is cited twice *(HS, 28 and 57)* underlines both Ullrich's quest for love and his failure to experience it; that the poem is not given to him to interpret underlines his exclusion. The eighth chapter includes three quotations from secondary literature on Hölderlin. Each is carefully related to Ullrich's current and future situation. 'Dichterisch war diese Periode sehr unproduktiv, schon weil Hölderlin noch im Bereich des "Abstrakten" angesiedelt blieb' *(HS, 54)*; this statement reinforces the connection between lack of productivity and abstraction, a motif which invokes the futility of Ullrich's academic work, as well as his later decision to abandon the abstract discussion of political ideology for the world of work.[14] The second quotation: 'Der Dichter versteht sich als Vorbote der kommenden Göttereinkehr' (*HS*, 55), underlines the utopian project which Ullrich pursues, while the final quotation refers only to Hölderlin's latter years and mental illness, betokening a failure to mediate between a highly personal vision and a mundane reality.

While the preoccupation with Hölderlin is ever-present in the first part of the novel, its importance gradually diminishes, without ever being totally expunged. When Ullrich escapes from Munich with Christa and they sit, dangling their feet in the river in Bamberg, a long quotation from the first section of Hölderlin's 'Brot und Wein' is interpolated. The rural idyll conjured up by the poem is matched by the potential fulfilment for Ullrich: 'Wir sollten hier bleiben, schlug Ullrich vor, irgendwo in einem Dorf übernachten' (*HS*, 86). Christa's refusal dissolves the dream, but the literary associations haunt their relationship: they met during a thunderstorm and an echo of Werther's meeting with Lotte is recognized by both of them. The Bamberg interlude closes with another literary association. Enquiring of Ullrich why he has suddenly decided to leave Munich and continue his studies in Hamburg, she utters the words: 'Und jedem Anfang wohnt ein Zauber inne', a line from Hermann Hesse's poem 'Stufen'.[15] She is clearly referring to Ullrich's hopes of a new beginning in Hamburg, rather than hinting of any new possibilities in their relationship. Ullrich is enough of a Germanist to spot that this iambic pentameter is literature, but his failure to identify the writer seems to mark the limits of their relationship:

> Schiller, fragte Ullrich.
> Nein, sie schüttelte den Kopf, kalt, sehr kalt sogar. Das ist aus einem Hesse-Gedicht. (*HS*, 93)

The involuntary humour of this misunderstanding should not be overlooked.[16]

The Hölderlin associations are taken up again when Christa leaves Ullrich's parents' house: Christa's perfume and its 'blumiger Geruch' bring to Ullrich's mind the third stanza of 'Die Liebe', which is cited in full (though the omission of 'doch' in the third line plays havoc with the metre).[17] Perhaps, the reader is invited to speculate, this relationship will bring the love that Ullrich is seeking. Although the Hölderlin associations which are paramount in the first part of the novel are largely absent in Parts Two and Three, Ullrich's sense of belonging and fulfilment when he participates in the SDS demonstration at the end of Part Two is also evoked by a quotation from 'Die Liebe'. Moreover, the lines quoted have appeared in *Heißer Sommer* twice before *(HS,* 28, 57) and now acquire a structural significance. Even the reader unfamiliar with Hölderlin's poetry will by now have been drawn into the process of reminiscence and will recall, on the second occasion, Ullrich's earlier sense of unfulfilment.[18]

If Hölderlin quotations (all clearly signposted by being placed in italics) predominate in Part One, Part Two is marked by a breaking down of the disparity between high and low culture, between literature and politics. As Ullrich continues his studies, attending a seminar on Kleist, he works on a seminar paper on Kleist's language. Only one italicized passage is devoted to Kleist: 'Auch Achill ist bewußtseinsabwesend, weil völlig gefühlsarm, ohne jeden Kontakt mit dem, was um ihn geschieht, nichts hörend ...' *(HS,* 126).[19] Here again, Achilles becomes a cipher to Ullrich in his as yet unfulfilled desire for access to the political activity which surrounds him in Hamburg. But, perhaps as evidence that Ullrich is neglecting his studies in favour of politics, Kleist disappears from the novel, to reappear only once more, in gold letters on the leather spine of an edition on the bookshelves of Christa's father. Even as Herr Carriere (the name a none too subtle hint of his function as a reproach to Ullrich) confesses that he reads Kleist 'auch heute noch mit Faszination und Gewinn', Ullrich is forced to recognize: 'Er würde den Schein nicht bekommen' *(HS,* 169). But dominating the early chapters of Part Two are six quotations from Herbert Marcuse, all taken from his two-volume collection *Kultur und Gesellschaft*.[20] His reading of Marcuse appears to be a crucial factor in the development of Ullrich's radical views, for Marcuse's arguments are placed in Ullrich's mouth as he debates ethics and revolution with Bungert (who advances the same positive views on Carl Schmitt which Marcuse attacks in his essay 'Der Kampf gegen den Liberalismus in der totalitäten Staatsauffassung' from the same volume). Two further sets of quotations characterize Part Two: subversive graffiti referring to Eiffe[21] der Bär, which are scattered throughout, and a series of instructions for demonstrators, which occupy only the last chapter of Part Two. Clearly, popular culture and a new critical approach to society mark this phase in Ullrich's development.

The third part of the novel is marked by a further shift of emphasis. The quotations are most frequently from pop music (Bob

Dylan, the Beatles and the Rolling Stones). Occasionally, Timm seems to be guessing at the words of the songs: 'I don't have the strings to get up' should clearly be 'the strength' *(HS, 207, 232)*, 'jealous' appears as 'jalous' *(HS, 207)* and Sergeant Pepper as 'Sargent' *(HS, 212)*. While the pop culture of the late sixties offers a kind of background music, it also has a thematic function; Ullrich is initially seduced by drugs and pop music into a phase of detached and self-indulgent indolence; as he emerges from this phase through his work in the factory, he becomes irritated by the very records which he had previously admired. Ullrich is now working on a third seminar paper: 'Die Arbeiterliteratur der zwanziger Jahre im Spiegel der Kritik' *(HS, 213)*, a paper which he again finds it impossible to complete, despite Petersen's helpful advice to base his conclusion on an essay by Johannes R. Becher.[22] The final set of quotations signals Ullrich's new-found political commitment to communism: Chapter Eleven contains four lengthy quotations *(HS, 279, 282, 291, 293)* from Lenin's essay *What is to be done?*, all of relevance to Ullrich's own predicament. Further references to Marx *(HS, 221)*, Mao *(HS, 292)* and to Markovic's *Dialektik der Praxis (HS, 273)* suggest that Ullrich is undergoing a political education which is more thorough-going than is explicitly stated in the novel. The reader, too, is given a vicarious political education by the inclusion of the snippets within the novel.

Timm uses quotation to convey to the reader the content of Ullrich's consciousness and the phases of his development and to evoke the cultural atmosphere of the late 1960s. Like Peter Handke he is concerned to register the multifarious information which streams in upon the consciousness; but unlike Handke, Timm attempts a political interpretation of that information. While Handke's goalkeeper seeks to relate signs to meaning, Timm's Ullrich is more concerned to explore the sociological and political implications of the cultural signs which surround him. In both cases the consciousness of the central character is used to register the confused data which the empirical world supplies, but while Handke's figure struggles to make sense of experience, Ullrich has no such difficulty; his problem is to deconstruct experience in order to reveal its ideological implications. Both writers present central characters who react to experience impulsively, but for different reasons: Handke's goalkeeper because he misinterprets signs, because he has lost the habitual and conventional confidence in signs; Timm's character, because he is aware of the fact that, behind the habitual and trivial, there lies an ideological manipulation. The moment in Handke's novel when Bloch murders the woman seems unmotivated, an 'acte gratuit': 'Plötzlich würgte er sie.'[23] Ullrich is equally sudden in his reactions, but for wholly different reasons. The adverb 'plötzlich' dominates the novel:

> Er hatte sie absichtlich verletzt, das wurde ihm plötzlich quälend bewußt (HS, 12)
> Er fühlte sich plötzlich beobachtet, wie im Zoo (HS, 20)
> Ullrich spürte plötzlich Hunger (HS, 22)
> Ullrich spürte, wie ihm plötzlich heiß wurde (HS, 22)
> Das plötzliche Würgen (HS, 41)
> Ullrich kam sich plötzlich lächerlich vor (HS, 56)
> Die Arbeit [. . .] war ihm plötzlich läppisch [. . .] vorgekommen (HS, 57)
> Ullrich mußte plötzlich alles rechtfertigen (HS, 144)
> Er kam sich plötzlich wie entblößt vor (HS, 149)
> Sie hatten sich plötzlich angeschrien, Ullrich und sein Vater (HS, 152)
> Ullrich lachte plötzlich, ein kurzes wütendes Lachen (HS, 166)
> Ullrich denkt plötzlich an Springer (HS, 200)

In many of these instances Ullrich's reaction is connected to social embarrassment, to anger at his own failure to see through the social mechanisms of oppression and manipulation. His sensitivity to shame and embarrassment makes him an ideal vehicle by which Timm can expose what he sees as the false consciousness of bourgeois society.

Heißer Sommer is a more ironic and funnier novel than many critics have been prepared to concede. The account of the sit-in, which occupies the second chapter of Part Two, is a sustained and witty exposé of the contradictions inherent in the student movement. Of the idealism of the young, their genuine belief in the utopian vision of 'ein realisierbares Glück für alle: Eine befriedete Welt, eine Welt ohne Ausbeutung und Unterdrückung' (HS, 160), there can be little doubt. But the idealism is so often juxtaposed with the tawdry realities of the everyday that it is relativized and undermined. The revolution remains a verbal one (as attested by the many quotations); direct action degenerates into farce. As they embark on their effort to set alight a car near the police station, they miscalculate grotesquely; the petrol bottle has too small a neck and takes an age to empty, the lookout suffers from an inability to whistle, and the getaway car fails to start. The net result is a lightly singed police car and the indignity of having to cut Bully's hair, so that when he turns up to reclaim the abandoned car he will not be taken for a student. Demonstrations become street theatre; street theatre replaces political activity; the reader is left wondering whether Ullrich's return to Munich and his decision to become a teacher will indeed resolve the tension between theory and practice. For all the irony of *Heißer Sommer*, Timm was later to concede that it sprang from his conviction that 'Literatur habe eine wichtige Bedeutung bei einer Veränderung der Gesellschaft zu mehr Gerechtigkeit, Gleichheit und Freiheit' (*EkE*, 111).

If parts of *Heißer Sommer* seemed to suggest that they were conceived as a literary response to Handke's *Die Angst des Tormanns beim Elfmeter*, then *Kerbels Flucht* (1980) could be seen as a counterpart to Handke's *Wunschloses Unglück* (1972). There are, of course, differences: Handke permits his narrator to recollect his mother's life after her suicide and to reflect on the process of writing as he turns her life and death into prose; Timm unites both functions in Christian Kerbel, who reflects on loss, after his relationship with K. comes to an end, but who is himself heading for suicide. He is both the narrator of loss and the person whose death will be recounted. Yet many of the concerns are shared: Kerbel's attempts to write about loss are, like Handke's narrator's efforts, self-centred: 'Ich will über sie schreiben, aber was mir einfällt, bin ich' (*KF*, 28). Handke's title is echoed on a number of occasions: Kerbel reports a fairy tale: 'Eines Nachts wachte ein Mann auf und, nachdem er zu Sinnen gekommen war, merkte er, daß ihm etwas fehlte. Man hat ihm seine Wünsche gestohlen' (*KF*, 91); and later in the text, under the title 'Wunschkonzert' the following: 'Der Wunsch, außer mir zu sein. Der Wunsch, in mir zu sein. Der Wunsch, da zu sein, wo ich (gerade) nicht bin' (*KF*, 164). The epigraphs which precede Handke's text are also echoed at the start of Timm's: Handke quotes Bob Dylan and the characteristic opening of Patricia Highsmith's *A Dog's Ransom*: 'It was just after 7 p.m., and the month was October.'[24] Timm ends his first section with: 'Es war kurz nach neun und der 19. April' (*KF*, 7), and loses no time in informing us that Karin 'wußte, als wir uns kennenlernten, jedes Lied von Bob Dylan auswendig' (*KF*, 10).

The echoes of Handke (and the counter-strategy of offering social or psychological explanation for what Handke viewed merely as semiotic) is but a part of the literary frame of reference. In keeping with what was a literary fashion[25] in the 1970s and early

1980s, Timm offers an impressive array of literary models and antecedents. If Hölderlin had been used in *Heißer Sommer* as a prefiguration of Ullrich's failure to come to terms with German society, at least in his early period in Munich, Kleist fulfils an analogous function in *Kerbels Flucht*. The Kleist allusions begin with the epigraph: 'Ein stiller Androgen fiel überall nieder', taken from Kleist's letter to Ulrike of 16 December 1801.[26] Not only does Timm echo this line in his text: 'Draußen aber war es wolkenverhangen und ein Landregen fiel' *(KF,* 124), but he also alludes to Kleist's situation in 1801. For Kleist the journey to Switzerland was 'wie ein Eintritt in ein anderes Leben' *(KF,* 5), much as Kerbel reflects on the possibility of escaping his emotional and professional crisis by living in a commune in the country. Kleist, at this time, seriously contemplated purchasing a small estate in Switzerland and devoting himself to a life of farming. After his final break with Karin, Kerbel seriously contemplates an apprenticeship as a furniture maker, much as Kleist did. Similarly, Kerbel's brief employment as editor of an in-house newspaper for a publisher seems a pale echo of Kleist's activities for the *Berliner Abendblätter*. Kerbel, like Kleist, is determined to evolve a 'Lebensplan', an alternative career, not least because he believes that a new set of ambitions will make him more attractive to Karin:

> Ich fragte mich, ob ich mir noch einmal eine Chance geben und irgend etwas neu anfangen sollte, beispielsweise ein Architekturstudium. Aber ich sagte mir, daß es ein kindlicher Glaube sei, alles durch die Wahl eines anderen Berufs ändern zu können. Auch als Architekt würde ich mir so, wie ich war, wieder begegnen. *(KF,* 77)

It is no coincidence that Timm includes in the narrative, at the point when Kerbel is introduced to the rural idyll in Franconia, a letter written by Kleist to Friedrich Wilhelm III, dated 17 June 1811.[27] Kleist's letter, a desperate plea for financial support so that he may achieve the 'Begründung einer unabhängigen Existence', immediately precedes the utopian scene in the commune and Kerbel's appointment to the publisher's press office. In Berlin Kerbel visits the graves of Brecht, Hegel and Hanns Eisler, but a much longer episode recounts the visit paid by Kerbel and Karin to Kleist's grave, where they are interrupted first by a school party and then by some troops on exercises in the woods. The noise of gunshots seems to give Kleist's suicide an immediacy, and it is in the immediate aftermath of the incident that Kerbel realizes that Karin has embarked on her new relationship as 'ein neuer Lebensentwurf' *(KF,* 96), echoing Kleist's constant quest for fulfilment. Although the parallels to Kleist predominate, there are allusions to other literary forebears, in particular Büchner's Lenz *(KF,* 167) and Goethe's Werther *(KF,* 163). The utopian ideal of the commune is associated with Schnabel's Insel Felsenburg *(KF,* 120); Kerbel's self-destructive behaviour with Rimbaud *(KF,* 67 and 157).

The narrative of *Kerbels Flucht* consists of a series of diary entries, dating from 19 April to 10 October in a single year, which are interspersed with autobiographical notes written by Kerbel at an earlier time and given to Karin, who leaves them in her room when she breaks off her relationship with him. These notes are, for the most part, reminiscences of Kerbel's childhood and adolescence. Virtually all the incidents are associated with anxiety or embarrassment, much of it sexual in origin. Kerbel himself wonders: 'Warum war ihm so wenig aus seiner frühen Kindheit in Erinnerung geblieben? Und warum war das, was er später erinnerte, meist mit dem Gefühl der Angst verbunden?' *(KF,* 119). The patterns of parenting which emerged in *Heißer Sommer* reappear: Kerbel's father, like Ullrich's, is an unsuccessful small businessman, resentful of the competition posed by supermarkets and larger chains of shops in the altered commercial world of the 1950s and 1960s. His values are authoritarian, yet his commercial failure deprives him of real authority over his son. Kerbel's autobiographical jottings are simultaneously an attempt to locate his own frustrations in the past, and the expression of an inchoate literary urge, a story-telling impulse which spills over into the novel, counteracting the sombre tenor of the text. The interpolated stories vary in tone and content. Some are significant shaping influences on Kerbel, like 'Der Klapperstorch' *(KF,* 22), 'Unter der Eisentralje' *(KF,* 28), 'Kerbels Verweichlichung' *(KF,* 32) or 'Vom Verlust der Unschuld' *(KF,* 52), which treat of sexual experiences. Others are more factual parts of family history, like 'Personalien des Vaters' *(KF,* 58–64) and the much more affectionate (though much shorter) 'Personalien der Mutter *(KF,* 65–6). Yet others are more whimsical stories, like 'Jan Mollsen' *(KF,* 24–5), or the comic tour de force 'Die Überquerung des Atlantiks und anderer Weltmeere' *(KF,* 54–6), expressive of that story-telling impulse which is, we feel, more Timm's than Kerbel's.

The opening section of the book – the page break alone signals the transition – recounts Kerbel's life in Munich between 19 April and 19 May. The following episode in Berlin is presented as a consecutive narrative, related from Kerbel's viewpoint in the first person. The third section, again marked by a page break, adopts the format of the first Munich section, except that the story-telling impulse disappears. There are, it is true, interruptions to the diary form: one interpolation, 'Der Orgeltraum' *(KF,* 103–5), recounts an incident during the student movement; for the rest, there are some factual 'Notizen' *(KF,* 108, 128) and quotations, from Marx's *Pariser Manuskripte (KF,* 139), from Bommi Baumann *(KF,* 153), from a dictionary definition of 'Kerbel' *(KF,* 161), from Büchner's *Lenz* (and there are two letters, one from Kleist to the Prussian king, the other a draft of a letter from Kerbel to Karin). The memories of the past are not completely absent, but they are reduced to a minimum: 'Alle Jahre wieder' *(KF,* 140) illustrates the tyranny of Kerbel's father, and 'Die Fahrt nach Wittenberge' *(KF,* 164) a brief happy memory. Only one episode invokes that story-telling which, we feel, might enable Kerbel to regain his equilibrium; 'Geschichtenball' *(KF,* 169) recalls a game in which, while a ball was kept in the air, the player would have to tell a story. Kerbel can, by this stage, not keep the ball in the air; his story will swiftly end. Even as the narrative loses its sense of consecutive time and the diary sections appear 'ohne Datum', a sudden shift of narrative voice occurs. The first-person narrative gives way to a third-person narrator: after the words 'ich ertappte mich mehrmals beim Selbstgespräch' *(KF,* 170), marking a retreat into solepsism, an editorial voice is heard, writing retrospectively about Kerbel's last weeks. Kerbel's final attempt to retreat to the commune is frustrated: the initial idealism of the alternative green economy has given way, in the meantime, to drug-dealing and cynicism. With this final possibility removed, Kerbel drives at speed towards a police road-block and is fatally shot. His death is not even the pretext for student protest. The radical idealism of the student movement has ended, first with a bang and then a whimper.

Uwe Timm succeeds beyond doubt in these two novels in conveying the rage, the idealism, and the sheer creative disruptiveness, of the student movement of the 1970s. He analyses more sharply than most the contradictions and compromises, the frustrations and the failures. But the question remains whether the novels are more than merely a historical record. Contemporary critical voices, especially from the Left, have questioned the subjectivity of his approach, his fondness for the outsider's perspective. With hindsight, his novels appear to be more central to what is going on in German literature in the 1970s than is first apparent. The 'Innerlichkeit' which marked the 1970s is present in Timm's writing, but in an unusual way: his central characters strive to realize their social vision, but they do so with the dim awareness that solutions have to be created, rather than discovered. This helps to explain Timm's fondness for literary models, particularly for those, like Kleist and Hölderlin, who come to grief because their vision cannot be realized in the society in which they find themselves. At the same time, Timm is sharply aware that our consciousness is structured by habitual expectations and mediated by the information industry. For all his irritation with Handke, he shares Handke's fascination with the manifestations of popular culture which obtrude upon our consciousness. Moreover, he shares Handke's fondness for literary characters which are vehicles for the disruption of our habits of perception. Yet for Timm, that is never quite enough; for him there must be a social resonance; the story must be told, but it must be told to some effect.

Notes

[1] Peter Handke, *Die Angst des Tormanns beim Elfmeter* (Frankfurt am Main, Suhrkamp, 1970), 35.

[2] Uwe Timm, 'Peter Handke oder sicher in die 70er Jahre', in *kürbiskern*, 1970, No. 4, 611–21 (here 611).

[3] Ibid., 617.

[4] *kürbiskern*, 1972, No. 1, 79–90.

[5] Ibid., 82.

[6] Ibid.

[7] Ibid, 86.

[8] Ibid., 88.

[9] Uwe Timm, 'Realismus und Utopie', in *kürbiskern*, 1975, No. 1, 91–101 (here, 95).

[10] See Rolf Hosfeld and Helmut Peitsch, '"Weil uns diese Aktionen innerlich verändern, sind sie politisch". Bemerkungen zu vier Romanen über die Studentenbewegung', in *Basis. Jahrbuch für deutsche Gegenwartsliteratur*, 8 (1978), 92–126.

[11] Manfred Jürgensen, in his essay 'Die dokumentierte Fiktion: *Heißer Sommer, Kerbels Flucht*. Uwe Timms Zeugenbericht auf Widerruf', in Keith

Bullivant, Manfred Durzak and Hartmut Steinecke (eds.), *Die Archäologie der Wünsche. Studien zum Werk von Uwe Timm*, (Cologne, Kiepenheuer & Witsch, 1995), 27–45, writes of 'Uwe Timms Variation des klassischen Bildungsromans' (33). In fact, the classical 'Bildungsroman' begins with the birth of the subject and traces the unfolding and self-cultivation of the central figure, abandoning him (it is invariably a male protagonist) on the threshold of active immersion in an adult world. Roy Pascal in his pioneering study *The German Novel* (Manchester, Manchester University Press, 1956), observes that the 'Bildungsroman' deals essentially only with 'the weaning of the heroes from their inwardness, with their spiritual preparation for social life, and stops or falters when they actually enter upon it' (229).

[12] Keith Bullivant in *Realism Today: Aspects of the Contemporary West German Novel* (Berg, Leamington Spa, 1987), complains of 'the lack of reality in this and other novels, above all the totally naïve hope for swift and radical social change' and of Timm's 'using the central character to put across an oversimplified view of the world' (113).

[13] Hölderlin, *Werke und Briefe*, ed. Friedrich Beißner and Jochen Schmidt, 3 vols (Munich, Insel, 1969), I, 89.

[14] Manfred Jürgensen (see note 12) relates this quotation to Ingeborg's abortion, though he concedes that 'die Abstrahierung des Sinnlichen und die Versinnlichung des Abstrakten sind das überragende Thema des Romans' (30).

[15] Hermann Hesse, *Gesammelte Werke in zwölf Bänden* (Frankfurt am Main, Suhrkamp, 1970), I, 119. If Christa is indirectly signalling her intention to put an end to any possible relationship with him, she could not have chosen a better literary model. The preceding lines run: 'Es muß das Herz bei jedem Lebensrufe / Bereit zum Abschied sein'.

[16] Manfred Jürgensen (see note 12) goes so far as to write of 'die Darstellung der deutschen Gesellschaft als kodifizierte Germanistik' (31).

[17] *HS*, 103 and Hölderlin, I, 73.

[18] That Hölderlin should have been chosen reflects his topicality in the early 1970s, stimulated, no doubt, by the two-hundredth anniversary in March 1970 of his birth and a spate of publications, biographies, critical works and literary works, such as Gerhard Wolf's *Der arme Hölderlin* (1972).

[19] The quotation is taken from Gerhard Fricke's essay on Kleist's *Penthesilea*, in the standard work Benno von Wiese (ed.), *Das deutsche Drama vom Barock bis zur Gegenwart* (Düsseldorf, August Bagel, 1958), 361–84 (here 368).

[20] The quotations on *HS*, 126, 129, 130, and 131 are from the essay 'Bemerkungen zu einer Neubestimmung der Kultur' in *Kultur und Gesellschaft*, II (Frankfurt am Main, Suhrkamp, 1965), 157, 159, 159 and 162 respectively; that on *HS*, 127 is taken from the essay 'Über den affirma-

tiven Charakter der Kultur', I, 68, and that on 139–40 is from 'Ethik und Revolution', II, 134.

[21] In his essay collection *Erzählen und kein Ende* Timm reports: 'In der Zeit gab es in Hamburg einen Graffiti-Künstler namens Eiffe, von dem in der Stadt Sprüche zu lesen waren, nicht nur in der Uni-Gegend, auch in den Vororten und in den U- und S-Bahnen' (41).

[22] The Becher essay is clearly 'Unsere Wendung. Vom Kampf um die Existenz der proletarisch-revolutionären Literatur zum Kampf um ihre Erweiterung', first published in *Die Linkskurve*, No. 10, 1931; see Johannes R. Becher, *Bemühungen, Reden und Aufsätze* (Berlin, Aufbau, 1970) 312–26.

[23] *Die Angst des Tormanns*, 23.

[24] *Wunschloses Unglück*, 7.

[25] Examples are Plenzdorf's *Die neuen Leiden des jungen W* (1973), Peter Schneider's *Lenz* (1973), and, most notably, Christa Wolf's *Kein Ort. Nirgends* (1979).

[26] See Heinrich von Kleist, *Sämtliche Werke und Briefe*, ed. Helmut Sembdner, 5th revised edition (Munich, Carl Hanser, 1970), II, 708. Incidentally, the same passage is woven into Christa Wolf's *Kein Ort. Nirgends* (Darmstadt and Neuwied, Luchterhand, 1981), 67.

[27] See *Sämtliche Werke und Briefe*, II, 869–71. Curiously, Timm addresses the letter to Friedrich Wilhelm II.

6

'Der Weg in die Zukunft':
Uwe Timm and the Problem of Political Ecology

COLIN RIORDAN

In tandem with German politics, German literature since the late 1970s has seen an exponential growth in the treatment of environmental themes. Among the exponents of this development are pre-eminent figures such as Günter Grass and Christa Wolf, who weave ecological issues into complex fictions with political implications which go far beyond the environmental agenda.[1] The sophisticated ambivalence of such texts is exceptional, however. Far more common is the kind of tendentiousness readily detectable in works by writers such as Gabriele Wohmann, Gudrun Pausewang and Carl Amery who have placed the environment so far in the foreground that it becomes the *raison d'être* of their work: literature as ecoprop. In such cases there is little room for ambivalence, let alone scepticism. Given that throughout Timm's work technology is viewed with varying degrees of suspicion, *Der Schlangenbaum* might easily be read as a standard warning against the dangers of progress and the prospect of ecological apocalypse. But it can also be argued that Timm's 1986 novel does show signs of ambivalence, and, moreover, that the concern with ecological issues in Timm's work goes back further than has hitherto been noted. In fact, the influence of ecological ideas can be detected in Timm's documentary novel *Morenga*, published in 1978, some years before the parliamentary success of *Die Grünen*.

Perhaps it is not surprising that *Morenga* should show signs of environmental awareness, given the enthusiasm for such ideas coupled with the anti-militarism which characterized the Federal Republic in the 1970s. As one might expect, for example, the German troops in the novel view the African landscape as an object for exploitation, and are on occasion defeated not by their human enemies, but by their own lack of sympathy with the environment in which they are fighting (*M*, 18, 36–7). But there is evidence of more specifically ecological awareness, including an incidental character who, while obviously a figure of fun, is also an early Green worried about a possible 'empfindliche[n] Störung des natürlichen Gleichgewichts' (*M*, 66) which might arise through the cremation rather than burial of fallen soldiers. Bezirksamtmann Schmidt is concerned that the natural fertility of the soil should be enhanced for future generations, and is decidedly against the use of artificial fertilizers. Such arguments in favour of sustainability are not, however, purely an example of 1970s environmentalism being imprinted on a novel set in the early years of this century. The first great wave of proto-environmentalism in Germany occurred in the late nineteenth and early twentieth century, even if it was frequently (as in this case) part of a more general antimodernist, nationalist stance. This is not to say that the dominant current of thought in Wilhelmine Germany is not represented in *Morenga*; messianic advocates of the power of technology are overwhelmingly present. The views of the surveyor Treptow can stand for those of many other characters in the novel, and indeed foreshadow the stance of Wagner at the beginning of *Der Schlangenbaum*: 'Treptow war von der bezwingenden Macht der Technik überzeugt. Wo die Natur noch Defekte zeigte, würde man sie über lang oder kurz mit technischen Mitteln beheben. Man würde Wüsten bewässern, Flüsse [...] regulieren, aufstauen oder umleiten. Alles war technisch machbar, und zwar so, daß es den Menschen zum Nutzen gereichen würde' (*M*, 256). Treptow, then is no less than 'ein technischer Fanatiker' (*M*, 256), who has plans to drain the Caspian Sea and to bring about local climate change in the Sahara by creating a vast lake.

Though entirely representative of contemporary notions of progress, such anthropocentrism does not go unchallenged in Timm's novel, for there is also clearly a focus on green alternatives in early twentieth-century German culture. We even encounter an appeal for animal rights which (as is also clear from the context) would have appeared decidedly unconventional at that time and might raise eyebrows even today: 'Freie Wahl und freie Entfaltung auch für die Tiere!' (*M*, 147). Similarly, the missionary Kraft is an evangelical vegetarian (*M*, 160),[2] while the (wholly fictitious) diary of the main character Gottschalk speculates on a future with more than a hint of ecological characteristics: 'Vielleicht wird es einmal selbstverständlich, jeder Kreatur zu helfen und ebenso den

Bäumen, Büschen und Blumen, ja sogar der Erde, der Landschaft. Der Garten Eden. Der Boden, auf dem ich liege, schwitzt, die Landschaft atmet, warm und feucht' (M, 349). But this Gaian lyricism is itself only part of a much more thorough political analysis, which derives from Gottschalk's study of Peter Kropotkin's *Gegenseitige Hilfe in der Entwicklung.*

This volume acts as a leitmotif in *Morenga* once Gottschalk has been presented with it by his colleague Wenstrup, a radical who subsequently deserts. Gottschalk carries the book everywhere with him, reading with such intensity that his colleagues assume him to be devoutly studying the bible (M, 142). Wenstrup has inscribed the volume with his own comments which are quoted throughout *Morenga*, as are Kropotkin's own words (the remark on animal rights quoted above is part of Wenstrup's marginalia). *Gegenseitige Hilfe* is of crucial importance as a structural and thematic element of *Morenga*: under its influence Gottschalk undergoes fundamental and important changes, acquiring anarchist and anti-imperialist views which, though they never challenge the overwhelming power of the existing state, are decidedly out of place for a soldier in the imperial army. The novel is indeed, as Jost Hermand comments, among other things 'ein bürgerlicher Entwicklungs- und Wandlungsroman'.[3] The question is, why should Timm have chosen this particular volume to be the text which both fascinates and transforms Gottschalk? While its anthropological relevance is important, as Keith Bullivant and others have pointed out,[4] Kropotkin's anarchism is the defining feature.

The association between anarchism and environmentalism, particularly in its historical context, might at first sight appear tenuous. In fact, the close relationship between anarchism and proto-ecologism in the early part of this century has been amply demonstrated by Ulrich Linse, who has documented in detail the early history of anarcho-socialist groupings and communes in Germany. In *Ökopax und Anarchie* Linse shows that figures such as Heinrich Vogeler, Paul Robien and Leberecht Migge were responsible for propounding a variant of revolutionary socialism which depended on respect for nature, the attempt to live in harmony with nature in a sustainable manner and small-scale communities using alternative, low-impact technologies. This involved the rejection not only of large-scale industry and the concomitant devastation of the environment, but also of the Marxist socialism which depended on the existence of industry. The principal theorist of this political philosophy (which we would now recognize as deep Green) was the anarcho-socialist Gustav Landauer. Landauer's non-Marxist, anti-industrialist socialism, formulated centrally in his tract 'Aufruf zum Sozialismus', formed a crucial theoretical underpinning to the anarcho-communism actually practised by Heinrich Vogeler and others. Landauer it was who translated Peter Kropotkin's *Mutual Aid* into German under the title *Gegenseitige Hilfe in der Entwicklung* in 1904.[5] The importance of this volume for the development of proto-Green communes in early twentieth-century Germany can hardly be overstated. As Linse puts it: 'Erst der optimistische Glaube an das allesdurchdringende Walten der "gegenseitigen Hilfe" ließ überhaupt das sozialistische Beginnen im Zeichen von Ökopax als praktikable Alternative erscheinen.'[6]

Ultimately it is Kropotkin's interpretation of Darwin that lies at the heart of his theory of mutual aid, and which therefore underlies notions of early ecosocialism. The whole thrust of Kropotkin's work is to focus on mutualism as the primary, though not the sole, factor in evolution.[7] Recognizing that Darwin had proposed for the first time a scientific theory which allowed a rational exposition of holism, or 'unity in nature'[8] as Kropotkin puts it, the anarchist geographer argued that practically all exponents of Darwinism, particularly in Britain, propounded the doctrines of competition and predation to the exclusion of other evolutionary factors. T. H. Huxley is taken as the prime advocate of such an approach, and it is he who is made responsible not only for the popularization but also the widespread distortion of the notion of 'survival of the fittest'. While 'fittest' was almost always taken to mean strongest, a more appropriate interpretation would be 'best adapted'. Mutualism, Kropotkin argued, figured far more often as a successful evolutionary adaptation than did competition.[9] Deriving this lesson from examples of evolutionary adaptation, Kropotkin applies it to the social organization of human beings. Once the premiss is accepted, the politico-constitutional logic is inescapable: the best behavioural adaptation for mankind is to live in small, cohesive communities in harmony with the environment.[10] Various examples are adduced to demonstrate this, including that of the Hottentots. Again there is a clear political implication of direct contemporary relevance: 'Unbridled individualism is a modern growth, but it is not characteristic of primitive mankind.'[11] Kropotkin displays many of the attitudes one might expect for a European of his era; the Hottentots, he agrees, are the 'filthiest animals'[12] who live in primitive conditions. Yet living off the land in close contact with the natural environment has its compensations in terms of mutual aid and tribal morality. He quotes P. Kolben in praise of the Hottentot manner: 'They know "nothing of the corruptness and faithless arts of Europe". "They live in great tranquillity and are seldom at war with their neighbours."'[13] The mutualist values of the Hottentots (and indeed of other 'savages') are described in *Mutual Aid* as exemplary for the nations of the world.

To what extent are such values critically reflected in Timm's *Morenga*? Gottschalk is understandably wary of referring to his subversive reading matter whilst a serving soldier in the Kaiser's colonial army, but does eventually explain in conversation the theory of mutual aid amongst animals which Kropotkin saw as the primary factor in evolution. The reaction of Gottschalk's interlocutor Oberarzt Haring is simultaneously predictable, ideological and political: 'er sei davon überzeugt, daß dieses Gesetz gilt: Der eine ist Amboß, der andere Hammer. Das sei ein universelles Gesetz: Der Wille zur Macht. Alles andere Philantropie' (*M*, 230). There can be no question of scientific objectivity; the political implications of mutual aid are such that German statist militarism can only oppose incomprehendingly. But it is in the lives led by the indigenous peoples in the novel that Kropotkin's ideas of mutual aid are most sympathetically demonstrated, and, by extension, in which the notion of proto-ecologist anarcho-communism most clearly emerges.

The fanatic of technology, Treptow, notes in a letter about the Hottentots that 'Es ist dies (der Kommunismus) eine eingebürgerte Sitte bei ihnen' (*M*, 269), and indeed it is clear that in Timm's representation the indigenous peoples do practise what amounts to a Kropotkin-style society including mutual aid, small-scale living, low to nil technology needs and therefore no economic growth beyond what is necessary.[14] An interpolated ethnological report notes that competition is the foundation of all economic development: 'Im Stammesverband der Hottentotten aber ist die Konkurrenz durch das Prinzip der gegenseitigen Hilfe außer Kraft gesetzt' (*M*, 320). Similarly, Gottschalk is later reported to have praised the natives' 'Friedfertigkeit, ihre gegenseitige Hilfe und die urkommunistischen Formen ihres Zusammenlebens' (*M*, 345). That Gottschalk is guided in the direction of ecosocialism by this model and by Kropotkin's theories seems clear from the last in his series of speculative sketches which began by depicting the kind of house he would like to live in with a putative family once having finally settled in German South-West Africa. This last sketch, illustrating the end-point of his political development, shows 'eine Art landwirtschaftlicher Genossenschaft oder Kommune, in der alle, die arbeiten, in ähnlichen Häusern untergebracht sind. Größere Hauskomplexe tragen Bezeichnungen wie: Schule, Leseraum, Bibliothek, Turnhalle' (*M*, 347). This drawing, reinforced by a quotation from Kropotkin asserting that human solidarity is a deep-rooted evolutionary feature, implies a social organization strongly resembling that which was shortly to be practised by Vogeler, Robien, Migge and others in Germany.

But of course, the sketch remains just that: an insubstantial dream of some unlikely future. In fact, the Hottentots lose the war against the Germans, being crushed by an overwhelming technological and numerical superiority. In the end the strongest do triumph. And Gottschalk, despite his transformation into a radical and despite his personal rebellions, is unable to draw the ultimate revolutionary conclusions from his inner debates. The reason for this is the deep-rootedness of the supremacy of technological progress, and of social Darwinism, in the society from which Gottschalk springs. Ironically, the interpretation placed on Darwin's theory of evolution, affording pride of place to competition and individualism in the evolutionary process, has almost entirely obscured the presence of mutualism as a factor. Ironic because it was only the advent of Darwin's theory of natural selection and its widespread popularity which allowed the science of ecology, fundamental to the ecological project, to blossom in the way it did from the early part of this century. The power of Gottschalk's cultural conditioning becomes evident when he finds himself in a position to put into practice an idea which has been growing in his mind since the anarchist Wenstrup deserted: to abandon his position and live among the Hottentots as a deserter. Thus he would be able to live out in a practical manner the theories of mutual aid to which he subscribes. What stops him is the cultural gap between himself and the Hottentots – which resembles the gap between Western technological society and the Green dream of thoroughgoing ecologism – and the impossibility of bridging it. He ponders that impossibility: 'Hätte er bleiben wollen, er hätte anders denken und fühlen lernen müssen. Radikal umdenken' (*M*, 375). That the impossibility of 'radikal umdenken' is couched in a socio-cultural context affords a crucial insight into the real obstacle to genuine ecological action: it demands too great a cultural shift.

What Timm has succeeded in doing with *Morenga* is to show precisely the problem faced by political ecology in the twentieth century. An episode towards the end of the novel offers a perfect model of the political will to change running into the sand. Meisel attempts to persuade Gottschalk to join him in exposing to the world the inhumane brutality with which the colonial masters treat the indigenous population. Gottschalk, however, has lapsed into apathy, and Meisel is astounded at his attitude: 'Eigentlich war er gekommen, Gottschalk für das zu gewinnen, was er den Aufstand des Gewissens nannte. Jetzt hatte er einen verstockten Vererinär getroffen, der von radikalen Mitteln im Kampf gegen das Unrecht redete, aber nur noch herumsaß, seinem Pfeifenrauch nachsah und vom Tanz der Hottentotten schwärmte' (*M*, 376). Almost symbolically, Gottschalk has become fascinated with cloud formations, as ephemeral and insubstantial as any dream of changing society. Though Gottschalk is entirely convinced of the need to bring about such social change, agrees that the prevailing system is entirely unjust and that only radical action can overcome it, he is unable to act. Gottschalk is simultaneously rejecting the role of Green pioneer with that of anarchist revolutionary. The fact that an individual might be convinced of the need for change cannot alone bring about the necessary social change. This is undoubtedly a reflection of Uwe Timm's own disillusionment with the DKP and the failed students' movement, amply reflected in *Kerbels Flucht* and other works. But the use of Kropotkin in *Morenga* illustrates the fault at the heart of political ecology: the very scientific revelations which gave birth to its fundamental tenets simultaneously prevent the social consequences of its implications from being carried through to fulfilment. The triumph of Huxleyan Darwinism over Kropotkin's interpretation has seen to that.

Far from being a form of eco-propaganda, then, *Morenga* implies the gloomiest prognosis for ecological politics. By contrast, *Der Schlangenbaum* does at first sight lend itself to interpretation as a standard attack on the anti-environmental stance of Western civilization in the mould of the eco-propagandists mentioned at the outset. As in Max Frisch's *Homo faber* (which is an obvious ancestor of Timm's novel), the main character, an engineer, apparently fails to comprehend that attempting to fight nature by literally imposing human structures on it is doomed to failure. Wagner, it seems, is forced to adjust his world-view to one which tends to reject technology and progress while embracing the power of nature. The native workers are wary of the consequences of ignoring traditions with respect to the natural environment. The local town even seems to be returning to the jungle: 'Auf den Dächern einiger Häuser wuchsen Büsche, und aus den oberen Fenstern krümmten sich kleine Bäume dem Licht entgegen. Es war, als wenn der Wald über die Dächer in die Stadt zurückkehren würde' (S, 159). There are even hints at Gaian mysticism: 'es schien, als atmeten die Bäume' (S, 170); 'nah und deutlich war das Glitzern der Sterne, als atme der Himmel' (S, 172). Furthermore, the novel ends with an almost apocalyptic scene where nature reclaims the human built environment; invading Wagner's house and apparently precipitating the imminent destruction of the compound in which he lives. This all takes place against the background of local political violence and unrest: Wagner, it appears, is forced to accept the superior forces both of nature and of a culture which he has not properly understood. Thus both Meyer-Minnemann and Niven argue that he undergoes a forced 'Lernprozeß',[15] though for Meyer-Minnemann the learning process has to do primarily with understanding the complexities and dangers of local politics. For Niven, by contrast, Wagner's abandonment of his previous attachment to progress is a positive development in an ecological sense; Wagner is furnished with an orientation towards a 'new set of values, values which I perceive to be essentially ecological'.[16]

The premiss of this argument is that, in effect, nature defeats Western attempts at economic and technological progress: 'Nature is to hold sway', as Niven puts it.[17] This view seems to be supported by the fact that Wagner is sent to Argentina to build a paper factory (which would result in continuous local deforestation), and Wagner does indeed deliberately fail to ensure that it will be soundly built. But the building of the factory fails because of local corruption and the defective concrete which is the result of that, not because the natural surroundings cannot be tamed. Steinhorst leaves Wagner in no doubt about this, on being asked how the building is going:

Es stimmt so ziemlich nichts.
Was stimmt nicht?
Gar nichts. Nicht der Beton, nicht die Arbeiter, nicht der Durchmesser der Bewehrung, nicht einmal der Baugrund.

Wieso?
Die Fabrik sollte eigentlich gut 500 Meter weiter westlich errichtet werden. (S, 48)

On discovering that this is an accurate representation, Wagner attempts to rectify the problem by redesigning the foundations; Bredow (who holds the purse-strings) is deeply reluctant, pointing out that 'Die Kalkulation für dieses Projekt ist extrem knapp' (S, 90). Even when Wagner does get the go-ahead to build his 'Kellerkasten' to secure the foundations, it transpires that the concrete used is defective. In a decisive turning-point near the end of the novel, Wagner takes the decision not to reject the defective material. But he takes this decision on neither engineering nor ecological, but rather on human and social grounds. If rejecting the cement would help the workers, he would do so, it appears (see S, 301). The change in Wagner has little to do with nature, or being green, and much to do with a personal crisis which the engineer is undergoing. He recognizes this himself: 'Irgendwie [...] waren ihm die Wünsche abhanden gekommen' (S, 268). The change he undergoes during the course of the novel is conditioned by his failure to understand the politics and culture of the country in which he is working. The experience of losing his way, being robbed, arrested and undergoing a terrifying forced anal search are all a result of that failure.

More particularly, the failure of the building is not a matter of nature reasserting itself, but of human choices and human decision-making. If the consistency of the ground on which the factory is to be built means that it is too expensive to pour secure foundations, then it means that the site was wrongly chosen, not that building on the site is inherently impossible. What both actuates and defeats technological projects in *Der Schlangenbaum* is economic calculation, fraud and bad decision-making, not the technical feasibility of the projects. The reason for the kidnapping of Ehmke, Wagner's predecessor, was specifically not 'um den Wald zu schützen' (S, 35) but in order to expose corruption. Indeed, Wagner himself says that when buildings fail 'der Grund ist dann immer: Schlamperei oder Korruption' (S, 313). Similarly, the abandoned motorway bridge in the jungle does not necessarily mean that connecting roads could not be built there, merely that the economic case is insufficiently compelling.[18] The history of humankind's impact on the world environment shows that where economic necessity and political will dictate, thoroughgoing transformations of the landscape can be and are undertaken, whatever the site. This is true of land reclamation in the Netherlands as it is of the deforestation of Europe or Australia and the urban development of Latin American countries. Wagner's conversion from a belief in progress does not translate to green fervour; rather he is succumbing to local conditions in much the same way as Gottschalk in *Morenga*.

But unlike in *Morenga*, where a deeply ecological alternative is at least present, even if it is crushed out of existence, in *Der Schlangenbaum* no such alternative is proposed. Far from being indigenous tribes living in close harmony with nature (which do of course exist in South America), the local population in *Der Schlangenbaum* is in many ways as out of place as Wagner himself. Not only are some of the workers Bolivian, but the language and culture of all the workers are the result of earlier colonizations of South America, even if they are nearly all ethnic 'Indios' (S, 184). It is true that they do have an understanding of the environment in which they live, expressed, for example, in their knowledge of how to extract a burrowing armadillo from the ground in order to supplement their meagre diet.[19] And, as Juan tells Wagner, they do not share his way of viewing the world as a logical calculation which can be resolved, everything which cannot be resolved being ascribed to chance (S, 190). According to Juan, the local workers have mystical rather than rational explanations for apparently fortuitous occurrences, explanations which lie 'in anders wirkenden Kräften, in dem Stein, in der Schlange, im Wald, der Sonne, dem Blitz, den Wolken, dem Regen' (S, 190). But this empathy with the environment does not extend to economic structures on which a society might be built. The workers remain dependent for their existence on industrial society, and are prepared to live in conditions of extreme poverty in order to earn the miserable wage of Wagner's company. They are, in fact, grotesquely alienated from the natural environment: an example of what happens to an undeveloped, but perhaps morally and ecologically superior society (such as the Hottentots) after prolonged contact with European industrialism.[20] Moreover, Timm goes to some lengths to undermine the notion that Wagner is purely a representative of European industrialism in contrast to a local population which lives in harmony with nature. There is only one glancing reference to a genuine indigenous jungle tribe, and that only to say that on contact with the outside world the tribe commits ethnic suicide by refusing to produce more children (see *S*, 126). Most of the people whom Wagner meets are either part of the expatriate European population or, like Sophie, Juan and others, the descendants of earlier waves of German colonization who have retained their own distinctive language and culture. They are representative of the overwhelming success of European, industry-based culture in colonizing the world. In a sense, then, all of the participants are anti-nature. There is no dichotomy here between Wagner the engineer on the one hand and indigenous cultures in harmony with nature on the other. The failure of adaptation which is at the root of the problem of political ecology is not just Wagner's, but that of all the characters.

Throughout the novel there are allusions to apocalypse, expressed in particular by Wagner's housekeeper Sophie, a 'Rußlanddeutsche' whose family, members of the 'Gemeinde des jüngsten Tages' (*S*, 295) had emigrated in the 1930s. Sophie is only articulate when she is relaying the beliefs of her religious sect in the form of eschatological biblical quotations, mostly from the Book of Revelation (see *S*, 118, 156, 174, 274, 295, 308). There can be no doubt that the systematic references to apocalypse do create an 'Endzeitstimmung', particularly since towards the end of the novel Sophie announces that the day of judgement has finally arrived. Here is sufficient proof, it might be argued, that the novel does act as a warning of future ecological disaster in the pattern of 1980s catastrophist literature. But Sophie's announcement of the end of the world is thoroughly undermined by its narrative context: 'Heute ist der Tag des Zorns und der Rache, sagte sie, ich habe Ihnen das Essen hingestellt' (*S*, 308). Moreover, there is an important difference between the biblical apocalypse with which Sophie is obsessed and some putative ecological catastrophe. Biblical apocalypse is a positive development, the Day of Judgement on which all will receive their just deserts, after which the righteous will enter the Kingdom of God. It portends new life, not disaster, for those who believe.

Crucially, therefore, it would be misleading to read *Der Schlangenbaum* as an unambiguous warning of coming ecological disaster or as a prescription of how people should behave in order to avoid apocalypse. That much is clear from the ambivalence of the ending, which contains frequent references to apocalypse, but couched in a form which is not susceptible to straightforward interpretation.

Against a background of local unrest, possibly a revolution in the making, Wagner's world appears on the point of collapse. But as Klaus Meyer-Minnemann points out, the fact that Wagner is obviously ill makes the version of events we read unreliable, since we have only his perception of events. Apocalypse is certainly prefigured, not least in a flood which washes away the neighbouring house. Nature begins to invade Wagner's home as the grammatical tense of the story switches to the present, emphasizing the immediacy and uncertainty of the events. The eruption of cockroaches through his bath-taps seems ominous, for cockroaches are the creatures best adapted to survive a world catastrophe. But these events clearly owe as much to Wagner's confused state of mind as to anything else; his perception of the swimming pool as full of ill-defined creatures is proof of that: 'Der Swimmingpool ist voller Kröten, aber auch Fische scheinen darin zu schwimmen, und machmal buckelt sich das Wasser dunkel auf' (S, 324). Just at the point when the confusion seems greatest, and Wagner sees the reflection of a great fire, the lights come back on. In the last paragraph of the novel they go out again, and an almost existential silence descends: 'Keine Schüsse, kein Schrei, auch die Tiere sind verstummt, als hielte die Welt den Atem an' (S, 325). The end of the world is here at least alluded to, but the point is that there is no unequivocal indication. Apocalypse may or may not be the result of the actions of humankind in fostering technology and economic progress. We cannot know, and, in particular, we can have no influence on the outcome. This novel is above all an expression of powerlessness. Far from being a warning, it is a resigned noting of the powerlessness not just of the individual but of humankind collectively to act in a manner which might influence our fate positively in the future.

And it is a sensation of existential powerlessness which most clearly defines the change wrought in Wagner by his experiences. Once he is making his way through the jungle on donkey-back, Wagner's inability to influence his fate propels him into a state of apathy: '[er fiel] in eine teilnahmslose Dumpfheit, eine Gleichgültigkeit gegenüber Ort und Zeit' (S, 274). Paradoxically, this is the inevitable consequence of Wagner's belief in the power of technology, or indeed of consumer capitalism. When Wagner goes to Hartmann's flat as part of his vain search for Luisa, the two men embark on a discussion of the conflict between economic growth and environmental protection. Wagner argues that since people possess a universal desire for personal comfort and enrichment, economic colonialism is not a matter of imposing industry and technology on an unwilling population:

> Es ist der Wunsch nach dem Anderen, nach einem Mehr, der Wunsch nach dem Transistor, nach dem Messer aus rostfreiem Stahl, nach der Coca Cola, es ist ein universeller Wunsch, der Wunsch des Genießens und der Bequemlichkeit. Niemand will mit der Hacke den Boden bearbeiten, wenn er einmal einen Motorpflug gesehen hat. [. . .] Ich bin ja dafür, [. . .] daß hier industrialisiert wird. Wo Menschen verhungern, ist das Entsorgungsproblem beim Atommüll eine recht akademische Frage. Ob der Müll noch hundert oder gar tausend Jahre strahlt, ist für denjenigen, der heute verhungert, ziemlich egal. (*S*, 226)

While it may be a commonplace to point out that short-termism and poverty are the enemies of environmental improvement, the argument is nevertheless at the heart of green debate. Moreover, the notion that underdeveloped countries should sacrifice the opportunity to catch up with the industrialized world in order to protect the environment, against which Wagner is here implicitly arguing, is one of the crucial obstacles to contemporary environmental reform. Global environmental action is only feasible if some way can be found of compensating such countries for the injustice caused by past imperial and present economic colonialism. This passage, then, encapsulates one of the central problems of contemporary political ecology: attitudes like Wagner's must be broken down if there is to be hope of ecological progress.

In response to Wagner, Hartmann contemptuously articulates the exploitative nature of such industrialization:

> Die Leute zahlen für alles. Wir geben ihnen die Kredite, bauen ihnen die Fabriken, liefern die Maschinen, holzen den Urwald ab und wischen uns dann mit dem Papier den Arsch ab. Was wir zurücklassen, ist eine rote Wüste, eine nutzlose Papierfabrik und Schulden. Und jetzt sagen Sie mir nicht wie neulich, daß Sie den Mond lieben. Der Mond ist unbewohnt. Hier aber leben Menschen. Er lächelte Wagner wie um Verzeihung bittend an: Ich bin dafür, daß die Fabrik im Schlamm versinkt, je schneller desto besser. (*S*, 226–7)

The fact that Wagner ultimately accepts the defective concrete, then, might seem a positive step. He even begins to express doubts about the value of progress *per se*: 'Er hatte sich immer in der Lokomotive des Fortschritts sitzen sehen, vielleicht galt es jetzt, in das Bremserhäuschen umzusteigen. Aber wie?' (S, 296). The last words are telling, for Wagner never embraces the ecological cause, while its advocate, Hartmann, reacts by resigning and returning to Germany. He abdicates responsibility, just as Gottschalk does in *Morenga*. Moreover, the circumstances which made the farcical building project possible remain: these are structural problems which will not be affected one way or the other. Wagner's crucial decision to accept the concrete was hardly an act of ecological sabotage; most of the damage was already done. In fact, it was merely a manifestation of Wagner's recognition that he was powerless to change things. And that is a profoundly depressing message for political ecology.

Thus an analysis which shows Timm's novels promoting ecology would be too simplistic. This is not part of some project on the part of Timm; indeed, there are reasons to believe that he is personally committed to the ecological cause. His books for children, for example, contain a number of worthy, or put more charitably, praiseworthy asides intended to help educate children about the undesirable, if not disastrous, effects of modern farming techniques on the world into which they are growing up.[21] But in the adult novels we find very little that is optimistic in an ecological sense. This view is reflected throughout Timm's work since the late 1970s, which repeatedly highlights the powerlessness not only of the individual but also of the collective to bring about significant change for the better. Timm's heroes make a series of disastrous errors but persist in their endeavours. Frequently they put their trust in technology which is unreliable or outdated, or become redundant themselves; Gottschalk recognizes that in an age of increasing mechanization, the days of the military veterinarian are numbered. They are essentially conservative, in that having once chosen a route they persist, even though they might manifestly be exploring a dead end. They find themselves fighting their way through the abandoned, overgrown branch lines of history. Though a passionate believer in technological progress, Schröder in *Der Mann auf dem Hochrad* is unable to force through his conviction that the high bicycle is innately superior to the newly invented safety bicycle and is, therefore, the means of transport of the future. Timm's characters attempt to control events but are led astray and are themselves subdued. Everything they touch goes wrong, with increasingly disastrous results; the frustration inflicted on such characters being perhaps most apparent in *Johannisnacht*. In both

Morenga and *Der Schlangenbaum* Timm structurally demonstrates the *failure* of humankind to grapple with the problem of its own treatment of nature, and so illustrates the real state of political ecology at an individual level. Though ecological disaster may well lie ahead, there seem to be no political means of avoiding it, whether on an individual or collective level. By way of conclusion, the resigned pessimism of these two novels is perhaps best represented in the television advertisement for his own company which Wagner sees on his arrival in Argentina:

> Dann kamen plötzlich Reklamespots, eine Whiskymarke, eine Kindercreme, ein Parfum, dann fielen nach rechts und links Bäume um, ein kolossaler Bulldozer bahnte sich einen Weg durch das Urwaldgestrüpp, sechs überschwere Planierraupen schoben einen kleinen Hügel beiseite, ein Berg flog in die Luft, in Zeitlupe wurden Felsbrocken in die Erde gewuchtet, hinter einer Planierraupe schob sich eine Teermaschine durch die Landschaft, dahinter rasten die Autos auf der fertigen Autobahn in das ovale Zeichen seiner Firma am Horizont, begleitet von Beethovens 'Freude, schöner Götterfunken'. Das also war der Weg in die Zukunft. (S, 41)

Notes

[1] See Günter Grass's *Unkenrufe* (1991) or Wolf's *Störfall* (1987), for example.

[2] Until he is forced to give up 'Lakto-Vegetarismus' after seriously poisoning himself (see *M*, 161).

[3] Jost Hermand, 'Afrika den Afrikanern! Timms *Morenga*', in Keith Bullivant, Manfred Durzak and Hartmut Steinecke (eds.), *Die Archäologie der Wünsche. Studien zum Werk von Uwe Timm*, (Munich, Kiepenheuer & Witsch, 1995), 47–64 (here 59).

[4] See for example, Keith Bullivant, 'The Writer as Anthropologist: The Works of Uwe Timm', in this volume.

[5] From the 1908 edition onwards the volume appeared under the title *Gegenseitige Hilfe in der Tier- und Menschenwelt*.

[6] Ulrich Linse, *Ökopax und Anarchie. Eine Geschichte der ökologischen Bewegungen in Deutschland* (Munich, dtv, 1986), 77.

[7] Only relatively recently has Kropotkin's pioneering work in this area received the recognition it deserves. The reason for this may be that 'a socio-political climate ripe for competitive or negative interactions may have subconsciously influenced the way in which ecologists formulate research problems in the first place'. See J. Vandermeer, 'The Evolution of

Mutualism', in B. Shorrocks (ed.), *Evolutionary Biology* (Oxford, Blackwell, 1984) 221–30 (221).

[8] Peter Kropotkin, *Mutual Aid: A Factor of Evolution* (London, Penguin, 1972), 83.

[9] Vandermeer confirms this analysis in 'The Evolution of Mutualism', 221.

[10] Kropotkin sees no necessary conflict between industrial progress and preservation of the natural order, reflecting the state of both political and scientific ecology at the time he was writing.

[11] Kropotkin, *Mutual Aid*, 92.

[12] Here Kropotkin is quoting Lubbock. See *Mutual Aid*, 93.

[13] Ibid., 93.

[14] While Kropotkin was not anti-technology, and not anti-industry, he nevertheless recommended their use on a small scale, anticipating the 1970s ideas of E. F. Schumacher.

[15] Klaus Meyer-Minnemann, 'Die fremde Logik und die Ordnung der Dinge. Uwe Timm, *Der Schlangenbaum*' in *Die Archäologie der Wünsche*, 119–42 (132), and Bill Niven, 'The Green *Bildungsroman*', in Colin Riordan (ed.), *Green Thought in German Culture: Historical and Contemporary Perspectives* (Cardiff, University of Wales Press, 1997), 198–209.

[16] Niven, 'The Green *Bildungsroman*', 198.

[17] Ibid., 206.

[18] The bridge was built with German and French loans to serve a mine which subsequently closed, and to celebrate the birthplace of a president who was subsequently toppled (see *S*, 140).

[19] The trick, apparently, is to insert a finger into the creature's anal passage, thus effecting a simple extraction from the ground (see *S*, 180). This episode is among other things clearly intended to pre-figure Wagner's forced anal examination by a police doctor (see *S*, 287).

[20] The description of the delegation which visits Wagner during the strike resembles those of photographs of Hottentots in *Morenga*: 'Sie standen da wie auf einer alten Photographie, die Strohhüte, die zerschlissenen Hemden, die weiten Leinenhosen' (*S*, 188).

[21] For more detail on this see Walter Seifert, 'Aufklärung und Komik. Uwe Timms Kinderromane', in *Die Archäologie der Wünsche*, 143–71 (153, 154–5).

7

'Die Wandlung des Alltags in Bedeutung': Social History and 'die Ästhetik des Alltags'

DAVID BASKER

In the series of lectures connected with his tenure of the 'Paderborner Gastdozentur für Schriftsteller', published under the title *Erzählen und kein Ende* (1993), Uwe Timm acknowledges that his views on the purpose of literature have undergone a change in the course of his career. He differentiates clearly between the novels that he wrote for the AutorenEdition and his more recent position:

> Ich überschätze die Möglichkeit der Literatur, Bewußtsein zu verändern, nicht. Sie ist äußerst begrenzt. Das habe ich nicht immer so gesehen. Früher, also beim Schreiben von *Heißer Sommer* und *Morenga*, war ich überzeugt, Literatur habe eine wichtige Bedeutung bei einer Veränderung der Gesellschaft zu mehr Gerechtigkeit, Gleichheit und Freiheit.
> Heute denke ich, daß ein wesentliches Kennzeichen von Literatur darin liegt, *überflüssig* zu sein. (*EkE*, 110–11)

Timm goes on in the course of the lectures to define his own set of aesthetics; his 'Ästhetik des Alltags' is a view of literature that has shaped all of his work since the early 1980s. Although that work has indeed moved away from the more obvious political commitment of the early novels,[1] Timm's categorization of his own work here can easily mislead. His contention that the capacity of literature to change the world is severely limited should certainly not be taken to mean that his more recent novels have nothing to say about the societies in which they are set. On the contrary, what is most fascinating about Timm's concentration on the unique, apparently insignificant details in the daily lives of the protagonists in his later work is the way in which those details intersect with more general social phenomena. Using the theoretical position outlined in *Erzählen und kein Ende* as a framework, this essay will investigate precisely this interaction between the specifically personal and the social in Timm's narrative approach since the 1980s. The study will focus on the three texts that could perhaps be termed Timm's most 'personal', in that they arise from the family backgrounds (very close to the author's own) of their respective narrators: *Der Mann auf dem Hochrad* (1984), *Die Entdeckung der Currywurst* (1993) and *Johannisnacht* (1996).

Der Mann auf dem Hochrad is the first text in which Uwe Timm turns directly to family history for inspiration. The narrator is a writer, the co-ordinates of whose biography overlap very closely with Timm's own, and he recounts episodes from the life of his great uncle, Franz Schröder, in Coburg during the second half of the nineteenth century. Two remarkable features of Uncle Franz's life provide the framework for the narration: his development of new techniques in the field of taxidermy, his chosen profession, and his introduction of the penny-farthing to Coburg.

The key to Uwe Timm's narrative approach in *Der Mann auf dem Hochrad* is the means by which the narrator gains access to the stories surrounding his uncle. In the first place, the family connections between the narrator and his subject are an obvious source of information. The narrator himself has some vague memories of his great uncle as an elderly man, since he and his mother had been evacuated from Hamburg to Coburg in the course of the Second World War. The act of writing itself unlocks these memories: 'In diese Schaffenszeit von Onkel Franz reicht meine Erinnerung, die, seitdem ich von ihm schreibe, reicher und bildengenauer geworden ist: Onkel Franz sitzt auf einem Bock an seinem Arbeitstisch und biegt an einem Drahtbein, das aus einem Stück Torf ragt' (*MH*, 214). On two occasions these early memories of Uncle Franz, specifically of his inventiveness, feed the narrator's dreams which are in turn incorporated into the text. The memories of other, older relatives are a further source of information for the account: the narrator's mother had given initial stimulus to the story when she happened to mention Uncle Franz to her son in passing, for example; and the elderly Tante Erna offers some insights into the later part of the taxidermist's career.

At the same time, direct memory of Franz is clearly insufficient to supply all the details of his life, since the story begins beyond the limits of living memory. The narrator proves to be an assiduous researcher, however, collecting documentary evidence that relates to the uncle's life and there are both private and public documents at his disposal. In the former category, he has a letter from Anna, Franz's wife, to her sister – who is also the narrator's grandmother – complaining about the restrictions on her cycling activities that pregnancy has brought; and he has the notes for a book which never reached the public domain that Franz and his fellow-cyclist Gützkow had planned to write about the pleasures of riding the penny-farthing. Written evidence that is public property includes a police report on the first meeting of the Coburg 'Gesellschaft zur Förderung des Radfahrens' (*MH*, 82), the minutes of a public debate concerning the respective merits of the penny-farthing and the newly introduced 'Niederrad', and newspaper articles covering a race between Franz and a rival intended to prove once and for all which of the two means of transport is superior. Photographs of certain events in Franz's life are also available to the narrator. The family photo of Franz and Anna standing proudly next to a penny-farthing is described in detail, for example, as is a picture of the young, adventurous Anna alone, an image that the narrator has difficulty reconciling with his own memory of the old woman whom he knew. The narrator is able to incorporate and interpret these documents and photographs at the appropriate point in his story; they act as conduits between the past and the narrative present.

Detailed and conscientious though the narrator's research is, it is clear that his account is much more than the piecing together of documentary sources. Memory, photographs and written evidence are useful guides, but they are not enough to complete the picture of Franz's life. The narrator's creative talents are also required for an account that is rich in specific detail of events for which, as far as we can tell, there is no supporting documentation or clear family recollections. The initial stimulus for the story suggests that the narrator's imagination will play a large part in the re-creation of Franz's life. The opening paragraphs of the text describe 'ein kleiner silberner Stab' (*MH*, 9) that the narrator keeps on his desk, the function of which no one is able to guess: the silver tube conceals a retractable tortoiseshell toothpick, 'ein Erbstück von meinem Großonkel Franz' (*MH*, 9). This object suddenly provides the key to a story:

> Bislang habe ich dabei nicht an Onkel Franz gedacht. Jetzt aber, seit dem Besuch meiner Mutter vor gut drei Wochen, die ganz zufällig auf Onkel Franz zu sprechen kam, ergibt das alles eine Geschichte: der

Zahnstocher aus Schildplatt, die Erinnerung meiner Mutter, meine Erinnerung an ihre Erzählung und an Onkel Franz, den Hochradpionier, den Erfinder des Klammer-Gepäckträgers und den Schöpfer des ausgestopften Riesengorillas im *Victoria and Albert Museum* zu London. (*MH*, 9–10)

The muted Proustian effect of a small, forgotten object unlocking a long and detailed story is one to which Timm returns on a number of occasions in later texts. The toothpick is what Timm defines in *Erzählen und kein Ende* as 'ein gezeichnetes Ding': 'Die gezeichneten Dinge, so will ich sie einmal nenne, also jene, die mit den Menschen in Kontakt kamen oder aber von ihnen hergestellt wurden, haben ihre Geschichte, die um so viel-sagender ist, je mehr diese Dinge durch Gebrauch abgenutzt, absichtlich oder unabsichtlich "verletzt" wurden' (EkE, 25). Here, the connections are both general and specific. On a general level, the toothpick leads to thoughts of Onkel Franz, which then leads to a dream, which in turn triggers the whole story; as a result, the toothpick changes its meaning for the narrator, who had previously used it simply to clean the keys of his typewriter.[2] Specifically, the origin of the toothpick is one episode upon which the narrator focuses in the course of his uncle's story. The object, he recalls, was a gift to Franz from Fräulein von Götze, an eccentric member of the Coburg aristocracy who secretly took lessons in penny-farthing cycling from Franz to help cure her digestive problems. Indeed, the detail surrounding the friendship between Franz and Fräulein von Götze illustrates clearly the way in which the narrator interweaves research and creative invention. He has a written record of a conversation between the two, which Fräulein von Götze had made at the time; but this simply provides a background to the narrator's precise re-creation of their lessons together. This description includes painful detail about Fräulein von Götze's long-term indigestion, her ten-year effort to translate one of Petrarch's sonnets into German, her affair with a court official, and an account of the cycling lessons themselves, in which Fräulein von Götze appeared dressed as a man. In such episodes, the narrator's insights extend to the thoughts, feelings and sense perceptions of the characters involved. When Fräulein von Götze first hears Franz talking about the benefits of cycling at the Coburg court, the narrator is able to tell us: 'Jedenfalls erschien ihr in diesem Moment der Präparator wie der Erlöser von all ihrem Ungemach, während die anderen, das hohe Paar eingeschlossen, diesen Mann eher kurios unterhaltsam fanden' (MH, 70); and during the cycling lesson, Franz's ambiguous thoughts about helping a woman other than his wife to learn to ride are exposed: 'Er dachte an Anna und an das Gerede in der Stadt. Andererseits bewunderte er den Einsatz, den Mut und die Begeisterung dieser Frau, die als Mann verkleidet das Rad bestieg [. . .]. Sie lag an seiner Schulter, und er roch einen unbekannten fernen Blütenduft und spürte kurz, aber deutlich weich ihre Nase an seiner Wange' (MH, 78).

Clearly this is much more than an account informed by memory and documentation alone. In such passages the narrator becomes omniscient, able to re-create not only precise, external detail but also the mental processes of those involved; and accordingly, the narrator frequently keeps the direct family connections at a distance by referring to his uncle not as 'Franz' but as 'Schröder'. Evidence of the same creative activity on the narrator's part abounds: at a public lecture on the dangers of cycling, he is able to describe the speaker even down to the foam moustache that his glass of beer leaves on his upper lip; and at the same meeting we are witness to Franz's agonizing over whether or not he is responsible for the injury sustained by an overweight pupil when he fell off the penny-farthing during a lesson. The narrator is even able to provide a detailed description of one of Anna's dreams, and of the subsequent discussion she and Franz had about it in bed together.

Further evidence of the narrator's imaginative re-creation of events emerges from the different layers of time built into the text. The chronological account of Franz's experiences with the penny-farthing and in his career provide a framework for the text; this account connects with the narrator in the 1980s and, through memory, with episodes from the period he spent in Coburg in the 1940s. The characters around Franz have their own stories, however, and a series of short digressions appears throughout the text, in which the narrator is able to go further into the past to offer insight into the earlier lives of incidental characters. As we have seen, most of Fräulein von Götze's biography is incorporated into the section in which she takes cycling lessons from Franz. In the same way, the narrator is able to go back into the years of study which the butcher, Schön, has put himself through in order to be able to recognize the best meat; and when the teacher and fellow-cycling enthusiast Gützkow arrives in Coburg, the narrator is in a position to fill in the detail as to the circumstances under which he was forced to leave his previous post in Kolberg in Pomerania. He is even able to recount some of the adventures leading up to the arrival in Coburg of Lord Hume, an African explorer, for whom Franz stuffs the gorilla.

Clearly, then, a large proportion of the episodes from Franz Schröder's life that constitute the text rely on the narrator recounting them in an imaginative way, as an omniscient narrator. At the same time, this omniscience has a counterbalance built into the text, which throws light on Timm's narrative approach. Repeatedly the reader is reminded of the fact that the narrator is inventing scenes by means of rhetorical expression of his own uncertainties: he asks himself what the characters in the story might have thought or how they might have acted, indicating that his account, however detailed, is simply a probable version. Franz's very first attempt to ride the newly delivered penny-farthing, and the resultant fall, set the tone: 'Was hat Onkel Franz in diesem Augenblick gedacht? Aufgeben? Einen anderen Übungsort ohne Zuschauer suchen? Und was hat Tante Anna gedacht? Überliefert ist, daß sie in jäher Wut gegen das kleine Hinterrad des Gefährts trat' (*MH*, 17). Subsequent episodes are punctuated by similar moments in which the narrator steps back from sections of the text that otherwise suggest omniscience, to speculate on what might have happened, to challenge his own version of events. To return to the incident where Franz teaches Fräulein von Götze to ride the penny-farthing, the passage in which the narrator is even able to reveal his uncle's reaction to the woman's perfume is introduced by two such rhetorical questions: 'Hat mein Onkel in diesem Moment an das Schicksal des Mannes [Götze's former lover] gedacht, von dem er doch sicherlich gehört hatte? Wußte er, in was er sich da von dieser exzentrischen Frau hineinziehen ließ?' (*MH*, 78). Similarly, the narrator's descriptions are modalized by the recurrence throughout the text of an introductory 'vermutlich' or 'vielleicht'. On his uncle's decision to accept the challenge of riding in the race against an ordinary bicycle, for example, the narrator comments: 'Vermutlich reagierte er ganz spontan und aus Lust an einer Wettfahrt' (*MH*, 160); and when the narrator sees the letter Anna wrote to his grandmother, he speculates: 'Vielleicht hat sie diesen Brief an eben diesem ersten Frühlingssonntag zu Hause geschrieben, während ihr Franz ins Freie hinausradelte' (*MH*, 153–4). The most striking example of the way in which the narrator's framework of speculation interposes itself between reader and description comes near the end of the text, as Franz, who has not ridden his penny-farthing for years, rides up to the castle on 11 November 1918, to witness Coburg's own November revolution:

> Andere behaupten, Schröder sei gar nicht auf dem Hochrad gefahren, er habe es nur geschoben. Aber das kann auch auf dem Rückweg gewesen sein, als er und Tante Anna gemeinsam nach Hause gingen. Warum also hat er das Rad aus dem Keller getragen und sich, was in seinem Alter und nach all den Jahren ohne Fahrpraxis doch recht mutig war, auf das Hochrad geschwungen? Sollte es eine Demonstration sein, und wenn ja, wofür? Glaubte er vielleicht, daß eine neue Zeit käme, wenn so begeisterte Fahrradfahrer wie sein früherer Schüler die rote Fahne auf dem Schloß hißten, die Zeit der Cyclisation? Aber er konnte doch vorher nicht wissen, daß Wachsmann [the ex-pupil] plötzlich oben auf dem herzoglichen Balkon stehen würde. Es gibt nur Vermutungen, keine Antworten. (*MH*, 210–11)

The effect of such passages is crucial, for they alter the reader's attitude to the whole text, not just to the episodes in which they appear: the narrator's omniscience, at times almost aggressive, can be seen in this light as a careful, imaginative attempt to re-create the probable course of events and pattern of motivations, conditioned by complete awareness that 'es gibt nur Vermutungen'. *Der Mann auf dem Hochrad* emerges as the working out of the theory of literature that Timm put forward explicitly, almost a decade later, in *Erzählen und kein Ende*. The fifth and final lecture in the series is entitled 'Das Geflüster der Generationen oder Der wunderbare Konjunktiv' and deals precisely with the question of re-creating episodes from the past in literary form, 'ein, wie man weiß, nur bedingt mögliches Verfahren' (*EkE*, 126). The story-teller, Timm contends in the essay, is not simply a chronicler of the past: 'Der Erzähler erzählt nicht nur nach, sondern neu und anders, nämlich wie es sein könnte, er erzählt eine andere Wirklichkeit' (*EkE*, 120). The statement accurately describes the narrator's approach in *Der Mann auf dem Hochrad*; even in his assiduous collection of written material, his method is not to assemble a piece of *Dokumentarliteratur*, but to work external evidence into an imaginative account of what *might* have happened in Uncle Franz's life.

It is this literary process that explains Timm's designation of the text as 'Legende'. The narrator has interpreted the details of Franz's life at his disposal and created a version of events from everyday detail that explains some remarkable things. *Der Mann auf dem Hochrad* creates a likely account of how the penny-farthing came to Coburg, of how Lord Hume's gorilla was stuffed. When the connection between Franz's daily routine and these unusual events begins to fade, the account draws to a close: 'Es bleibt nur noch wenig zu berichten. Mein Onkel führte über Jahre und Jahrzehnte ein auch für diese Stadt ganz normales Leben, das keinen Anlaß mehr zur Legendenbildung bot' (*MH*, 205).

The motivation for a narrative approach of this sort, Timm asserts in *Erzählen und kein Ende*, is a search for meaning not only in the lives of other individuals, but also on a more general level: 'Aus der Distanz zu sich selbst [that emerges in the act of writing], dem Zwiespalt, entspringt eine Frage, die das Erzählen bewegt, die Frage nach dem Sinn der eigenen Existenz, anderer Existenzen und damit implizit auch die Frage nach dem gesellschaftlichen Sinn' (*EkE*, 120). Connections with *Der Mann auf dem Hochrad* emerge on this latter point, too. For all that this is a highly personal and unique story, one rooted in private family history, the experiences of Franz Schröder and of those around him are presented in such a way that, implicitly at least, aspects of the development of German society in the late nineteenth century emerge. In the first place, Franz's story provides plenty of evidence of the growing fear of left-wing politics among those in power in Germany at the time. The Coburg aristocracy clings doggedly to the values of the feudal past and does everything in its power to protect the *status quo*. As the narrator discovers to his benefit, the police send their spies to the first meeting of his cycling club to monitor its politics, and keep a record of the meeting. The co-founder of the club, the teacher Gützkow, has been forced to come to Coburg in the first place because: 'Man hatte ihm Kontakte zu der verbotenen Sozialdemokratischen Partei nachgesagt' (*MH*, 39). Gützkow has, after all, got red hair, and when he sets up a 'Plattdeutsch' conversation circle for fellow exiles from the North, it too becomes the object of police surveillance: 'Man vermutete einen geschickt getarnten revolutionären Geheimbund [...]. Ein als Interessent getarnter Polizeispitzel verfolgte einen solchen Konversationsabend sprach- und verständnislos' (*MH*, 40).

The narrator notes in passing that Anna is the only female member of the 'Plattdeutsch' group. This is just one illustration of her unconventional behaviour which, in turn, highlights slowly changing social attitudes to women. She causes a storm of controversy by learning to ride the penny-farthing, not just because the activity *per se* is regarded as a male concern, one that could have dire medical consequences for a woman, but also because she is forced to offend against the prevailing dress code in order to be able to ride in the first place. Anna is just as enthusiastic as her husband in championing the virtues of the penny-farthing and having taught herself to ride in secret, she 'comes out' as a cyclist, asserting her right to enjoy the sport like any man. Franz's attitude changes gradually from resistance to his wife's participation, to pride and support for her determination not to be intimidated by prevailing opinions. When Anna defends her right to cycle in public, attitudes in the town as a whole undergo a change: 'Durch die Stadt ging nicht nur ein Riß, der die Velociped-Befürworter und die Velociped-Gegner trennte, sondern noch ein anderer, mit dem ersten durchaus nicht deckungsgleich, nämlich jener, der die Anna-Grüßenden von den Anna-Nichtgrüßenden scharf trennte. Der Riß kannte keine Konfession und keine Profession. Er trennte Gemeinden, Familien und Ehepaare' (*MH*, 140). Anna's personal stance, which comes from a simple but determined desire to learn to ride a penny-farthing, becomes a wider social issue, pointing to a slow change in gender roles in late nineteenth-century Germany.

Of course, the very fact that the penny-farthing has reached provincial Coburg in the first place is itself a sign of further social change. Technological advance is coming quickly to a country catching up with the leaders in the industrial revolution. The sight of the first penny-farthing, with Franz Schröder in the saddle, is a cause of fear, consternation and not a little hilarity. Yet the days of this latest invention are numbered, since it is soon to be replaced by the more practical and less dangerous 'Niederrad'. No matter how hard he tries to prove the superiority of the penny-farthing, Franz cannot resist the march of technological development. The narrator explicitly draws a wider conclusion from the race between penny-farthing and normal bicycle:

> Es begann ein Wettlauf um die Zeit, in den Fabriken, auf den Landstraßen, Ozeanen und in den Velodromen, um die berechenbare Zeit, eine Zeit in Minuten, Sekunden, in zehntel, hundertstel, tausendstel Sekunden, eine Zeit, die je kleiner, desto zeitloser wurde, weil sie um ihr Maß gekommen war. Und auch Onkel Schröder hat dazu sein Teil beigetragen. (*MH*, 161)

Sitting at his desk writing about Uncle Franz, the narrator cannot escape the evidence of how far this 'Wettlauf' has come, as the daily visit of two jet fighter planes rattles the glass in his windows.

Der Mann auf dem Hochrad is thus a highly personal story which deals with unique events in the life of Franz Schröder. These unique events nevertheless point to patterns of change throughout German society at the time. The narrator re-creates episodes from the life of his uncle using a combination of memory, documentary evidence and imagination. In so doing, he locates his uncle not just in his or her own particular spheres – taxidermy and cycling – but also against historical development. Through the connections across time, the narrator sets his own memories in historical context and 'das Ferne wird langsam nah' (*MH*, 215). As the rhetorical questions and modalizations indicate, the account is simply what might have happened; in re-creating what might have happened, however, the writer/narrator has brought his uncle into focus, uncovered the personal significance of the silver tube with the tortoiseshell toothpick, and revealed something of the society in which Franz Schröder lived.

Die Entdeckung der Currywurst first appeared in 1993 and carried the designation *Novelle*. To what extent Timm's categorization of the text in this way is justified has been a matter of some critical controversy. While it is not intended that this analysis should address that debate directly, reasons why Timm chose to connect his text with the tradition of the Novelle will emerge from a close examination of his narrative approach.

The story of the remarkable culinary discovery runs as follows: the narrator, a resident of Munich and the details of whose life once again match closely with Uwe Timm's, recounts the disappearance of his favourite Currywurst stand from his native Hamburg. His memory is that the owner of the stall, Lena Brücker, was the inventor of the dish and he embarks on research into the details of the invention. He tracks Lena down to an old people's home in Hamburg and visits her seven times. These visits consist of the now blind Lena eating cake, knitting a jumper, and recounting the episodes from her life, primarily from 1945 to 1947, which led to her creation of the dish and the successful establishment of her small business. A particular focus for these memories is a four-week affair she had with a sailor named Bremer who, having been conscripted to an anti-tank division in the last weeks of the war, deserted and hid in Lena's flat. Following the seventh visit to the old people's home, the narrator leaves on a trip to New York and only returns to Hamburg with his unanswered questions six months later, to discover that Lena has died. She has bequeathed to him the jumper that she had been knitting during their conversations and the original piece of paper bearing her recipe for Currywurst.

From the opening pages of the text, Timm's approach puts the process of telling a story into the foreground. His narrator is someone in search of a satisfying explanation for an event that has different possible histories, as the arguments he provokes among his friends by putting forward his version of the culinary invention illustrate. His first visit to Lena in the nursing home is intended to stimulate the story and he is desperately disappointed when she initially denies that she created the dish. The narrator's laconic 'Und wie?' (*EC*, 18) when Lena does admit her hand in the invention is the first of several questions that he directs at her in order to keep the story going; he even takes her back to the site of her stall to eat curried sausage from the modern fast-food van that has replaced it, in part at least to focus her mind on the story once again. The narrator's anxiety to get to the heart of the story is equally evident on the occasions when he mistakenly anticipates the end of Lena's account: Bremer's request for curry in his food, and the chef Holzinger's advice to Lena on restoring Bremer's sense of taste, which he mysteriously loses, with spicy food, are such red herrings for the narrator.

That is not to say, however, that the narrator is entirely dependent on Lena. Before he visits her in the nursing home, a partial version of the story exists in his mind. Thereafter, the text is more than just a written account of their conversations; there is ample evidence to suggest that the narrator has used his gifts as a storyteller to fill in scenes which Lena herself could not have witnessed, or to relate the thought processes of characters other than Lena. We are given insight, for example, into Bremer's troubled mind at the point of his decision to desert (*EC*, 45); and when Bremer loses his sense of taste, we are told what his mouth feels like: 'Es war eine eigentümliche Empfindung auf der Zunge und am Gaumen, etwas Pelziges, Stumpfes, so als sei ihm die Zunge eingeschlafen' (*EC*, 160). At times the narrator speculates openly about what characters in Lena's story might have been thinking, a technique familiar from *Der Mann auf dem Hochrad*. When Lena and Bremer first meet during an air-raid, for example: 'Der Luftschutzwart, mit seinem

Stahlhelm auf dem Kopf, kaute, sah zu ihnen herüber. Was wird er gedacht haben? Da hatte sich mal wieder eine reife Frau einen jungen Mann angelacht' (*EC*, 26); and when Bremer returns to bed following his decision to desert: 'Was dachte Hermann Bremer, als er wieder zu Lena Brücker ins Bett stieg? Hatte er Angst? Gewissensbisse? Zweifel? Dachte er, ich bin ein Verräter, ein Kameradenschwein?' (*EC*, 48). The tension between confident omniscience and uncertainty as to the story's progress is familiar from *Der Mann auf dem Hochrad* and, as in the earlier case, highlights the process of telling the story itself.

The effect of these narrative strategies – the narrator's anxiety to find a story, the conversations, the narrator's creative inventions and his uncertainties – is to make the account before the reader appear as a contingent *version* of the history of 'die Entdeckung der Currywurst', with its basis in the remarkably clear memories of Lena Brücker. We know from the reactions of the narrator's friends that other versions exist, perhaps that Currywurst was invented in Berlin. Similarly, the narrator turns on a number of occasions to sources other than Lena for further information, other versions of events. As elsewhere, his own family is tied in to the story and he is able to call on both his own early childhood memories and his mother's recollection of Lena to throw different light on her account. Lena remembers the resignation in the behaviour of the narrator's father when she involved him in her bartering scheme, for instance, a memory that ties in closely with the narrator's own childhood experience of his father. Likewise, his mother recalls:

> Und dann gab es da noch die Geschichte mit ihrem Mann. Frau Brücker war verheiratet? Ja. Sie hat ihn eines Tages vor die Tür gesetzt. Warum?
> Das konnte meine Mutter mir nicht sagen. (*EC*, 14)

The mystery surrounding the incident in the mother's eyes is one that will be cleared up from Lena's perspective nearly two hundred pages later in the text.

The narrator also turns to sources normally considered more reliable than memory for other perspectives on the story. When Lena recounts how Bremer was convinced of the beneficial psychological impact of eating curry, for example, the narrator consults an English friend who is an ethnologist and who supplies a mundane physiological explanation for the effects Bremer noted.

Then the narrator visits the Staatsbibliothek to consult the archive of the *Hamburger Zeitung* for articles from the period of the German surrender, noting the same sudden change in ideology that Lena recounts from her experiences with colleagues. In addition, he consults the Gestapo archives to investigate who was responsible for informing on Wehrs, a dock worker who lived in the same block of flats as Lena and who told jokes at the expense of the Nazis when drunk. This investigation uncovers the fact that it was not the hated air-raid warden Lammers who had been a Gestapo informant, but Frau Eckleben, a nosy but otherwise insignificant neighbour. This discovery puts the narrator in a position to interpret elements of Lena's story in a completely new way: Lammers, for all his commitment to the Nazi cause, turns out to have refused to inform on his neighbours, despite Lena's confident suspicions to the contrary; Frau Eckleben, whom he also visits, is exposed to him as a deceitful and vicious woman and her sudden friendliness towards Lena at the end of the war is revealed to be the result of her mistaken belief that Lena was hiding a Nazi from prosecution at the hands of the British. As in *Der Mann auf dem Hochrad*, the narrator's research is carefully interwoven into the re-creation of the characters' past. Crucial to Timm's narrative approach here is what the narrator does with the information he discovers: he does not attempt to correct or alter Lena's view of the past, indeed, as far as we know he never even tells her that he has visited Frau Eckleben; and he leaves a number of documents from the Gestapo archive unread. Interesting though these insights might be, what is important to the narrator is Lena's highly personal account of the episodes in her life, not the scientific or documentary evidence that might call that account into question. Lena's story consists of a series of what Timm defines in *Erzählen und kein Ende* as 'sprechende Situationen' which define an individual's existence: 'Wer sich selbst befragt, nicht abstrakt nach dem metaphysischen Sinn des Lebens, sondern allein auf seine eigene Existenz bezogen, der denkt – ich jedenfalls – in Situationen, die ihm in Erinnerung geblieben sind, die nicht ins Grau des Vergessens eingegangen sind, bestimmte herausgehobene Situationen, in denen sich sein Verhalten, sein Handeln regelrecht verdichten' (*EkE*, 66). These situations are 'true' in the sense that they represent an individual's conception of his own life, irrespective of how closely they correspond to documentary or other external evidence.

Thus, it is to Lena's perspective that the narrator consistently returns, for it is personal history that fascinates him. In contrast to the ethnologist's dry account of the origins and effects of curry, Lena's story is full of humour, chance and mystery.³ Everyday objects take on added significance as they recur through Lena's story and connect – for Lena, too – one episode in her life with another; they are 'gezeichnete Dinge'. Bremer's regulation groundsheet for example, in itself a connection with the military obligations that weigh so heavily upon him, is what brings him and Lena together in the first place, as they shelter under it from the rain; he leaves it behind in Lena's flat, such is his hurry to return home once he discovers the war really has ended; and it is then transformed by Lena into a waterproof covering for her sausage stall and is thus a fixed co-ordinate in the narrator's childhood memories. Similarly, the 'Reiterabzeichen' that Bremer wears is much more than an unusual medal for someone in the navy to have. It breaks the ice with Lena, so that she can learn in more intimate conversations with Bremer that it has also been a key to his relatively successful career in the navy; it, too, gets left behind when Bremer leaves and it then becomes a key element in the complex series of exchanges Lena embarks upon in order to set up her business: a British major who collects unusual German medals attaches to it the handsome price of '24 Festmeter Holz' (*EC*, 200).

The 'Reiterabzeichen' seems to have an almost mystical power to help the person who has it. Further elements of the mysterious and fantastic are connected closely to Lena's personal experience. One need only consider the unlikely list of characters and objects that, Lena tells the narrator at the outset, play a part in the discovery of the Currywurst. This is not the recipe one might expect: 'ein Bootsmann der Marine, ein silbernes Reiterabzeichen, zweihundert Fehfelle, zwölf Festmeter Holz, eine whiskytrinkende Wurstfabrikantin, ein englischer Intendanturrat und eine englische rotblonde Schönheit, drei Ketchupflaschen, Chloroform, mein Vater, ein Lachtraum und vieles mehr' (*EC*, 19–20). Even when the story behind most of these ingredients has been explained by Lena, the combination of events that leads directly to the culinary discovery is shaped by the most remarkable chance and coincidence. Having chosen, for no practical reason, to accept a tin of curry powder as part of the black-market deal, Lena trips going up the stairs to her flat, 'ausgerechnet sie, Lena Brücker, die Hunderte, Tausende von Malen die Treppen rauf- und runtergelaufen war' (*EC*, 211). Bottles of ketchup break, the lid of the curry powder falls off, and the resulting mess becomes a sauce which has miraculous powers. On tasting it, Lena goes from tearful despair to laughter, and the prostitutes who are her first customers at the stall are soon converted: 'Scheußlich, sagte Moni, aber dann, nach dem ersten Bissen, ein Schmecken, daß sie sich wieder spürte. Mann inner Tonne, sagte Moni. Das Grau hellte sich auf. Die Morgenkälte wurde erträglich' (*EC*, 215). The whole of Lena's account has led to the moment of discovery; 'Entdeckung' is an unusual but appropriate word to use in the context of an exotic dish which has miraculous effects and which, for the narrator, did not come into existence like others: 'bei der Currywurst ist es anders, schon der Name verrät es, er verbindet das Fernste mit dem Nächsten, den Curry mit der Wurst. Und diese Verbindung, die einer Entdeckung gleichkam, stammt von Frau Brücker und wurde irgendwann Mitte der vierziger Jahre gemacht' (*EC*, 12).

For all the mysterious, even fantastic elements of the story, the fact that the narrator is able to date the discovery of the Currywurst relatively precisely is itself important, for the historical background is crucial to Timm's narrative approach. The highly personal events of Lena's life do not take place in a social or historical vacuum, but against the backcloth of instantly identifiable events of twentieth-century history. That personal experience of history is a major concern of the text is obvious even from the timing of Lena's affair with Bremer. The four weeks they spend together correspond exactly to the momentous last weeks of the war, Hitler's suicide, the German surrender, and the British occupation of Hamburg. The text presents Lena's personal experience of these events, her version of them. Her individual, laconic reaction to the end of the Nazi regime is a case in point; she listens to public instructions over the radio, then: 'Lena Brücker nimmt ihre Tasche, darin ein Henkelmann mit Erbsensuppe, und sagt: Dann mal tschüs. So geht für sie das Tausendjährige Reich zu Ende' (*EC*, 105). On the one hand, she and Bremer are seen to act for purely personal reasons. As far as the motives behind Bremer's desertion are concerned, for example, Lena is lonely and enjoys his company, so encourages him to stay with her; he is understandably scared of joining the suicidal enterprise of fighting British tanks on foot. On the other hand, these personal decisions take place against the background of key public events in twentieth-century history. The post-war black-market economy is thus not just a set of historical details, but, as a result of what Lena tells the narrator, a matter of personal survival. Lena's story – admittedly highly subjective – depicts her as an ordinary, sceptical, non-Nazi, trying to survive the twelve years of National Socialist rule as best she could. She presents herself as being strongly opposed to war and by the end of the period, she contends, she would have been prepared to help anyone who wanted to desert. At the same time, her account does not appear to be an attempt to exonerate herself.[4] It gains considerable credibility through her reaction to the first newspaper pictures of the concentration camps after the war. Horror turns to anger at Bremer's insistence that the pictures are Soviet propaganda, then to a growing sense of guilt as she realizes – again, through very personal experience – that she, too, turned a blind eye. Her recollection of seeing Frau Levinson being taken away is particularly poignant: 'Ein SS-Mann nahm ihr [Frau Levinson] den Koffer ab, als sie auf den Laster stieg, von zwei behandschuhten Händen nach oben gezogen. Frau Levinson winkte ihr, schon auf dem Laster stehend, zu, so wie man winkt, wenn man wegfährt, aber verstohlen' (*EC*, 175).

What emerges through this personal account, therefore, is an individual perspective on the events surrounding the end of the Second World War and the subsequent period of occupation. Within this version of events, it is clear that characters in the story present their own versions of what is happening. The most obvious case here is Lena's elaborate set of lies to convince Bremer that the war is continuing and that he must stay with her. She tells him there are no newspapers because of a paper shortage, that her radio cannot be mended, and she feeds his imagination with news of a pact between Germany, Britain, and the United States against the Soviet Union, complete with details of the new allies' advances in the east, which the hapless Bremer draws into a school atlas. Troubled by her conscience at this deception, Lena repeatedly imagines telling Bremer the truth and plays out a series of possible versions of how this moment might run. Bremer, too, has given Lena only a version of his family circumstances; he denies that he is married, but Lena has seen a photograph of him with his wife and a child in his arms. Repeatedly we see that the events that befall Lena are susceptible to different interpretations. To Lena, we know, Lammers is a repellent, dangerous, interfering Nazi; the narrator has evidence of some noble qualities; and the opposite is true of Frau Eckleben. When Bremer loses his sense of taste, Lena interprets his lukewarm reaction to the food she has gone to such lengths to provide as criticism of her cooking. Bremer himself identifies various possible causes for his affliction: 'Vielleicht, dachte er, kommt es vom Rauchen, du rauchst zuviel, aber dann nistete sich sogleich der Gedanke ein, es ist nicht das Rauchen, sondern daß du dich hier von einer Frau verstecken läßt' (*EC*, 164). More disturbingly, when Lena sees the pictures from the death camps she recalls the evasions of which she too has been guilty: 'Und sie hatte sich natürlich gefragt, wohin die Leute kommen würden. Und jeder ahnte, irgendwo in den Osten, in Konzentrationslager. Dort verschwanden sie. Der Osten war weit. Lebensraum, das war der Ost-en' (*EC*, 175). Different versions of what might be happening to the deported Jews whom Lena knew from her daily life have covered over the terrible truth.

In fact, Lena's story reveals that not only do people tell stories to account for events in their personal lives, but governments and their representatives do the same to explain the public sphere. The historical setting – Nazism collapsing and being replaced by occupation – offers plenty of examples of how one interpretation of political necessity can replace another. In the newspaper archive, the narrator needs to check with the archivist that reports separated by only a few days but falling either side of the collapse of the Nazi state were really written by the same journalist, such is the ideological discrepancy. Lena's personal experience offers insight here, too. Betriebsführer Dr Fröhlich, head of the food supply authority in Hamburg during the war, trots out all the commonplaces of Nazi rhetoric to his employees. No sooner is the war over than Fröhlich is addressing his colleagues once again, urging them now to help pull Germany out of the mire into which the Nazis have driven it. Lena cannot restrain her indignation as Fröhlich nears the end of his speech: 'wir müssen jetzt arbeiten bis – da hielt es Lena Brücker nicht mehr, es platzte regelrecht aus ihr heraus – laut und deutlich: zum Endsieg. Endsieg, sagte er. Er stutzte, habe ich Endsieg gesagt, nein, sagte er, Neuanfang, natürlich, und Wiederaufbau' (*EC*, 135–6). Fröhlich is so skilled at adapting his views to the predominant ideological version of the world that, having passed quickly through the British denazification machinery, he returns as head of personnel to the food authority and takes his revenge on Lena by promptly giving her the sack.

In the private and the public spheres, then, Lena Brücker's story demonstrates how it is interpretations of the external world that affect people's lives; and her story is, in turn, an interpretation for the narrator of the mystery behind the 'Entdeckung der Currywurst'. Moreover, this story itself is brimming with other potential stories waiting to be told.[5] The anecdotal style is common to all three texts and opens up brief digressions into tangential events from the past. When Bremer gives Lena a very effective massage, for example, a brief excursion into Bremer's family history reveals how he learned his skills: his father was a vet and used the technique to treat injured horses. Likewise, we learn something of Holzinger's past, most notably his tendency to use his culinary skills to poison prominent Nazis and radio announcers whose job it was to announce German victories. Where such anecdotes risk taking the account too far away from the Currywurst, however, the narrator and/or Lena intervene to close off the digression. Bremer discovers love letters to Lena in the flat, but the story behind them is 'ne andere Geschichte. Hat nix mit der Currywurst zu tun' (*EC*, 112), the narrator is told, just as he had concluded when confronted with the evidence of Frau Eckleben's complicity in denouncing neighbours to the Gestapo. Even the narrator's personal schedule restricts the digressions. Since he soon needs to return to his family in Munich, he does not have time to hear Lena's account of how her husband invented a dance.

In these potential stories that are cut short one might identify a perhaps playful reason for Timm's choice of the Novelle form. The genre traditionally demands concentration on a single event and does not allow for digression; in pointing to, and yet restricting, possible digressions Timm emphasizes how stories are connected and reveals how heavily laden every story is with the potential for other narration. Timm himself exploits that potential elsewhere. *Der Mann auf dem Hochrad, Johannisnacht, Die Entdeckung der Currywurst,* and indeed the novels *Heißer Sommer* (1974) and *Kopfjäger* (1991) have in common figures and episodes from a family background in Hamburg very close to Timm's own. Most strikingly, here the narrator recalls that the first time he ate a Currywurst from Lena's stand he was with his Uncle Heinz, about whom he asks Lena for further information: 'Stimmt es, daß er die Herkunft von Kartoffeln schmecken konnte?', to which she replies 'Er war ein Kartoffelkenner, wie andere Leute Weinkenner sind' (*EC*, 70). It is Uncle Heinz's remarkable gift that provides the stimulus for *Johannisnacht*; the narrator of the later text even repeats Lena's words almost verbatim to explain Heinz's skill to an acquaintance.

The debate as to whether *Die Entdeckung der Currywurst* fits exactly into any definition of the Novelle is thus perhaps less important than the way in which aspects typical of the genre which appear in the text coincide with Timm's treatment of the interplay between personal and socio-political history. The narrator's rendition of Lena's account contains symbolism of everyday objects and stresses elements of the fantastic not because definitions of a Novelle say it should, but because these are aspects of personal experience which emerge when one person narrates a part of their life to another. It concentrates on one unusual event which has, nevertheless, actually happened because the narrator must at least try to keep the account within manageable limits and stop the sheer potential for other stories from overwhelming this one. Like Lena Brücker, Uwe Timm is not simply following a recipe in *Die Entdeckung der Currywurst*. Lena's everyday experiences of life at the end of the Second World War are remarkable components of a highly individual story; at the same time, they intersect with a more general social reality. What emerges is a humorous, moving, illuminating version of life for an ordinary but unique person living in Germany from 1945 to 1947.

Johannisnacht, Uwe Timm's most recent prose work of any length, has a number of points in common with *Die Entdeckung der Currywurst*. Most obviously, the spark for the story is, once again, research into the history of food, a history in which the narrator's family is also caught up. Here Timm has removed the (admittedly rather loose) strait-jacket of the designation Novelle, however, for in *Johannisnacht. Roman* he allows himself greater freedom to follow the unusual stories that chance throws across the path of his narrator. In the opening chapter of the text, the narrator, who is an author, succumbs to a mild case of writer's block and, for want of something better to do, he accepts a commission to write a magazine article on potatoes; there are some family connections to the article, but the task does not promise to be especially exciting. He sets off to spend three days in post-unification Berlin, apparently 'für eine ganz gewöhnliche Recherche' (J, 13). By the end of the text, he finds himself with badly cut, green hair on a dilapidated, ex-GDR train on the way to Leipzig, in the company of a former Russian opera singer, fleeing from a Bulgarian arms dealer, a Bedouin prince, and a failed Ph.D. student who makes money from telephone sex, about whose gender the narrator is far from certain – and he is several hundred marks worse off!

Die Wandlung des Alltags in Bedeutung 101

The discrepancy between original project and end result can be explained in terms of Timm's narrative strategy of exploring the unusual which hides behind the mundane. The narrator's research into the potato provides a loose framework to his time in Berlin; everyone he meets is tangentially connected with Rogler, a deceased East German academic who kept a potato archive, or with the narrator's desire to gain access to that archive. Yet he is constantly distracted by other people's unusual experiences, by objects behind which lie exotic stories, by curious incidents that befall him. Structurally, the result is a novel that, although it progresses chronologically over the three days in Berlin, is episodic, with divisions between chapters often representing a short leap in time and place. These episodes are so bizarre that they border on the fantastic. As the narrator is told on two separate occasions, he is in Berlin over the period of midsummer, 'Johannisnacht', a time when people's behaviour is subject to mysterious influences, when 'die Dinge zeigen sich von einer anderen Seite, wie auch die Menschen' (*J*, 221). The artist Christo is, after all, wrapping the Reichstag up in plastic. The narrator, too, is fully aware that he is behaving in ways he would never even contemplate at home in Munich: drinking dry Martinis during the day, visiting night clubs, running up 600 Mark bills on a telephone sex line. And yet, with the exception of an alcohol-induced dream, all of the events that befall him are part of the real world, no matter how bizarre. Behind the 'ganz gewöhnliche Recherche' lurks a very unusual story, but one located in the outside world.

Indeed, the subject of the narrator's research could hardly be more mundane and the ordinariness of the potato underlines the extraordinary nature of the narrator's experiences. The family connection points the way from the beginning and is one of the stories the narrator of *Die Entdeckung der Currywurst* chose to leave unexplored. It concerns the narrator's favourite uncle who, as well as being a good story-teller and an expert at blowing smoke rings, possessed the remarkable skill of being able to identify types of potato by their taste alone. Uncle Heinz emerges as an appealingly unconventional figure through the narrator's memories and immediately the reader is presented with an engaging story behind the unprepossessing façade of the potato. Other connections with the vegetable work in the same way. The narrator remarks laconically to his friend Kubin: 'Ich hab mich mal in eine Kartoffel verliebt', stimulating the description of 'eine unbeschreibliche Nacht'

(J, 17) he spent with a girl who attended a Fasching party dressed as a potato. Extracts from Rogler's archive take the reader into a variety of academic areas: the potato's part in demographic growth in the Europe of the eighteenth and nineteenth centuries, for example, and the sociology of its geographical spread; and the narrator has a series of anecdotes concerning everything from the potato in eighteenth-century German literature to its supposed aphrodisiac effect. Through Rogler, the potato has even led to the creation of a new area of vocabulary. Unlike wine critics who insist on making dubious comparisons between the bouquet of a wine and other familiar smells, Rogler invented his own terms to describe the taste of each type of potato and recorded them in the 'Geschmackskataloge' which the narrator goes to such lengths to recover.

The author continually comes across other apparently mundane 'gezeichnete Dinge' during his time in Berlin. On arrival in the city he stays with his friend Kubin, who, the narrator quickly discovers, has been suffering from insomnia. The cure, Kubin tells him, has been the purchase of a wonderful new bed; but when he sees it, the narrator notes only 'Das Bett war ein einfaches Feldbett' (J, 14). Ordinary appearances deceive, however, for this is 'der exakte Nachbau von Napoleons Feldbett' (J, 14) and Kubin is able to expand not only on Napoleon's sleeping habits, but also on the personal history of the beds he has tried out in an attempt to cure his insomnia. This includes a water bed that became infested with algae: 'das Bett roch plötzlich wie eine Grotte, und nach weiteren zwei Monaten wie ein Karpfenteich. Wir haben es heimlich in einen Wald gebracht, sozusagen als Kleinstbiotop' (J, 15). A detail of French history and an extremely unusual domestic incident thus hide beneath the 'einfaches Feldbett'. Likewise, on his search for the potato archive, the narrator comes across Spranger, a friend and former flat-mate of Rogler, who has an out-of-tune grand piano in his flat. Of course, there is a story behind it: 'Der Flügel ist ein Findelkind' (J, 61), we learn from Spranger, for it was dumped in front of the building in April 1945, presumably following an abortive attempt to rescue it from the advancing Red Army. A Russian colonel stationed in the flat after the war was responsible for having it brought inside. But the piano has still more to tell, specifically concerning the hole in its lid. The Russian colonel was an excellent shot and, after a few drinks, used to shoot champagne glasses out of the hand – or even off the head – of the unfortunate

'Kommerzienrat' who lived downstairs. One day he got so drunk that he missed, hitting the piano 'an dem gerade ein NKWD-Offizier eine Mazurka spielte' (J, 69) – and the colonel ended up 'strafversetzt' to Murmansk. In one sense, then, the story of the dilapidated piano takes the narrator away from his research into the potato; in another, it connects very closely with it as another unremarkable object that has a remarkable history.

Just as objects trigger fascinating digressions in the narrator's account, so the people whom he meets frequently have an unusual story to recount about their own lives or the lives of others around them. Of course, the narrator has already started the trend with his memories of his uncle's talents, and he has shown how complex the resulting levels of narration can be; he recalls how his uncle used to tell stories of a ship's stoker who used to tell stories of the Boxer rising. Of the people the narrator encounters in Berlin, Kramer, another flatmate of Rogler and the person responsible for making such a mess of the narrator's hair, has a series of anecdotes about his time as a barber in the GDR and the famous heads of hair he cut; Tina, the PhD student who now runs a telephone sex line, tells the narrator about her preference for older men, a confession that brings her to recount at length how her marriage broke up as a result of a series of migraine attacks and a course of swimming lessons; and, perhaps most remarkably, the narrator meets Herr Bucher, the husband of a West Berlin academic who had hoped to stage a potato exhibition in conjunction with Rogler. Bucher's marriage, too, has broken up, but under the most unusual circumstances. His wife went on holiday to the Sahara desert and made the acquaintance of Moussa, a Tuareg prince. Her throw-away European pleasantry 'Wenn Sie mal nach Deutschland kommen, besuchen Sie uns' (J, 174) is taken at face value by Moussa; he sells all his camels, buys a ticket for Germany and rings the Buchers from the airport. They are forced to take in the handsome African prince (the narrator mistakes him for a woman at first), and he becomes a local celebrity. On a trip to the island of Sylt, Frau Bucher, who has fallen in love with Moussa, tries to turn her feelings into actions, but is rejected by him; to Moussa, the rules of hospitality are sacred and they certainly do not include seducing one's married host. The distraught Frau Bucher leaves her husband and runs off to Paris, leaving Herr Bucher and Moussa to share the family home in Berlin. Herr Bucher's account, related to the narrator over two rounds of dry Martinis which themselves trigger a story concerning Rogler, is extremely detailed, and even includes its own digression: how Moussa comes to speak old-fashioned German with a Russian accent. It contributes nothing to the narrator's specific research into the potato, but reveals much of Timm's narrative approach of allowing the chance encounters of the narrator's journey to determine the direction of the novel.

That is not to say, however, that those encounters are so personal that they have significance only to the narrator, within the enclosed framework of the novel. Certainly, each digression contains very specific, often extremely intimate detail; but Timm goes a stage further, for, as in the other texts under discussion, personal experience is repeatedly seen to intersect with wider cultural, political and historical factors. Just as Lena Brücker's individual experience throws light on life in Hamburg under National Socialism and the British occupation, so the unique story of Moussa offers sociological insight into cultural differences, not least into the patronizing attitude of Europeans towards Africa. Likewise, Tina's experiences illuminate contemporary sexual mores; and Kramer's mutilation of the narrator's hairstyle appears to be part of a lifetime's practice of 'Allagssabotage'(J, 56), through which he had expressed his opposition to the worst abuses of the GDR and which he now unleashes on an unsuspecting 'Wessi' as a protest about unification. The stories triggered by objects work in the same way. The grand piano does not just have an unusual history, it reveals something of the Soviet occupation of Berlin and of disciplinary measures in the Red Army; and Kubin chooses to sleep on a camp bed not just because it suits him, but because Napoleon was able to conquer half of Europe while sleeping on an identical bed. Likewise, in a section that connects closely with *Der Mann auf dem Hochrad*, the narrator links together German political history, his unconventional uncle and the humble potato. Uncle Heinz's dying words were 'Roter Baum' and, at one level, the novel is an attempt to discover what those words mean. The narrator believes they refer to a type of potato, but no one he asks can confirm his supposition. At the end of the text, however, a song he hears triggers a different childhood memory; 'Roter Baum', he suddenly recalls, was the name of a pub at which his uncle's father, a farm worker in Mecklenburg, attended his first meeting of the Social Democratic Party, despite being warned by his employer that his action would have unpleasant consequences. Such was the hostility towards left-wing politics in the rural Germany of the mid-nineteenth century, the man was sacked immediately. The uncle then had to follow his father from town to town looking for occasional work, but the result of their impecunious existence was that the uncle developed his remarkable skill: 'So haben sie sich monatelang nur von Kartoffeln ernährt, die sie auf den Feldern heimlich ausgegraben haben. Und das Sonderbare ist, das sich der Onkel nicht übergessen hat, sondern, als Kind immer auf die Unterschiede achtend, die winzigen Varianten im Geschmack zu schätzen lernte' (J, 278–9). Via family connections the narrator's research into the potato thus exposes a significant feature in the political history of Germany in the second half of the nineteenth century.

Perhaps the most obvious way in which the narrator's experiences intersect with political issues is in the conflict between east and west which, five years after unification, is still simmering away in Berlin. Although he is nominally only interested in information about the potato, his sources for that information continually confront him with views on how unification has affected contemporary life in the reinstated German capital. Rogler, Rosenow, Spranger and Kramer are all former East Germans who have been forced to accommodate themselves, with varying degrees of success, to the western takeover. Rosenow, for example, has rapidly adopted all of the external mannerisms of a successful West German businessman in his new career as an estate agent: designer clothes, a stylish haircut, a BMW, a mobile phone. He tells the narrator, by contrast, that Rogler never truly fitted in to either society. Spranger, too, is a former East German academic; he now makes his living preserving and wrapping the flowers that are offered for sale every night in pubs and restaurants throughout Berlin. The elderly Kramer, meanwhile, lives largely in the past, telling stories of how he ruined the hairstyles of leading polit-bureau officials. The narrator's interaction with all four characters is unusual and specific, yet their stories reveal something of the general problems of daily survival in post-unification Berlin.

The series of rides in taxis which the narrator takes works in a similar way. He makes each journey for a very specific, even idiosyncratic purpose; yet his experiences with the taxi drivers point to endemic social tension. On his first trip to see Christo's activities at the Reichstag, for example, he hears the life story of a West Berlin taxi driver. The driver who, we discover, studied Romanistik and has written a travel guide to the Sahara, moved to Berlin long before unification to avoid national service. His attitude to the city has changed since the Wall came down: 'Nee, seit der Vereinigung gibts hier einen unglaublichen Aggressionsstau. [...] Jetzt kommen all die Jungs her, die ne schnelle Mark machen wollen. Ich überleg mir, ob ich nicht weggeh' (J, 23). Later, on a trip to the taxi lost-property office in the former East Berlin, a second western taxi driver is even more direct in expressing his suspicion of the east. To the narrator's question as to whether he often gets fares into the east of the city, the driver replies:

> Nee, [...] und wenn sichs vermeiden läßt, fahr ick ooch nich, kenn mich nich so jut aus, is doch ne fremde Stadt, andere Jebräuche, andere Sitten. Nee. Die Stimmung is, jeder soll ma hübsch bei sich bleiben. Ohne Mauer, det ist jut. Kenn Se den: Was ist der Unterschied zwischen einem Türken und einem Sachsen?
> Nein.
> Der Türke spricht Deutsch und arbeitet. (J, 95)

That a former West German can easily get into deep water in the east is a lesson the narrator has in fact already learnt, for he only has to visit the lost-property office in the first place because of an altercation with a taxi driver from former East Berlin. Having collected part of Rogler's potato archive, including the all-important 'Geschmackskataloge', the narrator discovers that getting a taxi at all is a problematic exercise in the east of the city. After a wait of almost an hour, a driver stops but, on seeing the documents in the cardboard box containing the archive and hearing that the narrator's destination is in the west, he jumps to the conclusion that the narrator is just another westerner out to exploit the east for financial gain. The result is a huge argument in which the narrator calls the driver a 'Straßenfaschist' (J, 76) and the driver simply hurls the contents of the archive on to the road and drives off. All three trips take the narrator, who is nominally interested only in completing his research on the potato, into the heart of the mutual suspicion and hostility that still governs relations between east and west Berliners in the mid-1990s.

The East German taxi driver's interpretation of the narrator's intent in taking the archive to the west links it to other episodes in the novel where characters only partly understand, or entirely misinterpret signals as a result of cultural interference; the eastern driver feels exploited by the west and leaps to the conclusion that he has one of the exploiters in his grasp. As the narrator then attempts to pick up the remains of Rogler's archive, others interpret his behaviour according to their own experience of life in the city: a man stops and asks him how much he charges for a box of 200 cigarettes; and his landlady, on seeing the now beaten cardboard box which houses the archive, asks him if he has been shopping in Aldi. Reactions to the narrator's extraordinary hairstyle work in the same way. In the trendy hairdressers' in West Berlin, the employees might be on the right track in suspecting that it is an act of revenge by an East German, but once it is coloured green people leap to conclusions about the narrator's profession: the composer who is staying in the narrator's hotel thinks he must be in advertising; and a man who writes speeches for funerals believes, partly correctly, that he is in some part of the entertainment industry, for 'wer so ne Frisur hat, kann nicht in der Bank arbeiten' (*J*, 257). What emerges is that people are constantly attempting to interpret signals in the world around them, to read stories into such signals that correspond to their own experience.

Such cultural assumptions and misunderstandings are not restricted to the divide between the two former Germanies. As we have already seen, Moussa interpreted Frau Bucher's words to be a genuine invitation to visit Germany which he would be rude not to accept, while for Frau Bucher they were little more than a polite commonplace. Similarly, the narrator is acutely aware after hearing Herr Bucher's story that, in accepting the gift of a ring from Moussa, he risks sending out a message in a different language: 'Diesen Ring als Geschenk anzunehmen, würde bedeuten, irgendwann eine Gegengabe machen zu müssen, etwas, was er dann ganz selbstverständlich einfordern würde, womöglich eine meiner Töchter, vielleicht, wer weiß' (*J*, 185–6). The fact that the narrator finds Moussa waiting for him in his hotel thus plays an important part in his decision to flee Berlin on the next available train. Another powerful reason to leave comes from a similar case of people speaking different languages, figuratively at least. In his attempt to recover the 'Geschmackskataloge' which went missing during the incident with the eastern taxi driver, the narrator places an advertisement in two newspapers, requesting anyone with any information to contact him. He gets a quick response and agrees to meet the respondent in the Hilton Hotel. To his horror, the narrator discovers that the two men who have replied to the advertisement are a Bulgarian arms dealer and his bodyguard; 'Kartoffel', it emerges, means 'mine' in the jargon of the illegal arms trade and the

Bulgarian has brought a glossy 'Katalog' from which the narrator can select his purchase. The narrator runs, leaving a bemused waiter with the words 'Der Waffenhändler zahlt!' (J, 209), and is forced to keep running until he leaves Berlin. The potential for such cultural misunderstandings is huge, in the narrator's experience over these few days, especially in the melting pot of post-unification Berlin.

In *Johannisnacht* Uwe Timm thus allows himself greater latitude to explore stories and incidents than is the case in *Die Entdeckung der Currywurst*. Although the narrator's activities are held together loosely by his research project on the potato, in practice he moves from one picaresque adventure to another, uncovering the stories behind the people and objects that happen to cross his path. From unprepossessing beginnings, the story quickly moves into the bizarre, almost into the fantastic. Berlin in midsummer seems a very strange place, and both literally and figuratively the narrator is not at home. The peculiar incidents and remarkable stories he comes across are, however, much more than an attempt by Timm to illustrate what a funny old world it is. However outlandish, not to say humorous they might be, the narrator's experiences intersect with historical and political issues, with the problems of living in multi-cultural post-unification Germany. The conclusion to the novel ties off the loose ends in a satisfying way. On the train with the Russian opera singer the narrator has managed to interpret his uncle's dying words, he has even learnt to blow smoke rings like Onkel Heinz, and he is able to assure his companion that his work is finished: 'Ich wollte eine Geschichte schreiben' (J, 274), he tells the Russian, and this is precisely what he has done as a result of his trip to Berlin. Narration for Timm consists in confronting everyday objects, incidents and people, uncovering the unusual stories concealed behind them, and hence revealing themes of more general significance. It is an act of interpretation of the outside world.

To return to the original distinction that Uwe Timm himself makes between the novels of the early part of his literary career and his later works, it is evident that none of the texts under discussion here has a clearly didactic intention. What interests the Timm of *Der Mann auf dem Hochrad*, *Die Entdeckung der Currywurst*, and *Johannisnacht* is the detail of everyday life. Using memory, documentary evidence, and personal experience as stimuli, the narrators – one might even suggest the identical narrator – of the three texts re-create episodes from their own past lives and from those of family members and friends. The creative act is built into each text and it is obvious that we are not simply dealing with *Dokumentarliteratur*; the texts are fictional versions of a given reality, no less 'true' for the fact that other versions might exist. People, objects, and events have their own hidden stories which the narrators set out to uncover and which drive the narration forward; 'gezeichnete Dinge' and 'sprechende Situationen' abound in Timm's conception of the world, even to the point that his narrators must restrain themselves from digressions that might take them too far from the original direction of each text. The stories that are stimulated by objects and situations in this way are, by definition, highly personal, for they belong to the individual experience of specific characters. Everyday detail might be mundane, but the stories hidden behind a toothpick, a ground-sheet or a potato are unusual, funny, even fantastic. In Timm's view, such stories represent authentic versions of how people experience their own lives. At the same time, it is clear that the texts are more than 'fly-on-the-wall' documentaries designed to satisfy prurient interest in the private lives of others. In each case, individual experience is set very clearly in a recognizable social and historical context. Specific stories thus have a significance which goes beyond the specific, as Timm is careful to emphasize in *Erzählen und kein Ende*: 'Und in diesen alltäglichen Geschichten drückt sich nicht nur der beliebige individuelle Kleinkram aus, sondern zugleich auch immer etwas von der Mentalität der jeweiligen Epoche, also von den die Gesellschaft bewegenden Problemen. Es sind Geschichten, die einmalig sind und doch allen gehören' (*EkE*, 103). The act of writing for Uwe Timm in the post AutorenEdition period thus consists in exploring the personal *and* the social meaning of the detail of people's lives. It is, as Timm puts it himself, 'die Wandlung des Alltags in Bedeutung' (*EkE*, 119).

Notes

[1] As Rhys W. Williams points out, the political concerns of *Heißer Sommer* and *Kerbels Flucht* are in any case tempered by highly personal ones. See Chapter 5 of this volume.

[2] Timm mentions the way in which the silver toothpick stimulated *Der Mann auf dem Hochrad* in *Erzählen und kein Ende* (*EkE*, 27).

³ Personal exeperience of fantastic events corresponds, of course, with literary features familiar from the Romantic tradition of the Novelle.

⁴ That individual, unexceptional biographies tend to exonerate the guilt for the crimes of National Socialism is a criticism familiar from reactions to the wave of texts designated as *Väterliteratur* from the 1970s and 1980s. In *Der Mann auf der Kanzel* (1979), for example, Ruth Rehmann builds the criticism into the text by having the narrator's son challenge her indulgent version of her father's experience of Nazi rule.

⁵ It is particularly on these digressions from a single event that critics have concentrated in challenging Timm's designation of the text as 'Novelle'. See for example Hartmut Steinecke, 'Die Entdeckung der Currywurst oder die Madeleine der Alltagsästhetik', in Keith Bullivant, Manfred Durak and H. Steinecke (eds.), *Die Archäologie der Wünsche. Studien zum Werk von Uwe Timm*, (Cologne, Kiepenheuer & Witsch, 1995), 217–30 (222). Timm himself defends the right of the material to break the form: 'Und es kommt gerade darauf an, sich von dem Herrschaftsanspruch der reinen Form abzuwenden und sich wieder auf die Eigentendenzen des Stoffes zu konzentrieren' (*EkE*, 121–2).

8

Bibliography

DAVID BASKER

CONTENTS

1. **Primary Literature**
1.a Prose works
1.b Anthologies of poems
1.c Edited volumes
1.d Prose extracts, poems and essays
1.e Films and radio plays
1.f Translations of Uwe Timm's work
1.g Interviews

Works are listed chronologically.

2. **Secondary Literature**
2.a General
2.b Individual texts

Books and articles are listed alphabetically, by author's name.

1. Primary Literature

1. a Prose works

1. *Das Problem der Absurdität bei Albert Camus* (Hamburg, Lüdke, 1971) [Geistes- und sozialwissenschaftliche Dissertation, 20].
2. *Heißer Sommer* (Munich, Gütersloh, Vienna, AutorenEdition bei C. Bertelsmann, 1974) [Lizenzausgabe: Berlin, Weimar, Aufbau, 1975; paperback editions: Reinbek, Rowohlt, 1977 [rororo 4094]; Cologne, Kiepenheuer & Witsch, 1985 [KiWi 70]].
3. *Morenga* (Munich, AutorenEdition, 1978) [Lizenzausgabe: Berlin, Weimar, Aufbau, 1979; paperback editions: Reinbek, Rowohlt, 1981 [rororo 4705]; Cologne, Kiepenheuer & Witsch, 1982 [KiWi 82]].
4. *Kerbels Flucht* (Munich, AutorenEdition, 1980) [Paperback editions: Munich, Deutscher Taschenbuch, 1983 [dtv 10143]; Cologne, Kiepenheuer & Witsch, 1991 [KiWi 232]].
5. *Die Zugmaus. Eine Geschichte*, illustrated by Tatjana Hauptmann (Zurich, Diogenes, 1981) [Paperback edition: Zurich, Diogenes, 1983 [kinder detebe 25073]].
6. *Die Piratenamsel*, illustrated by Gunnar Matysiak (Zurich, Cologne, Benziger, 1983) [Revised edition: Zurich, Frauenfeld, Nagel & Kimche, 1991; paperback edition: Munich, Deutscher Taschenbuch, 1986 [dtv 70088]; reprinted 1994 [dtv 70347]].
7. *Der Mann auf dem Hochrad. Legende* (Cologne, Kiepenheuer & Witsch, 1984) [Lizenzausgabe: Berlin, Weimar, Aufbau, 1985; paperback edition: Cologne, Kiepenheuer & Witsch, 1986 [KiWi 97]].
8. *Der Schlangenbaum* (Cologne, Kiepenheuer & Witsch, 1986) [Lizenzausgabe: Berlin, Weimar, Aufbau, 1985; paperback edition: Cologne, Kiepenheuer & Witsch, 1989 [KiWi 198]].
9. *Rennschwein Rudi Rüssel*, illustrated by Gunnar Matysiak (Zurich, Frauenfeld, Nagel & Kimche, 1989) [Paperback edition: Munich, Deutscher Taschenbuch, 1993 [dtv 70285]].
10. *Vogel, friß die Feige nicht. Römische Aufzeichnungen* (Cologne, Kiepenheuer & Witsch, 1989) [Paperback edition: Cologne, Kiepenheuer & Witsch, 1996 [KiWi 421]].
11. *Kopfjäger. Bericht aus dem Inneren des Landes* (Cologne, Kiepenheuer & Witsch, 1991) [Paperback edition: Cologne, Kiepenheuer & Witsch, 1993 [KiWi 320]].
12. *Erzählen und kein Ende. Versuche zu einer Ästhetik des Alltags* (Cologne, Kiepenheuer & Witsch, 1993).
13. *Die Entdeckung der Currywurst* (Cologne, Kiepenheuer & Witsch, 1993) [Paperback edition: Kiepenheuer & Witsch, 1995 [KiWi 380]].
14. *Der Schatz auf Pagensand* (Zurich, Frauenfeld, Nagel & Kimche, 1995).
15. *Johannisnacht* (Cologne, Kiepenheuer & Witsch, 1996).

1.b Anthologies of poems
1. *Widersprüche* (Hamburg, Neue Presse, 1971).
2. *Wolfenbütteler Straße 53* (Munich, Damnitz, 1977).

1.c Edited volumes
1. *Lesebuch 4. Freizeit. Texte zu einem schönen Wort und unserer Wirklichkeit*, with Uwe Friesel (Munich, Gütersloh, Vienna, Bertelsman, 1973).
2. *Auf Anhieb Mord. Kurzkrimis*, with Klaus Konjetzky, Dagmar Ploetz, Roman Ritter, Peter Stössel (Munich, Gütersloh, Vienna, AutorenEdition bei C. Bertelsmann, 1975).
3. *Kontext 1. Literatur und Wirklichkeit*, with Gerd Fuchs (Munich, AutorenEdition bei C. Bertelsmann, 1976).
4. *Deutsche Kolonien* (Munich, AutorenEdition, 1981) [Reprinted: Cologne, Kiepenheuer & Witsch, 1986]

1.d Prose extracts, poems and essays
1. 'Linguistik' [poem], *Frankfurter Allgemeine Zeitung*, 25 November 1967.
2. 'Wie treiben Filmkritiker Sozialkritik ab. Zu *Rosemaries* [sic] *Baby* von Roman Polanski, Besprechung in Heft 12/68 von Joachim von Mengershausen', *Film*, No. 2 (1969), 7–8.
3. 'Der Underground im Elfenbeinturm. Vom 2. Hamburger Filmfestival der Underground-Filmer', *Deutsche Volkszeitung*, 28 March 1969.
4. 'Rainer Maria Rilkes *Lieblingspark*. Eine Erzählung', *Frankfurter Allgemeine Zeitung*, 19 April 1969.
5. 'Gedichte' ['Jagdzeiten'; 'Verständnis für die Jugend'; 'Politische Argumentation'], *kürbiskern. Literatur und Kritik*, No. 2 (1969), 255–7.
6. 'Griechische Aspekte' [poem], *kürbiskern. Literatur und Kritik*, No. 3 (1969), 552.
7. 'Günter Grass oder Kräht der Hahn auf dem Mist, ändert sich das Wetter oder es bleibt, wie es ist', *Deutsche Volkszeitung*, 29 August 1969.
8. 'Alfred zum Beispiel' [story], in Joachim Fuhrmann and Klaus Kuhnke (eds.), *thema: arbeit. lyrik & prosa* (Hamburg, Neue Presse, 1969), 25–7.
9. 'Verständnis für die Jugend' [poem], in Joachim Fuhrmann (ed.), *agitprop. Lyrik, Thesen, Berichte. Kollektivausgabe*, (Hamburg, Quer-Verlag, 1969), 16–17.
10. 'Widersprüche' [poem], ibid., 19–20.
11. 'Jagdzeiten' [poem], ibid., 35.
12. 'Schutzhaft/Vorbeugehaft' [poem], ibid., 82–3.
13. 'Politische Argumentation' [poem], ibid., 143.
14. 'Relationen' [poem], ibid., 145–6.
15. 'Griechische Aspekte' [poem], ibid., 150.
16. 'Vorteile, die sich aus dem täglichen Hungertod von ca. 7000 Menschen in Biafra ergeben' [poem], ibid., 162–3.
17. 'Die Bedeutung der Agitprop-Lyrik im Kampf gegen den Kapitalismus oder Kleinvieh macht auch Mist', ibid., 209–11.

18. 'Kolle und die Folgen. Zum Beispiel Ehebruch, ein Film von Oswald Kolle', *Deutsche Volkszeitung*, 14 November 1969. [Reprinted in: *Film*, No. 12 (1969), 6–7.]
19. '"Ästhetische Linke" steht kopf. Der Film Z und seine Kritiker', *Deutsche Volkszeitung*, 20 February 1970.
20. 'Zeig mal dein Visum. Möglichkeiten der politischen Lyrik' [on F. C. Delius, *Wenn wir bei Rot*], *Deutsche Volkszeitung*, 27 March 1970.
21. 'Dokumentation eines Linksliberalen. *Die Ausgelieferten* von Per Olov Enquist', *Deutsche Volkszeitung*, 19 June 1970.
22. 'Agitprop-Stück gegen das technokratische Hochschulmodell' [with Roman Ritter], in Agnes Hüfner (ed.), *Straßentheater* (Frankfurt am Main, Suhrkamp, 1970), 88–106.
23. 'Peter Handke oder sicher in die 70er Jahre', *kürbiskern. Literatur und Kritik*, No. 4 (1970), 611–21.
24. 'Griechische Aspekte' [poem], in Hilde Domin (ed.), *Nachkrieg und Unfrieden. Gedichte als Index 1945–70* (Neuwied, Berlin, Luchterhand, 1970), 120.
25. 'Der entflohene Sklave. *Der Cimarrón* von Miguel Barnet', *Deutsche Volkszeitung*, 7 January 1971.
26. 'Sport in der Klassengesellschaft', *kürbiskern. Literatur und Kritik*, No. 4 (1971), 608–17.
27. 'Der Sport und seine tatsächliche Funktion', *Deutsche Volkszeitung*, 9 September 1971.
28. 'Emanzipation eines Verspäteten. *Emanzipation der Kunst* von Michael Scharang', *Deutsche Volkszeitung*, 14 October 1971.
29. 'Zwischen Unterhaltung und Aufklärung', *kürbiskern. Literatur und Kritik*, No. 1 (1972), 79–90.
30. 'Reflexion des Bewußtseins. Romane schreiben im Werkkreis Literatur der Arbeitswelt', *Deutsche Volkszeitung*, 18 May 1972.
31. 'Ein Denkmal stürzt' [extract from *Heißer Sommer*], *Deutsche Volkszeitung*, 8 June 1972.
32. 'Vilshofener Stichworte' [poem], *Literarische Hefte*, 11 No. 41 (1972), 42.
33. 'Die Rotts und die Rothschilds. Von einem, der glaubte, ohne zu arbeiten gut leben zu können' [review of Hermann Peter Piwitt, *Rothschilds*], *Deutsche Volkszeitung*, 30 November 1972.
34. 'Mitten im kalten Winter' [poem], in Uwe Wandrey (ed.), *Stille Nacht allerseits! Ein gartiges Allerlei* (Reinbek, Rowohlt, 1972), 52.
35. 'Frauenlob' [poem], in Joachim Fuhrmann (ed.), *Linke Liebeslyrik* (Hamburg, Neue Presse, 1972), 29.
36. 'Liebesgedicht' [poem], ibid., 29.
37. 'Lob der Idylle' [poem], in Uwe Friesel and Uwe Timm (eds.), *Lesebuch 4. Freizeit. Texte zu einem schönen Wort unserer Wirklichkeit* (Munich, Gütersloh, Vienna, Bertelsmann, 1973), 58–9.
38. 'Die Durchsuchung' [extract from *Heißer Sommer*], *kürbiskern. Literatur, Kritik, Klassenkampf*, No. 4 (1973), 672–82.

39. 'Herbstgedicht' [poem], *Literarische Hefte*, 11 No. 43 (1973), 44.
40. 'Aussichten' [poem], ibid., 45.
41. 'Der Glasbläser' [poem], *Literarische Hefte*, 12 No. 44 (1973), 31.
42. 'Edle Einfalt, stille Größe. Das Literaturmagazin, eine "Autorenzeitschrift" bei Rowohlt', *Deutsche Volkszeitung*, 17 January 1974.
43. 'Catch' [extract from *Heißer Sommer*], *Literarische Hefte*, 12 No. 46 (1974), 47–51.
44. 'Heißer Sommer' [extract from *Heißer Sommer*], *Deutsche Volkszeitung*, 22 August 1974.
45. 'Schriftsteller und Politik. Eine Umfrage der Deutschen Volkszeitung', *Deutsche Volkszeitung*, 14 November 1974.
46. 'Realismus und Utopie', *kürbiskern. Literatur, Kritik, Klassenkampf*, No. 1 (1975), 91–101.
47. 'Von den vielen kleinen Schritten' [poem], *Literarische Hefte* 13 No. 49 (1975), 31–2.
48. 'Die Barrikade' [story], *Deutsche Volkszeitung*, 26 June 1975.
49. 'Ringtail' [poem], *kürbiskern. Literatur, Kritik, Klassenkampf*, No. 4 (1975), 38–41.
50. 'Sensibilität für wen?', *kürbiskern. Literatur, Kritik, Klassenkampf*, No. 1 (1976), 118–22.
51. 'Realismus und Utopie', in Peter Laemmle (ed.), *Realismus – welcher? Sechzehn Autoren auf der Suche nach einem literarischen Begriff* (Munich, edition text + kritik, 1976), 139–50.
52. 'Von den Schwierigkeiten eines Anti-Realisten', ibid., 164–77.
53. 'Über den Dogmatismus in der Literatur', in Uwe Timm and Gerd Fuchs (eds.), *Kontext 1. Literatur und Wirklichkeit* (Munich, AutorenEdition bei C. Bertelsmann, 1976), 22–31.
54. 'Massa' [story], in *Warum wird so einer Kommunist? Erzählungen, Gedichte, Reportagen, Protokolle* (Munich, Damnitz, 1976), 166–76. [Reprinted in *Neue deutsche Literatur*, 24 No. 8 (1976), 27–36; extract reprinted in *Deutsche Volkszeitung*, 21 October 1976).]
55. 'Handkes entfremdete Schwester', *Stuttgarter Zeitung*, 20 August 1976.
56. 'Dalli, Dalli, Literatur! Der alte, neue Realismus (2)', *Stuttgarter Zeitung*, 21 August 1976.
57. 'Wo die Weißen schwarz sehen' [travel report from Namibia], *Konkret*, No. 9 (1976), 36–8.
58. 'Deutsche in Afrika' [extract from *Morenga*], Wespennest, No. 29 (1977).
59. 'Hosianna. Aus dem Roman *Morenga*', *kürbiskern. Literatur, Kritik, Klassenkampf*, No. 1 (1978), 24–40.
60. 'Wenstrups Verschwinden' [extract from *Morenga*], *Deutsche Volkszeitung*, 16 December 1978.
61. 'Meine Hottentotten oder Die verschwiegene Gewalt. Eine ärgerliche Anthologie südafrikanischer Prosa' [review of Peter Sulzer (ed.), *Südafrika*], *Deutsche Volkszeitung*, 18 May 1978.

62. 'Ich über mich: Uwe Timm' [on *Morenga*], *Buchreport*, 22, 2 June 1978.
63. 'Die Zeit der kleinen und der großen Kämpfe. Jurek Beckers neues Buch Schlaflose Tage', *Deutsche Volkszeitung*, 24 August 1978.
64. 'Der Tulpenbläser' [poem], *Neue deutsche Literatur*, 27 No. 6 (1979), 107–8.
65. 'Stenographische Mitschrift', in Heinar Kipphardt (ed.), *Aus Liebe zu Deutschland. Satiren zu Franz Josef Strauß* (Munich, AutorenEdition, 1980), 141–5. [Reprinted in *Die Tat*, 21 March 1980.]
66. 'Massa' [story], *Sonntag*, 21 March 1982.
67. 'Der Mann auf dem Hochrad' [extract from *Der Mann auf dem Hochrad*], *Deutsche Volkszeitung*, 28 September 1984.
68. 'Die Figuren behalten ihr Geheimnis' [review of Per Olov Enquist, *Auszug der Musikanten* and *Der Sekundant*], *Literatur Konkret*, No. 9 (1984–85), 92–3.
69. 'Wo die Weißen schwarz sehen. Eindrücke einer Recherchenreise nach Namibia im Jahre 1976', in *ARD Fernsehspiel. Jan Feb März 1985*, ed. im Auftrag der ARD von der Pressestelle des WDR (Cologne, 1985), 120–33.
70. 'Ein ganzes und ein halbes Huhn. Uwe Timm über Breyten Breytenbach: *Wahre Bekenntnis eines Albino-Terroristen*', *Der Spiegel*, 21 January 1985, 148–51.
71. 'Mitten im kalten Winter' [poem], *Westdeutsche Allgemeine Zeitung*, 30 November 1985.
72. 'Der Abflug' [from material for *Der Schlangenbaum*], in Brigitte Chowanetz (ed.), *Herzogenauracher Anthologie 3* (Herzogenaurach, 1985), 11–30.
73. 'Der Schlangenbaum' [extract from *Der Schlangenbaum*], *Deutsche Volkszeitung*, 17 October 1986.
74. 'Der Lauschangriff. Hörspiel', *Düsseldorfer Debatte*, No. 1 (1986), 63–75.
75. 'Das Hochrad' [extract from *Der Mann auf dem Hochrad*], *Deutsche Volkszeitung*, 16 December 1986.
76. 'Krieg am Ende der Welt. Uwe Timm über Antonio Lobo Antunes: *Der Judaskuß*', *Der Spiegel*, 27 April 1987, 243–7.
77. 'Der Mann auf dem Hochrad' [extract from *Der Mann auf dem Hochrad*], *Deutsche Volkszeitung*, 13 November 1987.
78. 'Reise nach Paraguay', in Armin Kerker (ed.), *Im Schatten der Paläste* (Frankfurt am Main, Athenäum, 1987), 105–18.
79. 'Mitten im kalten Winter' [poem], in *Westdeutsche Allgemeine Zeitung*, 19 December 1987.
80. 'Versuch über Seamus Heaney', *Volkszeitung*, 24 March 1989.
81. 'Der Blick über die Schulter oder Notizen zu einer Ästhetik des Alltags', in *Es muß sein. Autoren schreiben über das Schreiben* (Cologne, Kiepenheuer & Witsch, 1989), 186–208.
82. 'Von der Schönheit subventionierter Schnittblumen', *Volkszeitung*, 9 March 1990.

83. 'Versuch über eine Ästhetik des Spaghetti-Essens' [extract from *Vogel, friß die Feige nicht*], in Julia Bachstein (ed.), *Von Nudeln & Menschen* (Frankfurt am Main, Frankfurter Verlagsanstalt, 1991), 29–32.
84. 'Die Umbettung: ein halbherziges Spektakel. 17. August 1991', *Freitag*, 23 August 1991. [Reprinted in Inge Hoeftmann and Waltraud Noack (eds.), *Potsdam in alten und neuen Reisebeschreibungen* (Düsseldorf, Droste, 1992), 302–7.]
85. 'Mit einem Fluch in den Mund. Versuch über eine Ästhetik des Spaghetti-Essens' [extract from *Vogel, friß die Feige nicht*], *Der Tagesspiegel*, 23 August 1992.
86. 'Die Zeit vergeht anders, wenn jemand stirbt' [on Ludwig Fels receiving the Kranichsteiner Literaturpreis], *Freitag*, 30 October 1992.
87. 'Die Entdeckung der Currywurst' [extract from *Die Entdeckung der Currywurst*], in Hartmut Steinecke (ed.), *Literarisches aus erster Hand. 10 Jahre Paderborner Gast-Dozentur für Schriftsteller. Mit Texten von Max von der Grün, Erich Loest, Peter Rühmkorf, Peter Schneider, Eva Demski, Dieter Wellershoff, Herta Müller, Günter Kunert, Uwe Timm* (Paderborn, Igel, 1994), 225–39.
88. 'Im Laufe der Zeit oder Der schöne Überfluß' [extract from *Erzählen und kein Ende*], in Uwe Wittstock (ed.), *Roman oder Leben. Postmoderne in der deutschen Literatur* (Leipzig, Reclam, 1994), 245–64.
89. 'Der politische Ästhet. Alfred Andersch lesen', *Neue deutsche Literatur*, 42 No. 4 (1994), 168–75.
90. 'Die Abschiedsparade', *Freitag*, 24 July 1994.

1.e Films and radio plays

1. *Viele Wege führen nach Rom* [TV film], written and directed by Uwe Timm, first broadcast West 3, 19 March 1984.
2. *Der Lauschangriff* [radio play], Westdeutscher Rundfunk, 22 May 1984.
3. *Kerbels Flucht* [TV film], written by Uwe Timm, directed by Erwin Keusch, first broadcast ZDF, 29 May 1984.
3. *Die Zugmaus. Zeichentrickfilm nach dem Kinderbuch von Uwe Timm*, Gunnar Matysiak, first broadcast ARD, 23 September 1984.
4. *Morenga* [TV film], written by Uwe Timm and Egon Günther, directed by Egon Günther, first broadcast in three parts, ARD (WDR), 13, 17 and 20 March 1985. [Cinema version: West German entry to 35th Berlin Film Festival, screened 16 February 1985].
5. *Der Flieger* [film], written by Uwe Timm, directed by Erwin Kausch, first screened 25 October 1986.
6. *Rennschwein Rudi Rüssel* [film], written by Uwe Timm and Ulrich Limmer, first screened March 1995.
7. *Die Bubi Scholz Story* [television film], script by Uwe Timm (Berlin, Aufbau, 1998).

1. f Translations of Uwe Timm's works

Heißer Sommer

1. *Hete Zomer* [Dutch], translated by Gerrit Bussink (Amsterdam, van Gennep, 1975).
2. *Zarkoe Leto* [Russian], translated by V. Kupriyanov (Moscow, Molodaya Gvardiya, 1978).
3. *Horké léto* [Czech], translated by Zusana Krej ová (Prague, Svoboda, 1978).
4. *Spekotne Lito* [Ukrainian], translated by Yuri Mychaylyuk (Kiev, Vydavnyctvo CK LKSMU Molod', 1979].

Morenga

5. *Morenga* [Czech], translated by Rú ena Grebení ková (Prague, Svoboda, 1981).

Kerbels Flucht

6. *Olyan Sötét Volt Minden* [Hungarian], translated by Gergely Erzsébet (Budapest, Magvetö Kiadó, 1982).

Die Zugmaus

7. *El Ratón de Tren* [Spanish], translated by Mon Elsa Alfonso (Madrid, Ediciones Alfaguara, 1985).

Die Piratenamsel

8. *O melro Pirata* [Galician] (Vigo, Editorial Galaxia, 1992).

Der Mann auf dem Hochrad

9. *L'Homme au Vélocipède* [French], translated by Bernard Kreiss (Paris, Balland, 1986).
10. *A Velocipédes Ember* [Hungarian], translated by Gergely Erzsébert (Budapest, Magvetö Kiadó, 1988).
11. *L'Homme au Vélocipède* [French], (Paris, Editions du Seuil, 1995).

Der Schlangenbaum

12. *De Slangenboom* [Dutch], translated by Gerrit Bussink (Amsterdam, Amber, 1987).
13. *A Árvore da Serpente* [Portuguese], translated by Brigitte Baum (São Paolo, Marco Zero, 1988).
14. *The Snake Tree* [English], translated by Peter Tegel (London, Picador, 1988).
15. *The Snake Tree* [English], translated by Peter Tegel (New York, New Directions, 1990).
16. *Zemeinoe Derevo* [Russian], translated by V. Sedel'nika (Moscow, Raduga, 1990).

17. *Ormträdet* [Swedish], translated by Eva Liljegren (Stockholm, Natur och Kultur, 1992).

Rennschwein Rudi Rüssel
18. *O Cocho de Carreiras. Rudi Fuciños* [Galician], translated by Amelia Rodríguez San Martín (Vigo, Editorial Galaxia, 1990).
20. *Rudi Mutturko Txerri Lastercaria* [Basque], translated by Xabier Mendiguren Berenciarth (San Sebastian, Elkar, 1991).
21. *Historien om Thorkild Tryne* [Danish], translated by Franz Berliner (Copenhagen, Gyldendal, 1991).
22. *Kalle Knorr på Kapplöpningsbanan* [Swedish], translated by Birgit Lönn (Stockholm, Bergh, 1991).
23. [Japanese translation] (Kyoko Hirano, 1991).
24. *Pikasika Köpi Kärsäkäs* [Finnish], translated by Marja Kyrö (Helsinki, Juva, Söderström, 1992).
25. *Rudi la Truffe, Cochon de Course* [French], translated by Bernard Friot (Toulouse, Milan, 1993).
26. *Rudi Renvarken* [Dutch], translated by Roger Vanbrabant (Auerbode, Apeldoorn, Altiora, 1993).

Kopfjäger
27. *Headhunter* [English], translated by Peter Tegel (New York, New Directions, 1994).

Die Entdeckung der Currywurst
28. *The Invention of Curried Sausage* [English], translated by Leila Vennewitz (New York, New Directions, 1995).

1g Interviews

1. Zacharias, Carna, 'Er will kein Pascha sein. Uwe Timm schrieb seinen ersten Roman *Heißer Sommer*', *Abendzeitung*, 3 July 1974.
2. Anonymous, 'Interview mit einem Debütanten: Uwe Timm', *Sonntag*, 3 November 1974.
3. Reinhold, Ursula, 'Interview mit Uwe Timm', *Weimarer Beiträge*, 22 (1976), 49–59. [Reprinted in Ursula Reinhold, *Tendenzen und Autoren. Zur Literatur der siebziger Jahre in der BRD* (East Berlin, Dietz, 1982), 434–45.]
4. Zacharias, Carna, 'Uns kann keiner hineinreden. Die AutorenEdition macht sich jetzt selbständig', *Abendzeitung*, 31 March 1978.
5. Colberg, Klaus, 'Interview mit Uwe Timm', Süddeutscher Rundfunk, 2. Programm, 23 August 1978.
6. Krall, Günter, 'Man muß einen langen Atem haben', *Die Rheinpfalz*, 22 November 1980.
7. General, Regina, 'Wirklichkeitsausschnitte. Gespräch mit dem Schriftsteller Uwe Timm, BRD', *Sonntag*, 21 March 1982.

8. Zacharias, Carna, 'Onkel Franz auf dem Hochrad. Uwe Timm kam aus Rom mit einem neuen Blick zurück', *Abendzeitung*, 27 August 1984.
9. Brücker, Wolf-Dietrich, '*Morenga* – eine deutsche Biographie. Ein Gespräch mit Uwe Timm', in *ARD Fernsehspiel. Jan Feb März 1985*, ed. im Auftrag der ARD von der Pressestelle des WDR (Cologne, 1985), 126-7.
10. Stuber, Manfred, '"Ich möchte nicht ewig auf der gleichen Flöte blasen". Ein Gespräch mit dem Schriftsteller Uwe Timm, Mitbegründer der legendären "AutorenEdition" und erzählerischer Realist', *Mittelbayerische Zeitung*, 6 August 1986.
11. Zacharias, Carna, 'Die Gefahr hinter unserem Fortschritt. AZ-Gespräch mit Uwe Timm zu seinem Buch *Der Schlangenbaum*', *Abendzeitung*, 7 Septembr 1986.
12. Anonymous, 'Wir sprachen mit: Uwe Timm. Themen suchen ihn', *Süd-West-Presse*, 21 November 1986.
13. Greiwe, Uwe, 'Die Bücher brauchen Busse. Sympathie für Nicaragua: Autor Uwe Timm besuchte das Land', *Abendzeitung*, 5–6 August 1989.
14. Urbach, Karin, '"Es kann gar nicht genug Preise geben". Für sein literarisches Werk prämiert: Gespräch mit dem Münchner Schriftsteller Uwe Timm', *Münchner Merkur*, 17 May 1990.
15. Schmitt, W. Christian, 'So kam Uwe Timm zu seinem *Rennschwein Rudi Rüssel*. Deutscher Kinderbuchpreis – Gespräch mit dem Autor', *Saarbrücker Zeitung*, 8 November 1990.
16. Scharioth, Barbara, '"Ich schreibe mit der Stimme im Kopf"' [on *Rennschwein Rudi Rüssel*], *Börsenblatt*, No. 71 (1990), 2724-6.
17. Ten Doornkaat, Hans, '"Anschaulich und unterhaltsam". Uwe Timm für Kinder wie für Erwachsene', *Eselsohr*, 11 (1990), 27–9.
18. Colberg, Klaus, 'Interview mit Uwe Timm', Süddeutscher Rundfunk, 2. Programm, 22 August 1991.
19. Stuber, Manfred, '"Es würde mich schrecklich langweilen, Peter Handkes Bücher zu schreiben". Ein MZ-Interview mit dem Schriftsteller Uwe Timm anläßlich einer Lesung', *Mittelbayerische Zeitung*, 12–13 October 1991.
20. Feldmann, Joachim and Heinemann, Georg, '"Ich weiß, wenn ich an einem Roman schreibe, nie den Schluß". Ein Gespräch mit Uwe Timm', *Am Erker. Zeitschrift für Literatur*, No. 24, April 1992.
21. Durzak, Manfred, 'Die Position des Autors. Ein Werkstattgespräch mit Uwe Timm', in Keith Bullivant, M. Durzak and Hartmut Steinecke (eds.), *Die Archäologie der Wünsche. Studien zum Werk von Uwe Timm* (Cologne, Kiepenheuer & Witsch, 1995), 311–54.
22. Stehr, Ingo, '"A trip of discovery into my own consciousness." A conversation with Uwe Timm', translated by Ingo and Louise Stoehr, *Dimension* 2, 2 (1995), 4.
23. Adler, Sabine, 'Wie eine Cocktail-Party', *Tageszeitung* (Munich), 5-6 October 1996.

24. Weber, Antje, 'Warum die "Blaue Maus" so köstlich schmeckt. Der Schriftsteller Uwe Timm über Kartoffeln, Berlin und Ästhetik - und damit über seinen neuen Roman *Johannisnacht*', *Süddeutsche Zeitung*, 11 November 1996.

2. Secondary Literature

2.a General studies

1. Ackermann, Irmgard and Borries, Mechthild (eds.), *Uwe Timm* (Munich, Goethe-Institut, 1988).
2. Barner, Wilfried (ed.), *Geschichte der deutschen Literatur von 1945 bis zur Gegenwart* (Munich, Beck, 1994), 602-5.
3. Borries, Mechthild, 'Frauenbilder in Uwe Timms Romanen. Beobachtungen einer weiblichen Leserin', in Keith Bullivant, Manfred Durzak and Hartmut Steinecke (eds.), *Die Archäologie der Wünsche. Studien zum Werk von Uwe Timm* (Cologne, Kiepenheuer & Witsch, 1995), 291–310.
4. 'Uwe Timm' in Kurt Böttcher (ed.), *Lexikon deutschsprachiger Schriftsteller. 20. Jahrhundert*, (Hildersheim, 1993), 736-7.
5. Brosche, Wolfgang, 'Uwe Timms Gesellschaftskritik asl Schmuggelgut im Roman. Auftakt der 9. Gastdozentur für Schriftsteller an der Uni-GH', *Neue Westfälische*, 19 December 1991. [Reprinted in Hartmut Steinecke (ed.), *Literarisches aus erster Hand. 10 Jahre Paderborner Gast-Dozentur für Schriftsteller. Mit Texten von Max von der Grün, Erich Loest, Peter Rühmkorf, Peter Schneider, Eva Demski, Dieter Wellershoff, Herta Müller, Günter Kunert, Uwe Timm* (Paderborn, Igel, 1994), 246.]
6. Bullivant, Keith and Briegleb, Klaus, 'Die Krise des Erzählens – "1968" und danach', ibid., 328–330.
7. Bullivant, Keith, 'Literatur und Politik', in Klaus Briegleb and Sigrid Weigel (eds.), *Gegenwartsliteratur seit 1968* (Munich, Hanser, 1992), 288–91.
8. ———, *Realism Today: Aspects of the Contemporary West German Novel* (Leamington Spa, Berg, 1987).
9. ———, *The Future of German Literature* (Oxford, Berg, 1994).
10. ———, 'Uwe Timm und die Ästhetik des Alltags', in Keith Bullivant, Manfred Durzak and Hartmut Steinecke (eds.), *Die Archäologie der Wünsche. Studien zum Werk von Uwe Timm* (Cologne, Kiepenheuer & Witsch, 1995), 231–43.
11. Drews, Jörg, 'Ein paar notwendige Anmerkungen zu Uwe Timms "Realismus und Utopie"', in Peter Laemmle (ed.), *Realismus – welcher? Sechzehn Autoren auf der Suche nach einem literarischen Begriff* (Munich, edition text + kritik, 1976), 178–83.
12. ———,'Wider einen neuen Realismus ', ibid., 151–63.

13. Durzak, Manfred, 'Ein Autor der mittleren Generation', in Keith Bullivant, M. Durzak and Hartmut Steinecke (eds.), *Die Archäologie der Wünsche. Studien zum Werk von Uwe Timm* (Cologne, Kiepenheuer & Witsch, 1995), 13–25.
14. Hagestedt, Lutz, 'Von essenden Sängern und singenden Ochsen. Sprechsituationen bei Uwe Timm', in Keith Bullivant, Manfred Durzak and Hartmut Steinecke (eds.), *Die Archäologie der Wünsche. Studien zum Werk von Uwe Timm* (Cologne, Kiepenheuer & Witsch, 1995), 245–66.
15. Kesting, Hanjo, 'Uwe Timm', in Heinz Ludwig Arnold (ed.), *KLG. Kritisches Lexikon zur deutschsprachigen Gegenwartsliteratur (KLG)* (Munich, edition text + kritik, 1989), 31. Nlg.
16. Kirchner, Doris, 'Timm, Uwe', in Walther Killy (ed.), *Literaturlexikon. Autoren und Werke deutscher Sprache*, vol. 11 (Munich, 1991), 374.
17. Kraft, Thomas, 'Timm, Uwe Hans Heinz', in Dietz-Rüdiger Moser (ed.) *Neues Handbuch der deutschen Gegenwartsliteratur seit 1945* (Munich, Nymphenburger, 1990), 613–5.
18. Norris, Ted, 'Literatur und Ethnologie des 20. Jahrhunderts: Hubert Fichte, Bruce Chatwin und Uwe Timm', in Keith Bullivant, Manfred Durzak and Hartmut Steinecke (eds.), *Die Archäologie der Wünsche. Studien zum Werk von Uwe Timm* (Cologne, Kiepenheuer & Witsch, 1995), 267–89.
19. Offergeld, Rüdiger, 'Schreiben können: ein Privileg. Vom Kürschner zum Autor: Uwe Timm', *Welt der Arbeit*, 6 August 1981.
20. Reinhold, Ursula, 'Vom Wert eigener Erfahrungen', *Weimarer Beiträge* 22 (1976), 60–8. [Reprinted in Ursula Reinhold, *Tendenzen und Autoren. Zur Literatur der siebziger Jahre in der BRD* (East Berlin, Dietz, 1982), 445–54.]
21. ———, 'Nachtrag 1980', in U. Reinhold, *Tendenzen und Autoren. Zur Literatur der siebziger Jahre in der BRD* (East Berlin, Dietz, 1982), 454–60.
22. Schütt, Peter, 'Romanprojekte. Gesellschaftskritische Erkenntnisse werden gestaltet', *Deutsche Volkszeitung*, 27 April 1972.
23. Seifert, Walter, 'Aufklärung und Komik. Uwe Timms Kinderromane', in Keith Bullivant, Manfred Durzak and Hartmut Steinecke (eds.), *Die Archäologie der Wünsche. Studien zum Werk von Uwe Timm* (Cologne, Kiepenheuer & Witsch, 1995), 143–69.

2.b Individual Texts
On *Widersprüche*
1. Ritter, Roman, 'Herrschaftssprache und Gegenrede', *Deutsche Volkszeitung*, 31 August 1972.
2. Schütt, Peter, 'Das Maß ist die Realität. Uwe Timms politische Texte', *Die Tat*, 20 May 1971.

On *Heißer Sommer*

3. Anonymous, 'das neue buch – Uwe Timm: *Heißer Sommer*', *Darmstädter Tagblatt*, 20 December 1974.
4. ——, '*Heißer Sommer*', *Frankfurter Neue Presse*, 5 February 1975.
5. ——, 'Von der Verweigerung zur bewußten Opposition', *Die Tat*, 12 October 1974.
6. Becker, Peter von, 'Thema versimmelt. Uwe Timms Roman über die Studentenrevolte', *Süddeutsche Zeitung*, 5–6 October 1974.
7. Beha, Erdmute, 'Ullrich Krauses Weg in die Politik. Roman über die Studentenbewegung', *Badische Zeitung*, 5 October 1974.
8. ——, 'Man muß etwas tun. Uwe Timms Roman über die Studentenbewegung', *Deutsche Volkszeitung*, 10 October 1974.
9. Bleisch, Ernst Günter, 'Revolution und Rolling Stones. Uwe Timm liest aus seinem Buch *Heißer Sommer*', *Münchner Merkur*, 27 November 1974.
10. Bullivant, Keith, *Realism Today. Aspects of the Contemporary West German Novel*, (Leamington Spa, Berg, 1987), 109ff.
11. Buselmeier, Michael, 'Nach der Revolte. Die literarische Verarbeitung der Studentenbewegung', in W. Martin Lüdke (ed.), *Literatur und Studentenbewegung. Eine Zwischenbilanz* (Opladen, Westdeutscher, 1977), 158–85.
12. Cramer, Sibylle, 'Revolution als Mode. Zwei Romane – zwei mißlungene Emanzipationsversuche' [review of *Heißer Sommer* and Anja Lundholm, *Zerreißprobe*], *Bücherkommentare*, No. 6 (1974).
13. Fleischer, Wolf and Krull, Wilhelm, 'Rosen für das Proletariat. Die Studentenbewegung als literarisches Sujet', *Einundzwanzig*, No. 10 (1979), 108–45.
14. Gerhard, Marlis, 'Schwache Arbeit über Hölderlin. Uwe Timms *Heißer Sommer* – ein APO-Roman ohne Dogma', *Stuttgarter Zeitung*, 4 January 1975. [Reprinted in Irmgard Ackermann and Mechthild Borries (eds.), *Uwe Timm* (Munich, Goethe-Institut, 1988), 7.]
15. Götze, Karl-Heinz, 'Gedächtnis. Romane über die Studentenbewegung', *Das Argument. Zeitschrift für Philosophie und Sozialwissenschaften*, 23 (1981), 367–82 (369–76).
16. Greiner, Ulrich, 'Allem Anfang woht ein Zauber inne. Uwe Timms *Heißer Sommer*: der erste Roman über die Studentenbewegung', *Frankfurter Allgemeine Zeitung*, 8 October 1974. [Reprinted in Irmgard Ackermann and Mechthild Borries (eds.), *Uwe Timm* (Munich, Goethe-Institut, 1988), 8–9].
17. Hosfeld, Rolf and Peitsch, Helmut, '"Weil uns diese Aktionen innerlich verändern, sind sie politisch". Bemerkungen zu vier Romanen über die Studentenbewegung', *Basis. Jahrbuch für deutsche Gegenwartsliteratur*, 8 (1978), 92–126 (115–20).
18. Hubert, Martin, 'Literatur der Studentenbewegung. Zur Neuauflage von Uwe Timms Roman *Heißer Sommer*', *Deutsche Volkszeitung*, 27 September 1985.

19. Jurgensen, Manfred, 'Die dokumentierte Fiktion: *Heißer Sommer, Kerbels Flucht*. Uwe Timms Zeugenbericht auf Widerruf', in Keith Bullivant, Manfred Durzak and Hartmut Steinecke (eds.), *Die Archäologie der Wünsche. Studien zum Werk von Uwe Timm* (Cologne, Kiepenheuer & Witsch, 1995), 27–45.
20. Kelber, Ulrich, 'Ein Roman aus der Studentenbewegung', *Neue Hannoversche Presse*, 9 November 1974.
21. Martin, Beate, '*Heißer Sommer*', in Bernd and Jutta Gräf (eds.), *Der Romanführer. Der Inhalt der Romane und Novellen der Weltliteratur*, vol. 19, *Inhalte erzählender deutscher Prosa aus den Jahren 1974 bis 1985. Zweiter Teil: L–Z* (Stuttgart, Hiersemann, 1988), 271.
22. Pasinato, Antonio, 'Contestazione e tradizione nel '68. *Heißer Sommer* di Uwe Timm', *ACF. Annali della Facolta di Lingue e Litterature Straniere di Ca'Foscari*, 23 No. 2 (1984), 195–211. [Reprinted in *L'immagine riflessa. Rivista quadrimestale di sociologica dei testi*, 10 (1987), 63–88.]
23. Piwitt, Hermann Peter, 'Rückblick auf heiße Tage. Die Studentenrevolte in der Literatur', in Hans Christoph Buch (ed.), *Literaturmagazin 4. Die Literatur nach dem Tod der Literatur. Bilanz der Politisierung*, (Reinbek, Rowohlt, 1975), 35–46. [Reprinted as 'Rückblick auf heiße Tage. Romane der Studentenbewegung', in H. P. Piwitt, *Boccherini und andere Bürgerpflichten* (Reinbek, Rowohlt, 1976), 93–109.]
24. Prinz, Alois, *Der poetische Mensch im Schatten der Utopie. Zur politisch-weltanschaulichen Idee der 68'er Studentenbewegung und deren Auswirkung auf die Literatur* (Würzburg, Königshausen & Neumann, 1990), 150–211.
25. Püschel, Ursula, 'Von Mühe und Lust des Begreifens. Gerd Fuchs, *Beringer und die lange Wut*, Uwe Timm, *Heißer Sommer*, Aufbau-Verlag Berlin und Weimar', *Neue deutsche Literatur*, 24 No. 8 (1976), 152–8.
26. Rauh, Inge, 'Denkmal für die APO', *Nürnberger Nachrichten*, 23 November 1974.
27. Rieger, Manfred, 'Eigentlich sollte Ullrich über Hölderlin schreiben. Literarische Nachlese der Studentenbewegung', *Rhein-Neckar-Zeitung*, 10–11 May 1975.
28. ——, 'Flucht mit dem "Genossen Frust". Uwe Timm: literarische Nachlese der Studentenbewegung', *Westdeutsche Allgemeine Zeitung*, 15 March 1975.
29. Schachtsiek-Freitag, Norbert, 'Unkritische Parteinahme', *Frankfurter Hefte*, 30 No. 6 (1975), 66–8.
30. Schultz-Gerstein, Christian, 'Wetterberichte von der Apo-Front. Ein Roman um die Studentenbewegung herum', *Die Zeit*, 1 November 1974.
31. Schwerter, Werner, 'Der APO-Sommer', *Rheinische Post*, 7 December 1974.
32. Thomas, Christian, 'Uwe Timm: *Heißer Sommer*', *Stadtblatt* (Münster), No. 14–15, 13 July–9 August 1985.

33. Wallesch, Friedel, 'Timm, Uwe. *Heißer Sommer*', in Kurt Böttcher (ed.), *Romanführer A–Z*, vol. 3, *20. Jahrhundert. Der österreichische und schweizerische Roman. Romane der BRD* (East Berlin, Volk und Wissen, 1980), 384–6.

On *Kontext 1. Literatur und Wirklichkeit*

34. Buch, Hans Christoph, 'Hetze, daß die Fetzen fliegen', *Pardon*, No. 10 (1976). [Reprinted as 'Neuer literarischer Sansculottismus. Die schrecklichen Vereinfacher aus dem Hause Bertelsmann', in H. C. Buch, *Das Hervortreten des Ichs aus den Wörtern. Aufsätze zur Literatur* (Munich, Hanser, 1978), 87–92.]
35. Geissler, Heinrich, 'Theorie der AutorenEdition. Periodikum *kontext* erschienen', *Die Tat*, 10 December 1976.
36. Hage, Volker, 'Realismus – wo denn? welcher? von wem? für wen? *kontext 1* und anderes zu der Frage, was realistische Literatur sein kann oder sein soll', *Frankfurter Allgemeine Zeitung*, 7 December 1976.
37. Piwitt, Hermann Peter, 'Über *Kontext 1*', Sender Freies Berlin, 1. Programm, 6 November 1976.

On *Morenga*

38. Anonymous, '"Deutsch-Südwest"-Bewältigung. Kolonialgeschichte als Roman', *Die Presse*, 24–25 June 1978.
39. ——, 'Guerilla in Deutsch-Südwest. Als das Reich noch Kolonien hatte – Ein Roman', *Kronen Zeitung* [Vienna], 1 July 1978.
40. ——, 'Menschlichkeit und ein bedrückendes Schweigen. Timms Roman *Morenga* zeichnet sich durch Mut aus', *Ruhr-Nachrichten*, 2 June 1978.
41. ——, '*Morenga* – Kleinbürgerlich anarchistische Theorien über die Befreiung des Menschen', *Kommunistische Volkszeitung*, 5 February 1979.
42. Booß, Rutger, 'David, Goliath und die Hottentotten', *Rote Blätter* July–August, 1978.
43. Busche, Jürgen, 'Ein deutsches Vietnam in Südwest? *Morenga*, Uwe Timms historischer Roman über den Kolonialkrieg in Afrika', *Frankfurter Allgemeine Zeitung*, 18 April 1978.
44. Bullivant, Keith, *Realism Today. Aspects of the Contemporary West German Novel* (Leamington Spa, Berg, 1987), 152ff.
45. Chotjewitz, Peter O., 'Das liest sich alles, als wäre es so gewesen. Uwe Timms *Morenga* – ein großer Roman über die Aufstände der Hereros und Hottentotten', *Deutsche Volkszeitung*, 6 April 1978. [Reprinted in Irmgard Ackermann and Mechthild Borries (eds.), *Uwe Timm* (Munich, Goethe-Institut, 1988), 13–15.]
46. Dede, H. E., '"Bis das Land den Menschen gehört". Uwe Timms Roman *Morenga* – Widerstand im ehemaligen "Deutsch-Südwest-Afrika"', *Unsere Zeit*, 15 July 1978.

47. Figge, Klaus, 'Film über Uwe Timms *Morenga*', Südwestfunk Baden Baden, 1 June 1978.
48. General, Regina, 'Ein Kapitel Großdeutscher Träume', *Sonntag*, 5 October 1980.
49. Giordano, Ralph, 'Der Sieger wird *Morenga* heißen', in *ARD Fernsehspiel. Jan Feb März 1985*, ed. im Auftrag der ARD von der Pressestelle des WDR (Cologne, 1985), 128–32.
50. Gurlit, Marion, 'Uwe Timm, *Morenga*, Verlag Kiepenheuer & Witsch, Köln, 1985', in Gesellschaft für entwicklungspolitische Bildungsarbeit (eds.), *EPK. Entwicklungspolitische Korrespondenz*, No. 1 (March 1991).
51. Hermand, Jost, 'Afrika den Afrikanern! Timms *Morenga*', in Keith Bullivant, Manfred Durzak and Hartmut Steinecke (eds.), *Die Archäologie der Wünsche. Studien zum Werk von Uwe Timm* (Cologne, Kiepenheuer & Witsch, 1995), 47–63.
52. Herrmann, Ludolf, 'Phantasien über Namibia', *Deutsche Zeitung / Christ und Welt*, 20 October 1978.
53. Holzinger, Lutz, 'Der Alltagskolonialismus', *Volksstimme*, 21 July 1978.
54. Horn, Peter, 'Fremdsprache und Fremderlebnis. Dr Johannis Gottschalks Lernprozeß in Uwe Timms *Morenga*', *Jahrbuch Deutsch als Fremdsprache*, 14 (1988), 75–91.
55. ——, 'Über die Schwierigkeit, einen Standpunkt einzunehmen. Zu Uwe Timms *Morenga*', in Keith Bullivant, Manfred Durzak and Hartmut Steinecke (eds.), *Die Archäologie der Wünsche. Studien zum Werk von Uwe Timm* (Cologne, Kiepenheuer & Witsch, 1995), 93–118.
56. Kersten, Paul, 'Uwe Timm, *Morenga*', Norddeutscher Rundfunk, 2. Programm, 1 July 1978..
57. ——, 'Uwe Timm, *Morenga*', *Stern*, 1 June 1978
58. Kipphardt, Heinar, 'Laudatio auf Uwe Timm (*Morenga*)' [speech given on the occasion of Timm receiving the Bremer Literaturpreis, 26 January 1979], in H. Kipphardt, *Ruckediguh, Blut ist im Schuh. Essays, Briefe, Entwürfe*, vol. 2, *1964–82* (Reinbek, Rowohlt, 1989), 261–5. [Abridged version, as 'Kolonisation als Geschäftsvorgang', in Wolfgang Emmerich (ed.), *'Bewundert viel und viel gescholten . . .' Der Bremer Literaturpreis 1954–1987. Reden der Preisträger und andere Texte* (Bremerhaven, Wirtschaftsverlag NW, 1988), 233–4.
59. Krall, Günter, 'Rückzug auf das Ich', *Die Rheinpfalz*, 20 July 1978.
60. Krause, Christine, 'Uwe Timm, *Morenga*', Radio Bremen, 2. Programm, 24 February 1979.
61. Kußler, Rainer, 'Interkulturelles Lernen in Uwe Timms *Morenga*', *Acta Germanica*, 21 (1992), 201–27. [Reprinted in Keith Bullivant, Manfred Durzak and Hartmut Steinecke (eds.), *Die Archäologie der Wünsche. Studien zum Werk von Uwe Timm* (Cologne, Kiepenheuer & Witsch, 1995), 65–91.]
62. Neukirchen, Alfons, 'Besprechung von Uwe Timms *Morenga*', Süddeutscher Rundfunk, 2. Programm, 23 July 1978.

63. ——, 'Die Legende von Südwest. Uwe Timms Buch über den deutschen Kolonialismus', *Rheinische Post*, 27 May 1978.
64. Oberprieler, Gudrun, 'Gottschalks Entwicklungsprozeß oder der gescheiterte Versuch, einen fremdkulturellen Kode zu erlernen. Eine Untersuchung zu Uwe Timms Roman *Morenga*', *Acta Germanica*, Beiheft 2 (1991), 167–83.
65. Ortlepp, Gunnar, 'Orlog in Südwest', *Der Spiegel*, 31 July 1978.
66. Pakendorf, Gunther, '*Morenga* oder Geschichte als Fiktion', *Acta Germanica*, 19 (1988), 144–58.
67. Scheller, Wolf, 'Ein afrikanischer Che Guevara in Deutsch-Südwest', *Bücherkommentare*, No. 4 (July–August, 1978).
68. ——, 'Ein edler Kämpfer? Uwe Timm über den Rebellen Morenga', *Kölner Stadt-Anzeiger*, 2 September 1978.
69. ——, 'Epos über angemaßte Herrschaft', *Mannheimer Morgen*, 28 September 1978.
70. ——, 'Schicksalskampf eines afrikanischen Volkes. Uwe Timms Roman über den Hottentottenführer Morenga', Deutsche Welle, Deutsches Programm, 19 May 1978.
71. ——, 'Uwe Timm, *Morenga*', Sender Freies Berlin, 1. Programm, 13 July 1978.
72. Schmidt, Jürgen, 'Herrenmenschen in Südwest. Uwe Timms Rebellen-Roman *Morenga*', *Stuttgarter Zeitung*, 3 February 1979.
73. Sperr, Monika, 'Als die Deutschen Sklaven hatten. Uwe Timms Roman *Morenga* schildert den Freiheitskampf der Schwarzen in Afrika', *Abendzeitung*, 2 September 1978. [Reprinted in Irmgard Ackermann and Mechthild Borries (eds.), *Uwe Timm* (Munich, Goethe-Institut, 1988), 16.]
74. ——, 'Deutsche Glorie auch zu den Hereros. Mit *Morenga* gelang Uwe Timm ein spannender und weitgehend dokumentarischer Roman', *Vorwärts*, 19 October 1978.
75. ——, '*Morenga*, Roman von Uwe Timm', *Die Zeit*, 20 October 1978.
76. ——, 'Rebellen von Namibia. Uwe Timms Schilderung des Freiheitskampfes im ehemaligen Deutsch-Südwestafrika', *Nürnberger Nachrichten*, 29 December 1978.
77. ——, 'Vor Ort', *Basler Zeitung*, 27 December 1978.
78. Streese, Konstanze, '*Cric?*' – '*Crac!*' *Vier literarische Versuche, mit dem Kolonialismus umzugehen* (Bern, Berlin, Frankfurt am Main, Lang, 1991), 65–100.
79. Traber, Margrit, 'Kolonisatoren in Südwestafrika', *Neue Zürcher Zeitung*, 28 July 1978.
80. Ueding, Gert, 'Uwe Timm, *Morenga*', Deutschlandfunk, 30 July 1978.
81. Vormweg, Heinrich, 'Uwe Timms *Morenga*', Hessischer Rundfunk, 26 July 1978.
82. Walser, Martin, 'Kropotkin bei den Hottentotten', *Konkret*, No. 7 (1978).

83. Zahl, Peter-Paul, 'Widerstandskämpfer – die kollektive Persönlichkeit. Uwe Timms Roman über Südwestafrika', *Frankfurter Rundschau*, 19 December 1978.
84. Zeller, Eva, 'Uwe Timms Roman *Morenga*, vorgestellt von Eva Zeller', RIAS Berlin, 2. Programm, 5 July 1978.

On *Kerbels Flucht*

85. Bosch, Manfred, 'Die Revolution frißt ihre Kinder. Zu Uwe Timms Roman *Kerbels Flucht*', *Die Horen*, 25 No. 120 (1980), 201–2.
86. ——, 'Flucht und (erzählerischer) Neubeginn', *Basler Zeitung*, 12 July 1980.
87. Bullivant, Keith, 'Möglichkeiten eines subjektiven Realismus – zur Realismusdiskussion der siebziger Jahre, zu Peter Handkes *Die Stunde der wahren Empfindung* und Uwe Timms *Kerbels Flucht*', in K. Bullivant and Hans Joachim Althof (eds.), *Subjektivität – Innerlichkeit – Abkehr vom Politischen? Tendenzen der deutschsprachigen Literatur der 70er Jahre. Dokumentation der Tagungsbeiträge des Britisch-Deutschen Germanistentreffens in Berlin vom 12.04–18.04.1982* (Bonn, DAAD, 1986), 19–34.
88. ——, *Realism Today: Aspects of the Contemporary West German Novel*, (Leamington Spa, Berg, 1987), 188ff.
89. Goetz, Rainald, 'Keine Lust auf nichts. Uwe Timms Porträt einer Generation', *Süddeutsche Zeitung*, 23–24 August 1980.
90. ——, 'Uwe Timm, *Kerbels Flucht*', Sender Freies Berlin, 1. Programm, 22 September 1980.
91. Götze, Karl-Heinz, 'Gedächtnis. Romane über die Studentenbewegung', *Das Argument. Zeitschrift für Philosophie und Sozialwissenschaften*, 23 (1981), 367–82 (376–8).
92. Hage, Volker, 'Auf der Flucht', in V. Hage (ed.), *Die Wiederkehr des Erzählers. Neue deutsche Literatur der siebziger Jahre* (Frankfurt am Main, Ullstein, 1982), 160–2.
93. Hosfeld, Rolf, 'Uwe Timm, *Kerbels Flucht*', Westdeutscher Rundfunk, 3. Programm, 30 October 1980.
94. Kämper-van den Boogaart, Michael, *Ästhetik des Scheiterns. Studien zu Erzähltexten von Botho Strauß, Jürgen Theobaldy, Uwe Timm* (Stuttgart, Metzler, 1992), 117–44.
95. Kesting, Hanjo, 'Die alten Leiden des neuen Werther', *Frankfurter Rundschau*, 9 September 1980.
96. Krall, Günter, 'Porträt einer lustlosen Generation', *Die Rheinpfalz*, 30 October 1980.
97. Müller, Roland, 'Schöne Helden bleiben auf der Strecke. Uwe Timm mit zwei Romanen aus der Marktwirtschaftsszene' [*Kerbels Flucht* and *Kopfjäger*], *Neues Deutschland*, 25 October 1991.
98. Reinhardt, Stephan, 'Mutlosigkeit', *Frankfurter Hefte* No. 1 (1981), 71–3.
99. Retzlaff, Randolf, 'Nur noch ein Leben als Zuschauer. Seinem Helden läßt der Autor keine Chance', *Die Tat*, 25 July 1980.

100. Rieger, Manfred, 'Erstarrt und mit atemloser Unruhe. Uwe Timms Roman über die 68er Generation', *Rheinische Post*, 27 March 1981.
101. Schütze, Peter, 'Unlust als Todesursache', *Deutsche Volkszeitung*, 17 April 1980.
102. Stratz, Erika, 'Jugend ohne Hoffnung', *Neue Ruhr-Zeitung*, 3 December 1981.
103. Traber, Margrit, '*Kerbels Flucht*', *Neue Zürcher Zeitung*, 15 November 1980.
104. Zacharias, Carna, 'Am Rand des Abgrunds', *Abendzeitung*, 18 April 1980. [Reprinted in Irmgard Ackermann and Mechthild Borries (eds.), *Uwe Timm* (Munich, Goethe-Institut, 1988), 11.]
105. Zeller, Michael, 'Nicht einmal eine Bombe wert. Uwe Timms Aussteiger-Roman *Kerbels Flucht*', *Frankfurter Allgemeine Zeitung*, 18 April 1980

On *Die Zugmaus*
106. Anonymous, '*Die Zugmaus*', *Frankfurter Allgemeine Zeitung*, 13 February 1982.
107. ——, 'Hutzel, Zottel, Zugmäuse und Menschen. Geschichten von Otfried Preußler und Uwe Timm', *Deutsche Volkszeitung*, 3 December 1981.
108. ——, 'Richard Hughes: *Der Wunderhund* [. . .] / Uwe Timm: *Die Zugmaus*', *Süddeutsche Zeitung*, 6 October 1982.

On *Deutsche Kolonien*
109. Anonymous, 'Der Zusammenprall verschiedener Kulturen', *Badisches Tagblatt*, 15 February 1982.
110. ——, 'Die härtesten Herren', *Der Spiegel*, 7 December 1981.
111. ——, 'Posen deutscher Kolonialherren', *Bremer Nachrichten*, 19 December 1981.
112. ——, 'Von Kaiserreich und Kolonisierten', *Nordwest-Zeitung*, 19 January 1982.
113. Behrendt, Meike 'Deutsche Tropen', *Die Zeit*, 8 May 1987.
114. Schaper, Michael, 'Schnaps, Tand und etwas Geld', *Stern*, 17 December 1981.
115. Schätzle, Egon, 'Uwe Timm: *Deutsche Kolonien*', Norddeutscher Rundfunk, 1. Programm, 23 August 1987.
116. Thorn-Prikker, Jan, 'Patriarchalische Geste', *Evangelische Kommentare*, No. 5 (1982) 10.
117. Van der Heyden, Ulrich, 'Uwe Timm: *Deutsche Kolonien*. Köln: Verlag Kiepenheuer & Witsch 1986', *Asien – Afrika – Lateinamerika. Zeitschrift des Zentralen Rates für Asien-, Afrika- und Lateinamerikawissenschaften in der DDR*, 17 No. 1 (1989) 12.

On *Die Piratenamsel*
118. Anonymous, 'Die Abenteuer des Vogels Padde', *Kieler Nachrichten*, 7 October 1983.
119. ——, 'Die Piratenamsel. Uwe Timms zweites Reisetier', *Deutsche Volkszeitung*, 25 November 1983.
120. ——, 'OttoKar wird langsam alt. Tierbücher, spaßig und traurig', *Saarbrücker Zeitung am Wochenende*, 8–14 October 1983.
121. Lohr, Ines, 'Schlauer Beo. Stationen einer Weltreise', *Der Tagesspiegel*, 1 March 1992.
122. Pluwatsch, Petra, 'Fee Franziskas Zauber-Zucker. Lesenswerte Geschichten bekannter Autoren. Neues von Nöstlinger, Ende und Timm', *Kölner Stadt-Anzeiger*, 6–7 July 1991.
123. Schüler, Ursula, 'Uwe Timm. Die Piratenamsel', *Jugenbuchmagazin*, 34 No. 3 (1984), 158.

On *Der Mann auf dem Hochrad*
124. Ackermann, Paul Kurt, 'Uwe Timm. Der Mann auf dem Hochrad', *World Literature Today: Literary Supplement of the University of Oklahoma*, Winter 1986.
125. Anonymous, 'Radelnde Lebenskunst', *Westfälische Rundschau*, 29 October 1984.
126. Beckelmann, Jürgen, 'Der Don Quichotte einer deutschen Kleinstadt', *Mannheimer Morgen*, 3 January 1985.
127. ——, 'Onkel Franz, Don Quichotte von Coburg', *Volksblatt Berlin*, 17 October 1984. [Reprinted in Irmgard Ackermann and Mechthild Borries (eds.), *Uwe Timm* (Munich, Goethe-Institut, 1988), 22–3.]
128. Bielefeld, Claus-Ulrich, 'Die legendäre Sinnschärfmaschine', *Frankfurter Allgemeine Zeitung*, 28 August 1984.
129. Fischbach, Ute, 'Ein Leben auf dem Hochrad. Uwe Timms historischer Familien-Roman', *Münchner Merkur*, 4 October 1984.
130. General, Regina, 'Fahrversuche. Uwe Timm: *Der Mann auf dem Hochrad*, Roman, Aufbau-Verlag, Berlin und Weimar', *Sonntag*, 15 June 1986.
131. Grumbach, Detlef, 'Welt verändern, weil ich LUST hab', *Hamburger Rundschau*, 4 October 1984.
132. Jokostra, Peter, 'Bewegte Stille', *Rheinische Post*, 13 October 1984.
133. ——, 'Uwe Timm: *Der Mann auf dem Hochrad*', Österreichischer Rundfunk, 10 March 1985.
134. Kaiser, Johannes, 'Uwe Timm: *Der Mann auf dem Hochrad*', Hessischer Rundfunk, 15 May 1985.
135. Lettau, Annette, 'Der Traum vom Fortschritt', Bayerischer Rundfunk, 1. Programm, 1 December 1984.
136. ——, 'Neumodisches Teufelswerk', *Westermanns Monatshefte*, No. 12 (1984), 55.

137. Reinhardt, Stephan, 'Vom Farbenreichen. Uwe Timms neue Prosa', *Frankfurter Rundschau*, 3 October 1984.
138. Ritter, Roman, 'Drahteseleien eines Tierpräparators', *Konkret*, No. 9 (1984), 90–2.
139. ——, 'Pedaltreter der Zukunft. Uwe Timms amüsante Familienlegende aus Coburg: *Der Mann auf dem Hochrad* – Pionier neuer Beweglichkeit', *Nürnberger Nachrichten*, 20 August 1984. [Reprinted in Irmgard Ackermann and Mechthild Borries (eds.), *Uwe Timm* (Munich, Goethe-Institut, 1988), 20–1.]
140. Rohde, Hedwig, 'Onkel Franz auf dem Hochrad. Uwe Timm las im Buchhändlerkeller aus seinem neuen Roman', *Der Tagesspiegel*, 26 January 1985.
141. Schlodder, Holger, 'Der halsstarrige Erfinder', *Hannoversche Allgemeine Zeitung*, 25 November 1984.
142. ——, 'Vom Fortschritt überrollt', *Darmstädter Echo*, 20 October 1984.
143. Siegler, Beate, 'Uwe Timm: *Der Mann auf dem Hochrad*, vorgestellt von Beate Siegler (mit Zitaten aus dem Roman)', RIAS Berlin, 2. Programm, 12 February 1985.
144. Springer, Michael, 'Stabil nur durch Bewegung. Uwe Timms Legende vom Hochrad', *Deutsche Volkszeitung*, 5 October 1984.
145. Tantow, Lutz, 'Hochrad kommt vor dem Fall. Spannung, Nachdenken und Spaß mit Uwe Timm', *Saarbrücker Zeitung*, 11 March 1985.
146. Vormweg, Heinrich, 'Aus dem frühen Alltag des Fortschritts. Wie Uwe Timms Großonkel die Coburger für das Hochrad begeistern wollte', *Süddeutsche Zeitung*, 7 November 1984. [Reprinted in Irmgard Ackermann and Mechthild Borries (eds.), *Uwe Timm* (Munich, Goethe-Institut, 1988), 19–20.]
147. Weiler, Klaus, 'Ein Ästhet der Bewegung', Deutsche Welle, 24 September 1984.

On *Der Schlangenbaum*

148. Anonymous, 'Allmacht der Technik hat an Kraft verloren. Geschichte eines Ingenieurs im Dschungel Lateinamerikas. Uwe Timm las aus dem Roman *Der Schlangenbaum*', *Westdeutsche Allgemeine Zeitung*, 7 November 1986.
149. Bärenbold, Kuno, 'Germanistenliteratur. Uwe Timm erzählt', *Die Tageszeitung*, 5 December 1986.
150. Bauer, Michael, 'Flucht, Macht, Magie', *Neue Zürcher Zeitung*, 15 November 1986. [Reprinted in Irmgard Ackermann and Mechthild Borries (eds.), *Uwe Timm* (Munich, Goethe-Institut, 1988), 25.]
151. Breitinger, Eckhard, 'Auf dem Vulkan', *Stuttgarter Zeitung*, 13 December 1986.
152. Busch, Frank, 'Hoch- und Tiefbau', *Die Zeit*, 7 November 1986.

153. Drewitz, Ingeborg, 'Das Elend im Urwald. Anklage gegen die neue Ausbeutung: Zu Uwe Timms Roman *Der Schlangenbaum* – Beklemmende Bilder', *Nürnberger Nachrichten*, 22 August 1986.
154. ——, 'Wagners Abenteuer', *Deutsches Allgemeines Sonntagsblatt*, 14 September 1986.
155. Ebel, Martin, 'Homo Faber und der Urwald', *Badische Zeitung*, 18–19 October 1986.
156. Ehret, Eva, 'Reise in das Chaos', *Mannheimer Morgen*, 30 September 1986.
157. Ernst, Gustav, 'Uwe Timm: *Der Schlangenbaum*', Österreichischer Rundfunk, 8 February 1987.
158. Friedrich, Volker, 'Ein Snob im Dschungel', *Stuttgarter Nachrichten*, 1 October 1986.
159. Fuld, Werner, 'Die Sandbank im Regenwald', *Frankfurter Allgemeine Zeitung*, 29 September 1986.
160. Großmann, Thomas, 'Von der Dingen und Menschen fremden Logik', *Listen. Zeitschrift für Leserinnen und Leser*, No. 6 (Winter 1986).
161. Grumbach, Detlef, '*Der Schlangenbaum*', *Die Wahrheit*, 13–14 September 1986.
162. Hartl, Edwin, 'Fiasko der Tüchtigkeit. Postkoloniale Verblendung', *Die Presse*, 31 January–1 February 1987.
163. Hebel, Franz, 'Technikentwicklung und Technikfolgen in der Literatur. Timm, *Der Schlangenbaum* / Eisfeld, *Das Genie* / Dürrenmatt, *Der Auftrag* / Wolf, *Störfall*', *Der Deutschunterricht*, 41 No. 5 (1989), 35–45.
164. Hegmanns, Dirk, 'Ungeeignet zum Export. Europäische Werte', *Neue Westfälische*, 10 December 1986.
165. Hesse, Hans, '*Der Schlangenbaum*', in Bernd and Jutta Gräf (eds.), *Der Romanführer. Der Inhalt der Romane und Novellen der Weltliteratur*, vol. 28, *Deutschsprachige Prosa aus den Jahren 1986 bis 1992. Zweiter Teil: L–Z* (Stuttgart, Hiersemann, 1994), 265–6.
166. Jelend, Wolfgang, 'Wagners Wandlung', *Westermanns Kulturmagazin*, No. 9 (1986), 70.
167. Klimm, Annemarie, '*Der Schlangenbaum*', in Bernd and Jutta Gräf (eds.), *Der Romanführer. Der Inhalt der Romane und Novellen der Weltliteratur*, vol. 19, *Inhalte erzählender deutscher Prosa aus den Jahren 1974 bis 1985. Zweiter Teil: L–Z* (Stuttgart, Hiersemann, 1988), 272.
168. Kreimeier, Klaus, 'Katharsis eines Bauingenieurs', *Frankfurter Rundschau*, 6 December 1986. [Reprinted in Irmgard Ackermann and Mechthild Borries (eds.), *Uwe Timm* (Munich, Goethe-Institut, 1988), 26–7.]
169. Lettau, Annette, 'Der Urwald verschlingt die Fabrik', *Hannoversche Allgemeine*, 4–5 October 1986. [Reprinted in Irmgard Ackermann and Mechthild Borries (eds.), *Uwe Timm* (Munich, Goethe-Institut, 1988), 28–9.]

170. Lohmann, Carl-Wilhelm, 'Uwe Timm: *Der Schlangenbaum*', Norddeutscher Rundfunk, 22 September 1986.
171. Meyer-Minnemann, Klaus, 'Die fremde Logik und die Ordnung der Dinge. Uwe Timm, *Der Schlangenbaum*', in Keith Bullivant, Manfred Durzak and Hartmut Steinecke (eds.), *Die Archäologie der Wünsche. Studien zum Werk von Uwe Timm* (Cologne, Kiepenheuer & Witsch, 1995), 119–42.
172. Bill Niven, 'The Green *Bildungsroman*', in Colin Riordan (ed.), *Green Thought in German Culture. Historical and Contemporary Perspectives* (Cardiff, University of Wales Press, 1997), 198–209.
173. Oehlen, Martin, 'Es knirscht im Getriebe. Geschichte eines Aussteigers in Südamerika', *Kölner Stadt-Anzeiger*, 18–19 October 1986.
174. Reck, Hartmut, 'Ohnmacht im Dschungel', *Westdeutsche Allgemeine Zeitung*, 6 October 1986.
175. Sars, Paul, 'Uwe Timm: *Der Schlangenbaum.* Roman', *Deutsche Bücher*, 16 (1986), 275–6.
176. Schmitz-Albohn, Thomas, 'Zivilisation und ihre Grenzen: Im Urwald ist Europa mit dem Latein schnell am Ende. Uwe Timm erzählt in seinem neuen Roman *Der Schlangenbaum* von einem gescheiterten Projekt', *Oberhessische Presse*, 13 March 1987.
177. Schneider, Michael, 'Homo Faber im Regenwald', *Konkret*, No. 12 (1986).
178. Sedel'nik, V. [review of *Der Schlangenbaum*], *Sovremennaya chudozestvennya literatura za rubezon* [Moscow], No. 4 (1987), 81–3.
179. Stuber, Manfred, 'Ein Kreuzfahrer der Zivilisation erleidet Schiffbruch. Uwe Timms neuer Roman *Der Schlangenbaum* erzählt vom Scheitern eines deutschen Ingenieurs in Südamerika', *Mittelbayerische Zeitung*, 28 November 1986.
180. Tantow, Lutz, 'In den Fallen der Fremde. Uwe Timms Südamerika-Roman *Der Schlangenbaum*', *Saarbrücker Zeitung*, 25 November 1986.
181. Thomas, Christian, 'Ein Vorposten des Fortschritts', *Stadtblatt Münster*, 27 December 1986–23 January 1987.
182. Vormweg, Heinrich, 'Auf Wasser gebaut. Vorzüglich nur im Handwerklichen: Uwe Timms neuer Roman', *Süddeutsche Zeitung*, 1 October 1986.
183. ——, 'Uwe Timm, *Der Schlangenbaum*', Deutschlandfunk, 30 September 1986.
184. Wick, Ingeborg, 'Südamerikanische Odyssee', *Deutsche Volkszeitung*, 3 October 1986.

On *Vogel, friß die Feige nicht*
185. Bauer, Michael, 'Privates, allzu Privates', *Neue Zürcher Zeitung*, 9 August 1989.
186. Grieger, Manfred, 'Fremdheitssuche im fernen Rom', *Unsere Zeit*, 23 June 1989.

187. Grumbach, Detlef, 'Alltag einer fremden Stadt', *Deutsches Allgemeines Sonntagsblatt*, 2 June 1989.
188. Hielscher, Martin, 'Subversives Pfeifen. Auch Uwe Timm in Rom', *Frankfurter Allgemeine Zeitung*, 13 March 1989.
189. Mack, Gerhard, 'Ein Hauch vom Paradies. Uwe Timms Rom-Skizzen', *Die Tageszeitung*, 5 February 1990.
190. Mohr, Peter, 'Ein sympathisches Streben nach Utopien. Humoristische Miniaturen von Uwe Timm aus dem Wallfahrtsort deutscher Literaten', *Eßlinger Zeitung*, 1 September 1989.
191. ——, 'Gegen die Vergangenheit anschreiben. Uwe Timms Luftholen in Rom', *Die Presse*, 12–13 August 1989.
192. ——, 'Subtile Suche eines Spät-68ers', *Schwäbische Zeitung*, 6 October 1989.
193. Müller, Roland, 'Rom ganz anders. Uwe Timm auf Reisen', *Stuttgarter Zeitung*, 7 July 1989.
194. Pickerodt, Gerhart, 'Die Außenhaut der Dinge', *Deutsche Volkszeitung*, 14 April 1989.
195. Sanna, Simonetta, 'Eigenes und Fremdes, Lust und List. Uwe Timms römische Aufzeichnungen', in Keith Bullivant, Manfred Durzak and Hartmut Steinecke (eds.), *Die Archäologie der Wünsche. Studien zum Werk von Uwe Timm* (Cologne, Kiepenheuer & Witsch, 1995), 171–87.
196. Schirnding, Albert von, 'Wiedergewinnung des Tastsinns. Uwe Timms römische Erkundungen', *Süddeutsche Zeitung*, 5 April 1989.
197. Tantow, Lutz, 'Zum Beispiel das Spaghetti-Essen. Ein Deutscher sieht Italien – und damit sich', *Saarbrücker Zeitung*, 20 September 1989.

On *Rennschwein Rudi Rüssel*
198. Anonymous, 'Spaß mit dem Rennschwein', *Kölner Stadt-Anzeiger*, 25–26 May 1989.
199. ——, '*Rennschwein Rudi Rüssel*', *Badische Zeitung*, 29 June 1989.
200. Frisé, Maria, 'Rudi Rüssel, das Glücksschwein', *Frankfurter Allgemeine Zeitung*, 10 April 1990.
201. Grumbach, Detlef, 'Was man in der Realität nicht schafft, schafft man in der Literatur. Uwe Timm wird für seine Geschichte *Rennschwein Rudi Rüssel* mit dem Deutschen Jugendbuchpreis – Sparte Kinderbuch ausgezeichnet', *Volkszeitung*, 20 July 1990.
202. Klimmer, K.-H., 'Uwe Timm. *Rennschwein Rudi Rüssel*', *Jugendbuchmagazin*, 41 No. 1 (1991), 50.
203. Lohr, Ines, 'Das Schwein im Mittelpunkt', *Der Tagesspiegel*, 2 July 1989.
204. Müller, Trude, 'Uwe Timm. *Rennschwein Rudi Rüssel*', *Jugendbuchmagazin*, 43 No. 4 (1993), 208.
205. Offermann, Waltraud, 'So sauber ist (k)ein Schwein!', *Eselsohr*, No. 8 (1989), 12.

On *Kopfjäger*

206. Albers, Wolfgang, 'Quasselkunst', *Stuttgarter Zeitung*, 6 December 1991.
207. Amor, Manuel José, 'Ein Leben ohne Geldsorgen. *Kopfjäger*: Wirtschaftskrimi mit Sozialkritik', *Westfälische Rundschau*, 23 November 1991.
208. Anonymous, 'Atemberaubende Lust am Fabulieren', *Gießener Anzeiger*, 5 February 1994.
209. ——, 'Ein literarisches Puzzle mit wenig spannendem Stoff', *Badisches Tagblatt*, 19 December 1991.
210. ——, 'Fluchtziel: Osterinsel. Auf der Flucht vor der Justiz', *Neue Osnabrücker Zeitung*, 30 December 1991.
211. ——, 'Headhunter by Uwe Timm', *The New Yorker*, 2 May 1994, 109.
212. ——, 'Headhunter. By Uwe Timm', *Washington Post. Book World*, 20 February 1994.
213. ——, '*Kopfjäger* fing das Publikum ein. Uwe Timms Roman zeichnet eine feine Ironie und überraschende Pointen aus', *Nordsee-Zeitung*, 29 January 1992.
214. ——, 'Timm, Uwe. Headhunter', *Kirkus Reviews*, 1 November 1993.
215. Bawer, Bruce, 'It's dog-eat-dog in Deutschland. *Headhunter* by Uwe Timm', *The Wall Street Journal*, 28 February 1994.
216. Bittrich, Dietmar, 'Ein fröhlicher Betrüger', *Spiegel Special. Bücher '91*, No. 3 (October 1991).
217. Boedecker, Sven, 'Eine Flucht aus Deutschland. Zu Uwe Timms neuem Roman *Kopfjäger* – Die Wandlung eines Betrügers zum "Vogelmenschen"', *Nürnberger Nachrichten*, 19 September 1991.
218. ——, '"Einer, der zum Reden geboren, aber auch verdammt ist". Roman über die Geschichten, die das Leben ausmachen', *Oberhessische Presse*, 7 December 1991.
219. ——, 'Mit Geschichten Geschäfte machen. Uwe Timms neuer Roman *Kopfjäger*: Balance zwischen Unterhaltung und Aufklärung', *Der Tagesspiegel*, 13 October 1991.
220. Brender, Irmela, 'Uwe Timm: *Kopfjäger*', Süddeutscher Rundfunk, 1. Programm, 25 August 1991.
221. Bullivant, Keith, *The Future of German Literature* (Oxford, Berg, 1994), 109ff.
222. Byrne, Jack, 'Uwe Timm. Headhunter', *Review of Contemporary Fiction*, Summer 1994, 220.
223. Derbacher, Mark, 'Ein Makler erzählt Geschichten. Zeitanalyse', *Fränkischer Tag*, 16 November 1991.
224. Grumbach, Detlef, 'Die Suche nach dem König der Osterinsel', *Hannoversche Allgemeine Zeitung*, 21 December 1991.
225. ——, 'Uwe Timm: *Kopfjäger*', Deutschlandfunk, 28 September 1991.
226. Günther, Wolfgang, 'Abenteuer Geld', *Neue Westfälische*, 17 October 1991.

227. Hagestedt, Lutz, 'Ausgleichende Ungerechtigkeit. Kurzweilige Geschichten', *Wiesbadener Kurier*, 12 June 1992.
228. Holzinger, Lutz, 'Vom Mehrwert des Geschichtenerzählens', *Salto*, 13 December 1991.
229. Horn, Anette and Peter, '"Poesie heißt nämlich nichts anderes als Schöpfung durch Verlust". Die "chaotische" Zirkulation der Zeichen in Uwe Timms Roman *Kopfjäger*. Bericht aus dem Inneren des Landes', in Keith Bullivant, Manfred Durzak and Hartmut Steinecke (eds.), *Die Archäologie der Wünsche. Studien zum Werk von Uwe Timm* (Cologne, Kiepenheuer & Witsch, 1995), 199–215.
230. Kehrer, Jürgen, '*Kopfjäger*. Uwe Timms Roman dreht sich um den Kern aller Dinge: Geld', *Stadtblatt* [Münster], No. 2, February 1992.
231. Kief, Dieter, 'Der Autor als Kopfjäger. Spannend: Uwe Timms Roman aus dem Wirtschaftsleben', *Main-Echo*, 10 August 1992.
232. ——, 'Der Autor als Kopfjäger. Uwe Timm über das Wirtschaftsleben der Bundesrepublik', *Südkurier*, 2 March 1992.
233. Kiesel, Helmuth, 'Warentermin', *Frankfurter Allgemeine Zeitung*, 8 October 1991.
234. Koch, Uwe, 'Die Lust des Erfinders', *Freitag*, 13 September 1991.
235. Kracht, Christian, 'Wie die Schuhe, so der Dichter. Als Stilist und Erzähler sucht Uwe Timm in Deutschland seinesgleichen. Auch mit dem Roman *Kopfjäger* dreht er beim Leser an den richtigen Knöpfen', *Tempo*, No. 12 (December 1991).
236. Langner, Rainer-K., 'Der Roman aus dem Laptop', *Neue deutsche Literatur*, 40 No. 1 (1992), 157–60.
237. Loimeier, Manfred, 'Die Jagd nach Geschichten', *Mannheimer Morgen*, 11 October 1991.
238. Mazenauer, Beat, 'In den Niederungen der grossen Geschäfte. Uwe Timms neuer Roman gibt einen spannungsvollen Einblick in die Wirtschafts-Wunder-Welten', *Der Landbote*, 8 February 1992.
239. Melchert, Rulo, 'Heutiger Alltag mit gewöhnlichem Betrüger', *Sächsische Zeitung*, 27 September 1991.
240. Mohr, Jens [= Peter Mohr], 'Wenn der Jäger zum Gejagten wird', *Unsere Zeit*, 13 December 1991.
241. Mohr, Peter, 'Ein Held der schiefen Bahn. Abenteuer statt Milieustudie – das Leben eines Betrügers', *Deutsches Allgemeines Sonntagsblatt*, 6 December 1991.
242. ——, 'Wenn der Jäger zum Gejagten wird', *Aargauer Tagblatt*, 1 February 1992.
243. ——, 'Wenn der Jäger zum Gejagten wird', *Luxemburger Wort*, 23 January 1991.
244. ——, 'Wenn der Jäger zum Gejagten wird. Spannend: Uwe Timms Roman *Kopfjäger*', *Bonner General-Anzeiger*, 15–16 February 1992.
245. ——, 'Wenn der Jäger zum Gejagten wird. Uwe Timms Geschichte eines Kriminellen', *Die Presse*, 19–20 October 1991.

246. Nagel, Wolfgang, 'Das Manager-Tabu', *Manager Magazin*, No. 11 (November 1991).
247. Oehlen, Martin, 'Zielort Osterinsel', *Kölner Stadt-Anzeiger*, 27 September 1991.
248. Perina, Udo, 'Die Lust an Lug und Trug. Uwe Timms spannender Wirtschaftsroman *Kopfjäger*', *Die Zeit*, 11 October 1991.
249. Piwitt, Hermann Peter, 'Zur Seele vom Geschäft', *Frankfurter Rundschau*, 5 October 1991.
250. Puhl, Widmar, 'Whiskyglas mit Dekolleté. Zwischen Geschäft und Gaunerei', *Die Welt*, 25 April 1992.
251. Reim, Dagmar, '*Kopfjäger* von Uwe Timm', Norddeutscher Rundfunk, 2. Programm, 1 September 1991.
252. Ries, Harald, 'Ein Aufsteiger im Kannibalismus des Kapitalismus', *Westfalenpost*, 3 December 1991.
253. Rottensteiner, Franz, 'Deutsches Wirtschaftswunder-Dschungelbuch', *Der Standard* [Vienna], 25 October 1991.
254. Rumler, Andreas, 'Ein moderner Märchen-Erzähler', Deutsche Welle, 2 April 1992.
255. Schlodder, Holger, 'Der Traum vom schnellen Geld. Uwe Timms aufregender Roman aus dem Wirtschaftsleben', *Darmstädter Echo*, 9 November 1991.
256. Schulze-Reimpell, Jesko, 'Aufstieg eines Sprachkämpfers. *Kopfjäger*: Ein unterhaltsamer Schelmenroman von Uwe Timm', *Thüringer Tagblatt*, 6 December 1992.
257. Spiegel, Hubert, 'Denn wer über die Sprache verfügt . . . Uwe Timm und sein neuer Roman *Kopfjäger*', *Badische Zeitung*, 7 October 1991.
258. Steuhl, Wolfgang, 'Der Abenteuertrieb der Börsenwelt. Uwe Timms Roman *Kopfjäger*: Ein unvergessliches Sittengemälde des Wirtschaftsmilieus', *Die Weltwoche*, 10 October 1991.
259. Stuber, Manfred, 'Kannibalismus durch Sprache. Die Erotik des Tauschs. Der Autor Uwe Timm las im Regensburger Dollingersaal', *Mittelbayerische Zeitung*, 7 October 1991.
260. Vormweg, Heinrich, 'Ein Broker macht Geschichten', *Süddeutsche Zeitung*, 5–6 October 1991.
261. ——, 'Ein Laptop als Blechtrommel. Uwe Timms Bericht aus dem Inneren des Landes', in Keith Bullivant, Manfred Durzak and Hartmut Steinecke (eds.), *Die Archäologie der Wünsche. Studien zum Werk von Uwe Timm* (Cologne, Kiepenheuer & Witsch, 1995), 189–98.
262. ——, 'Uwe Timm: *Kopfjäger*', Westdeutscher Rundfunk, 3 September 1991.
263. Weidner, Wolfram, 'Absahner aus Zufall', *Südwest Presse*, 27 January 1992.
264. ——, 'Anlagebetrüger mit literarischen Ambitionen', dpa. *Deutsche Presse Agentur*, 25 November 1991.

265. Weinhart, Martin, 'Uwe Timm: *Kopfjäger*', Bayersiches Fernsehen, 11 September 1991.
266. Zacharias, Carna, 'Leben ist wie Monopoly. Uwe Timms raffinierter Gesellschafts-Roman *Kopfjäger*', *Abendzeitung*, 5 December 1991.
267. Zimmermann, Ulf, 'Uwe Timm. *Kopfjäger*', *World Literature Today. A Literary Quarterly of the University of Oklahoma*, Summer 1992.
268. Zulauf, Jochen, 'Im Reich der Börse. Antiroman', *Sozialmagazin. Die Zeitschrift für soziale Arbeit*, No. 4 (April 1992).
269. ——, 'Uwe Timm: *Kopfjäger*', Sender Freies Berlin, 3. Programm, 16 December 1991.

On *Erzählen und kein Ende*
270. Bernhard, Hans Joachim, 'Der wunderbare Konjunktiv. Uwe Timm: *Die Entdeckung der Currywurst* und *Erzählen und kein Ende*, beide Verlag Kiepenheuer & Witsch, Köln', *Neue deutsche Literatur*, 42 No. 1 (1994), 168–71.
271. Gesing, Fritz, 'Gewürzte Wurst. Uwe Timms Versuche zu einer Ästhetik des Alltags', *Die Zeit*, 12 November 1993.
272. Harig, Ludwig, 'Vom Füttern und Tränken der Triebe. Uwe Timms Paderborner Poetikvorlesungen', *Süddeutsche Zeitung*, 22 September 1993. [Reprinted in Hartmut Steinecke (ed.), *Literarisches aus erster Hand. 10 Jahre Paderborner Gast-Dozentur für Schriftsteller. Mit Texten von Max von der Grün, Erich Loest, Peter Rühmkorf, Peter Schneider, Eva Demski, Dieter Wellershoff, Herta Müller, Günter Kunert, Uwe Timm* (Paderborn, Igel, 1994), 247.]
273. Kiesel, Helmuth, 'Der Computer dichtet mit. Und andere Überlegungen zu einer neuen Poetik von Uwe Timm', *Frankfurter Allgemeine Zeitung*, 15 July 1993.
274. Magenau, Jörg, 'Erfindung der Wirklichkeit. Über die Poetik-Vorlesungen von Uwe Timm und seine Novelle *Die Entdeckung der Currywurst*', *Freitag*, 8 October 1993.
275. Reinhold, Ursula, 'Vom Erfindungsgeist der kleinen Leute. *Die Entdeckung der Currywurst* und ein Essayband von Uwe Timm', *Neues Deutschland*, 5 October 1993.
276. Wurzenberger, Gerda, 'Erzählen heute. Uwe Timms Paderborner Poetikvorlesungen', *Neue Zürcher Zeitung*, 28 July 1993.

On *Die Entdeckung der Currywurst*
277. Anonymous, 'Die Currywurst und ihr Bezug zu Braunschweig', *Braunschweiger Zeitung*, 12 January 1994.
278. ——, 'Die Lüge bedeutet das Ende der Liebe . . . Autorenlesung mit Uwe Timm am Freitag', *Westfälische Zeitung*, 19 October 1993.
279. ——, 'Matratzenfloß statt Panzerfaust. Süßlich-scharfe Anarchie zwischen Trümmern und Neubeginn', *Handelsblatt*, 4–5 March 1994.

280. ——, 'Umwege zur Erkenntnis', *Allgemeine Zeitung* [Mainz], 9 October 1993.
281. ——, 'Uwe Timm: *Die Entdeckung der Currywurst*', *Der Bund*, 13 November 1993.
282. Antl, Herbert, 'Uwe Timm: *Die Entdeckung der Currywurst*', Süddeutscher Rundfunk, 1. Programm, 12 September 1993.
283. Ascher, Rupert, 'Aromen und Leckerbissen aus der Kriegsküche', *Der Standard* [Vienna], 22 October 1993.
284. Bauer, Michael, 'Uwe Timm: *Die Entdeckung der Currywurst*', Deutschlandfunk, 8 November 1993.
285. Baum, Hans-Ulrich, 'Currywurst und Eichelkaffee – Novelle aus der Nachkriegszeit', *dpa. Deutsche Presse Agentur*, 1 November 1993.
286. ——, 'Vom Überleben nach dem Krieg mit Courage und Eichelkaffee: Kleines Glück ohne große Moral', *Oberhessische Presse*, 13 January 1994.
287. ——, 'Zeit für Eichelkaffee. Hamburger Uwe Timm schrieb Novelle aus Nachkriegszeit', *Nordsee-Zeitung*, 17–18 November 1993.
288. Berke, Bernd, 'Am Fenster sehen Krieg und Frieden völlig anders aus', *Westfälische Rundschau*, 6 September 1993.
289. Boedecker, Sven, 'Das Paradies auf der Zunge', *Berliner Zeitung*, 11 March 1994.
290. ——, 'Lena verschweigt das Ende des Krieges. Uwe Timms Novelle über die Currywurst fördert eine Lebensgeschichte zutage', *Saarbrücker Zeitung*, 4–5 December 1993.
291. Campe, Joachim, 'Kopfjäger Erinnerung', *Frankfurter Rundschau*, 23 November 1993. [Reprinted in Franz Josef Görtz (ed.), *Deutsche Literatur 1993. Jahresüberblick* (Stuttgart, Reclam, 1994), 228–31.]
292. Damm, Steffen, 'Gefangenschaft in der Wohnung der Geliebten. Uwe Timm erzählt von einer Fahnenflucht und vertieft sich in die Frühgeschichte der Fastfood / Die Currywurst – eine Hamburger Erfindung?', *Der Tagesspiegel*, 20 March 1994.
293. Dattenberger, S., 'Schatz', *Münchner Merkur*, 2 September 1993.
294. Doerry, Martin, 'Liebesnest mit List. Eine Novelle auf der Suche nach der verlorenen Zeit', *Spiegel Special. Bücher '93*, No. 5 (October 1993).
295. Fuld, Werner, 'Affäre fürs Leben. Uwe Timms süß-scharfe Geschichte', *Frankfurter Allgemeine Zeitung*, 2 October 1993.
296. Gesing, Fritz, 'Gewürzte Wurst. Uwe Timms Versuche zu einer Ästhetik des Alltags', *Die Zeit*, 12 November 1993.
297. Grumbach, Detlef, 'Uwe Timm: *Die Entdeckung der Currywurst*', *Die Woche*, 9 December 1993.
298. ——, 'Uwe Timm: *Die Entdeckung der Currywurst*', Ostdeutscher Rundfunk Brandenburg, 7 November 1993.
299. Günther, Wolfgang, 'Liebe ohne Helden', *Neue Westfälische*, 4 November 1993.
300. Haase, Wolf, 'Lebensmut und Currywurst. Novelle vom Wert der Erinnerungen', *Sächsische Zeitung*, 11 February 1994.

301. Hansen, W., 'Futschikato en Schikkimicki. Uwe Timm over de gechiedenis van de Currywurst', *De Volkskrant*, 5 November 1993.
302. Hanuschek, Sven, 'Die Entdeckung der Currywurst. Buchtip', *Quer. Monatszeitung für Arbeitslose*, No. 12 (December 1993).
303. Herwig, Oliver, 'Dem Erzählen auf der Spur . . .', *Mittelbayerische Zeitung*, 20–21 November 1993.
304. Hoven, Herbert, '"Ein Gewürz gegen die Schwermut". Uwe Timms Buch *Die Entdeckung der Currywurst* handelt vom Essen und vom Genießen', *Landshuter Zeitung*, 22 October 1993.
305. Höving, Elisabeth, 'Bittersüß', *Westdeutsche Allgemeine Zeitung*, 18 November 1993.
306. Howald, Stefan, 'Leib- und Magenfrage', *Tages-Anzeiger* [Zurich], 11 January 1994.
307. Jäger, Monika, 'Scheherezade in Hamburg. Uwe Timms wunderschöne Novelle *Die Entdeckung der Currywurst*', *Mindener Tageblatt*, 9 December 1993.
308. Jokostra, Peter, 'Denkmal für ein mutiges Frauenleben', *Rheinische Post*, 30 October 1993.
309. ——, 'Uwe Timm: *Die Entdeckung der Currywurst*', Österreichischer Rundfunk, 10 October 1993.
310. ——, 'Uwe Timm: *Die Entdeckung der Currywurst*', RIAS Berlin, 20 December 1993.
311. Kanold, Jürgen, 'Was der Mensch braucht oder *Die Entdeckung der Currywurst*. Der Schriftsteller Uwe Timm und seine pointenreiche Novelle', *Sudwest-Presse*, 12 November 1993.
312. Kant, Hermann, 'T. und G.', *Konkret Literatur*, No. 18 (1993–4).
313. Kanthak, Dietmar, 'Lenas Bootsmann', *Hannoversche Allgemeine Zeitung*, 8 January 1994.
314. ——, 'Süßlichscharfe Anarchie. Uwe Timm weiß, wer die Currywurst erfunden hat', *Bonner General-Anzeiger*, 6 October 1993.
315. Kappel, Sonja, 'Uwe Timm: *Die Entdeckung der Currywurst*', Südwestfunk, 2. Programm, 27 October 1993.
316. Kopplin, Wolfgang, 'Es geht um die Currywurst', *Bayernkurier*, 11 June 1994.
317. Kracht, Christian, '*Die Entdeckung der Currywurst*', *Tempo*, No. 9 (September 1993).
318. Kraft, Thomas, 'Die Liaison zerbricht, die Geschichten gehen weiter. Wer nur das Rezept will, wird nicht bedient', *Stuttgarter Nachrichten*, 5 October 1993.
319. ——, 'Erzählen um zu überleben. Mehr als ein Appetithäppchen: Uwe Timms *Die Entdeckung der Currywurst* – Lesung in Nürnberg', *Nürnberger Nachrichten*, 4 November 1993.
320. ——, 'Wer erzählt, der überlebt. Der neue Roman von Uwe Timm verfolgt deutsche Geschichte auf der Spur eines kulinarischen Leitfossils', *Rheinischer Merkur*, 17 September 1993.

321. Linden, Thomas, 'Schlemmerkost für einen Matrosen. Der Kölner [sic] Uwe Timm schrieb das verblüffend-vergnügliche Buch über *Die Entdeckung der Currywurst*', *Kölnische Rundschau*, 4 November 1993.
322. Lorenz, Dagmar, 'Die Entfernung zwischen zwei Enden einer Wurst. Uwe Timms Novelle auf Zeitreise in die 50er Jahre / Eine Biographie', *Wiesbadener Kurier*, 7 October 1993.
323. Moers, Peter and Papenbroock, Frank, 'Uwe Timm: *Die Entdeckung der Currywurst*', ARD, 30 September 1993.
324. Mohr, Peter, 'Die Soße der frühen Jahre', *Deutsches Allgemeines Sonntagsblatt*, 8 October 1993.
325. ———, 'Timms Novelle über Herkunft der Currywurst', *Stadtspiegel Wattenscheid*, 6 October 1993.
326. ———, 'Uwe Timms Novelle *Die Entdeckung der Currywurst*', Ruhrwelle Bochum, 7 November 1993.
327. Nievergelt, Gery, 'Am Anfang steht die Wurst, doch am Ende siegt die Liebe. Warum Uwe Timms Novelle *Die Entdeckung der Currywurst* auch hierzulande Beachtung verdient', *Sonntagszeitung* [Zurich], 24 October 1993.
328. Oehlen, Martin, 'Hamburger Glück', *Kölner Stadt-Anzeiger*, 30 November 1993.
329. Ottevaere, E., 'De oorlog en de kerrieworst', *De Standaard* [Belgium], 5–6 March 1994.
330. Papendieck, Hans-Anton, 'Curryexperte. Eine Lesung von Uwe Timm', *Hannoversche Allgemeine Zeitung*, 30 October 1993.
331. Peuker, Elisabeth, 'Vergnügliche Begegnung mit einer Curry-Circe. Uwe Timm fühlt sich in die Lebensphilosophie einer Frau ein, die Ersatzlösungen durch eigenes Zutun zu Vollwertigem macht', *Mitteldeutsche Zeitung*, 3 November 1993.
332. Prugger, Irene, 'Süßlichscharfe Anarchie. Uwe Timm erzählt von Currywürsten und Trümmerfrauen', *Wiener Zeitung*, 8 October 1993.
333. Reichart, Manuela, 'Uwe Timm: *Die Entdeckung der Currywurst*', Radio Bremen, 12 October 1993.
334. ———, 'Uwe Timm: *Die Entdeckung der Currywurst*', Sender Freies Berlin, 3. Programm, 14 December 1993.
335. Röder, Hendrik, 'Marktwirtschaft und Currywurst. Uwe Timm zu Gast bei Wist & Ressel', *Potsdamer Neueste Nachrichten*, 1 October 1993.
336. Schaber, Susanne, 'Scharfe Entdeckung. Uwe Timm und seine Currywurst-Novelle', *Die Presse*, 18 September 1993.
337. Schneider, Anette, 'Uwe Timm: *Die Entdeckung der Currywurst*', Norddeutescher Rundfunk, 2 September 1993.
338. Siedenberg, Sven, 'Drei-Sterne-Lese-Kulinarik. Uwe Timms Novelle vom Geschmack der Erinnerung', *Stuttgarter Zeitung*, 3 December 1993.
339. Steinecke, Hartmut, 'Die Entdeckung der Currywurst oder die Madeleine der Alltagsästhetik', in Keith Bullivant, Manfred Durzak

and H. Steinecke (eds.), *Die Archäologie der Wünsche. Studien zum Werk von Uwe Timm* (Cologne, Kiepenheuer & Witsch, 1995), 217–30.
340. Steinert, Hajo, 'Falscher Hase', *Die Zeit*, 12 November 1993.
341. Surminski, Arno, 'Als Deserteur in Liebeshaft bei Mutter Courage. Wenn die Helden ans Überleben denken – Kriegsende für einen Marinesoldaten', *Welt am Sonntag*, 3 October 1993.
342. Wurzenberger, Gerda, 'Wurstnovelle', *Neue Zürcher Zeitung*, 29 October 1993.

On *Johannisnacht*
343. Altmann, A., 'Ein Kartoffel-Krimi rund um die Wiedervereinigung. *Johannisnacht*, der neue Roman des Münchner Dichters Uwe Timm', *Abendzeitung* (Munich), 2 September 1996.
344. Ammann, Ludwig, 'Allerlei Raffiniertes rund um die Kartoffel. Uwe Timms Roman *Johannisnacht*', *Hannoversche Allgemeine Zeitung*, 10 May 1997.
345. ——, 'Im Zeichen der Kartoffel. Uwe Timms zauberhafter Roman *Johannisnacht*', *Badische Zeitung*, 3 September 1996.
346. Anonymous, 'An der unsichtbaren Berliner Mauer. Berlin: Deutschsprachige Autoren über das Stadtleben nach der Ostöffnung', *Oberösterreichische Nachrichten*, 5 February 1997.
347. ——, 'Die launige Lust an Alltagsgeschichten. Uwe Timm philosophiert im neuen Roman *Johannisnacht* über die Kartoffel', *Kieler Nachrichten*, 31 October 1996.
348. ——, 'Lust am Fabulieren. Ein Berliner Sommernachtstraum', *Nordsee-Zeitung*, 23 November 1996.
349. ——, 'Zu den Wurzeln der Kartoffel. Uwe Timms *Johannisnacht*, der Großstadtdschungel und das neue Deutschland', 6 September 1996.
350. Arend, Ingo, 'Angedeutete Genüsse. Berliner Kartoffelsalat: Uwe Timms neuer Roman *Johannisnacht*', *Freitag*, 6 September 1996.
351. Barthelemy, Andrea, 'Abenteuer in der Johannisnacht', *Frankfurter Neue Presse*, 10 September 1996.
352. ——, 'Auf den Spuren einer tollen Knolle. Ein Berliner Sommernachtstraum: Uwe Timms neuer Roman *Johannisnacht*', *Südwest Presse*, 4 December 1996.
353. ——, 'Ein Spiel um Schein und Sein in der Johannisnacht. Schauplatz Berlin. Uwe Timm beweist wieder sein Talent als Geschichtenerzähler', *Mitteldeutsche Zeitung*, 2 October 1996.
354. ——, 'Fälschung als neues Spiel. Uwe Timm auf Recherche in Ost und West', *Schweriner Volkszeitung*, 14 September 1996.
355. ——, '*Johannisnacht*: Von Kartoffeln und mehr. Ein Journalist auf Recherchetour', *Ruhr Nachrichten*, 20 December 1996.
356. ——, 'Sommernachtstraum. Uwe Timms Berliner *Johannisnacht*', *Heilbronner Stimme*, 14 September 1996.

357. Basler, Daniel J., 'Merkwürdige Begegnungen. Uwe Timms fulminante Satire *Johannisnacht*', *Mittelbadische Presse*, 8 February 1997.
358. Bothe, Petra, 'Christo und die Knolle. Berichte von verrückten Berliner Begegnungen', *Sächsische Zeitung*, 7–8 September 1996.
359. Dotzauer, Gregor, 'Uwe Timm, *Johannisnacht*', *Die Woche*, 4 October 1996.
360. Endres, Elisabeth, 'Puk, ein Hairstylist in Berlin. Mit Uwe Timm rein in die Kartoffeln und auch wieder raus', *Süddeutsche Zeitung*, 6 November 1996.
361. Grumbach, Detlef, 'Roter Baum und Fürstenkrone. Uwe Timms famos fabulierte *Johannisnacht*', *Die Zeit*, Messebeilage, 4 October 1996.
362. Gutschke, Irmtraud, 'Das wunschlose Glück. Uwe Timm sucht nach Kartoffeln und findet Geschichten – burlesk und bitter', *Neues Deutschland*, 6 December 1996.
363. Hagestedt, Lutz, 'Die Realität als Nachtschattengewächs. Uwe Timm erzählt der Kartoffel nach', *Frankfurter Rundschau*, 14 December 1996.
364. Halter, Martin, 'Kartoffelauflauf in Berlin. Uwe Timms Roman *Johannisnacht*', *Tagesanzeiger* (Zurich), 18 November 1996.
365. Hawes, James, 'The German storyteller', *Prospect* (June 1997), 10–11.
366. Helling, Reinhard, 'Was hat die Kartoffel mit deutscher Mentalität zu tun? Erzählerische Entdeckungsreise: Der Schriftsteller Uwe Timm über sich und seinen neuen Roman *Johannisnacht*', *Die Welt*, 14 January 1997.
367. Hinck, Walter, 'Schwer geackert. Uwe Timm treibt Kartoffelkunde', *Frankfurter Allgemeine Zeitung*, 17 August 1996.
368. Hock, Rotraut, 'Kartoffelforschung im wiedervereinigten Berlin. Buntes Panoptikum: Uwe Timms *Johannisnacht*', 30 November 1996.
369. Ihlefeld, Claudia, 'Tiefenangst oder Spurensuche in Berlin. Uwe Timm und die Erzählkunst als demokratischer Akt: eine Odyssee während der Reichstagsverhüllung', *Heilbronner Stimme*, 5 December 1996.
370. Kemper, Hella, 'Berliner Kartoffeln. Uwe Timms neuer Roman *Johannisnacht*', *Neue Westfälische*, 23 October 1996.
371. Kornemann, Alfred, 'Geschichten um die Kartoffel. *Johannisnacht* schildert drei Berliner Tage zur Zeit der Reichstagsverhüllung', *Der Patriot*, 3 September 1996.
372. Kraft, Thomas, 'In kleinen Dingen steckt das pralle Leben. Uwe Timm begibt sich als Kartoffelforscher nach Berlin und reflektiert über die deutsche Einheit', *Landshuter Zeitung*, 18 September 1996.
373. ——, 'Prolet unter den Gemüsen. In seinem neuen Roman erhebt der literarische Entdecker der Currywurst die Kartoffel zu poetischen Ehren. Uwe Timm / *Johannisnacht*', *Rheinischer Merkur*, 11 October 1996.

374. ——, 'Überlegene Kartoffelsorte als Errungenschaft. Berlin im Umbruch – Uwe Timms jüngster Roman *Johannisnacht'*, *Stuttgarter Zeitung*, 22 November 1996.
375. Krall, Günter, 'Ein Abenteuer rund um die Kartoffel. Uwe Timms frühes Alterswerk *Johannisnacht'*, *Die Rheinpfalz*, 28 September 1996.
376. Krass, Stephan, 'Sättigungsbeilage. Uwe Timm macht die Kartoffel literaturfähig', *Neue Zürcher Zeitung*, 1 October 1996.
377. Kunze, Rolf-Ulrich, '*Johannisnacht*, Uwe Timm', *Stadtblatt* (Osnabrück), No. 219 (April, 1997).
378. Ladenthin, Volker, 'Würfelspiel oder Sommernachtstraum? Ilja Trojanow: *Die Welt ist groß und Rettung lauert es überall*, Carl Hanser Verlag, München; Uwe Timm, *Johannisnacht*, Verlag Kiepenheuer & Witsch, Köln; beide 1996', *Neue deutsche Literatur*, 41 No. 2 (1997), 27–8.
379. Liersch, Werner, 'Knolle', *Berliner Morgenpost*, 28–29 September 1996.
380. Linden, Thomas, 'Nach Berlin der Kartoffeln wegen. Bissig erzählt: Uwe Timms Roman *Johannisnacht'*, *Kölnische Rundschau*, 2 August 1996.
381. ——, 'Was die Pasta für die Italiener ... Uwe Timms Roman rund um die Kartoffel', *Berliner Zeitung*, 24–25 August 1996.
382. Mazenauer, Beat, 'Die Sache mit der Kartoffel – Das Erzählen, eine Lust. Uwe Timms Roman *Johannisnacht* – ein wucherndes Kompendium von Geschichten und Geschichten', *Der Landbote*, 30 October 1996.
383. ——, 'Flunkern und fabulieren über das Kartoffelgeheimnis. Uwe Timm: *Johannisnacht*, ein Roman aus dem Nachwende-Berlin', *Neue Luzerner Zeitung*, 5 December 1996.
384. Meissner, Toni, 'Die Rauchringe des faulen Onkels. Uwe Timms [sic] liest heute aus *Johannisnacht'*, *Abendzeitung* (Munich), 10 October 1996.
385. Meyhöfer, Annette, 'Komik aus Christo-Tagen', *Spiegel extra*, No. 9 (September 1996), 9.
386. Michels, Dietmar, 'Im Dickicht der Großstadt. Uwe Timm schickt eine Sonde ins Labor der deutschen Einheit', *Der Tagesspiegel*, 2–3 October 1996.
387. Mohr, Peter, 'Niveauvoll unter Niveau', *Schwäbische Zeitung*, 13 December 1996.
388. Müller-Zech, Fritz, 'Kartoffelgeschichten', *Am Erker. Zeitschrift für Literatur*, 19 No. 32 (Winter 1996–7), 15.
389. Odenwald, Andreas, 'Die Droge Berlin in Überdosis genossen. Der Schriftsteller Uwe Timm und seine gerade erschienene Erzählung *Johannisnacht'*, *Die Welt*, 13 September 1996.
390. Pittler, Andreas P., 'Der literarische Nährwert einer hochpolitischen Knolle. Uwe Timm, *Johannisnacht'*, *Der Standard* (Vienna), 16 August 1996.
391. Rabenstein, Edith, 'Ein Tor ohne Tiefgang. Uwe Timm schrieb einen Berlinroman *Johannisnacht'*, *Passauer Neue Presse*, 23 January 1997.

392. Rack, Monika, 'Magie der Kartoffel. Uwe Timms Roman *Johannisnacht*', *Südkurier*, 24 October 1996.
393. Roufs, Peter, 'Lauter kleine Verlierer. *Johannisnacht* von Uwe Timm', *Stadtmagazin Mönchengladbach*, No. 4 (1997).
394. Schlodder, Holger, 'Deckname "Kartoffel". Uwe Timms Roman *Johannisnacht* bei Kiepenheuer & Witsch', *Mannheimer Morgen*, 5 December 1996.
395. ——, 'Im Zeichen der braunen Knolle. Uwe Timms *Johannisnacht* macht Appetit, sättigt aber nicht', *Darmstädter Echo*, 23 September 1996.
396. Schmidt, Gudrun, 'Midsummer in Berlin', *Berliner Lesezeichen* (September 1997), 12–13.
397. Schmitz-Albohn, Thomas, 'Kartoffeljagd im Dämmerzustand zwischen Wachen und Träumen. Die mißlungene *Johannisnacht* von Uwe Timm sollte man schnell überschlafen', *Gießener Anzeiger*, 8 March 1997.
398. Seibel, Wolfgang, 'Berliner Sättigungsbeilage. Uwe Timms Geschichten rund um die Kartoffel', *Die Presse* (Vienna), 11 January 1997.
399. Weber, Mareike, 'Suche nach der Knolle. Uwe Timms *Johannisnacht* als Berliner Sommernachtstraum', *Lübecker Nachrichten*, 17 September 1996.
400. Wester, Christel, 'Von Kartoffelgeschmackskatalogen, germanistischem Telefonsex und ... Uwe Timms neuer Roman *Johannisnacht*', *Stadtrevue* (Cologne), No. 11 (November 1996).
401. Zenker-Baltes, Inge, 'Im Wendekreis der Kartoffel. Timms *Johannisnacht* ist ein Loblied auf die Knolle', *Bremer Nachrichten*, 24 October 1996.

On films of Uwe Timm's work
402. Gotthold, Monika, 'Flucht aus dem Liebesschmerz' [on *Kerbels Flucht*], *Westfälische Rundschau*, 31 May 1984.
403. Mack, Günther, '*Morenga* ohne Morenga', *Die Zeit*, 8 March 1985.
404. Pawek, Karl, 'Gewöhnlicher Kolonialismus. Die Verfilmung von Uwe Timms Roman *Morenga*', *Deutsche Volkszeitung*, 8 March 1985.
405. Schulze, Hartmut, 'Wie Wespen' [on TV film of *Morenga*], *Der Spiegel*, 11 March 1985.
406. Visarius, Karsten, 'Wirre Gefühle und Empfindungen. Fernsehspiel *Kerbels Flucht*', *Frankfurter Allgemeine Zeitung*, 1 June 1984.
407. Wienert, Klaus, 'Tragödie des Verlassenwerdens. *Kerbels Flucht* nach Uwe Timms Roman im ZDF', *Der Tagesspiegel*, 27 May 1984.

Index

Adorno, Theodor 21
Amery, Carl 66
Andersch, Alfred 21
APO (Außerparlamentarische Opposition) 30, 42
AutorenEdition 19–21, 82

Baumann, Bommi 61
Beatles 57
Becher, Johannes R. 57
Benedict, Ruth 38
Biermann, Wolf 20
Böll, Heinrich 21, 29
Brecht, Bertolt 21, 60
Büchner, Georg
  Lenz 61, 62

Carpentier, Alejo 10
Chamisso, Adalbert von 13, 15
Chatwin, Bruce 39
Chotjewitz, Peter O. 19
Christo 101, 105
Clausewitz, Karl von 34
Clifford, James 41
Cook, James 4, 12
Cortázar, Julio 10

Darwin, Charles 69, 71
Das Problem der Absurdität bei Albert Camus 18
Delius, Friedrich Christian 17
Der Mann auf dem Hochrad 22, 23, 24, 42, 45, 79, 83–91, 93, 94, 99, 104, 108
Der Schatz auf Pagensand 24
Der Schlangenbaum 1, 22, 35–6, 41–2, 45, 66, 67, 72–80
Die Entdeckung der Currywurst 23–4, 43, 45, 83, 91–100, 101, 108
Die Grünen 66
Die Piratenamsel 24

Die Zugmaus 24
Deutsche Kolonien 21, 41
DKP (Deutsche Kommunistische Partei) 20, 29, 72
Dutschke, Rudi 20, 50
Dwinger, Edwin Erich 52
Dylan, Bob 56–7, 59

Eichmann, Adolf 37
Eisler, Hans 60
Ellis, Bret Easton 37
Erzählung und kein Ende 24, 39, 43, 44, 45, 82–3, 85, 88, 89, 94, 109
Evans-Pritchard, Edward 38

Fanon, Franz 2
Fassbinder, Rainer Werner 31
Fichte, Hubert 39
Fischer, Michael M. J. 42
Forster, Georg 4, 7, 12
Friesel, Uwe 19
Frisch, Max
  Homo faber 72
Fuentes, Carlos 10

García Márquez, Gabriel 10
Goethe, Johann Wolfgang von 52
  Die Leiden des jungen Werther 61
Gonzaléz y Haedo, Filipe 4
Gramsci, Antonio 23
Grass, Günter 29, 35, 66
Guevara, Che 2

Handke, Peter 47–9, 57–9, 63
  Die Angst des Tormanns beim Elfmeter 47–8, 57–8, 59
  Wunschloses Unglück 59

Hegel, Georg Wilhelm Friedrich 60
Heißer Sommer 2, 20, 21, 42, 47, 49–59, 60, 61, 82, 99
Hesse, Hermann
 'Stufen' 55
Hey, Richard 19
Heyerdahl, Thor 7–8, 14
Highsmith, Patricia 59
Hitler, Adolf 96
Hölderlin, Friedrich 51, 53–6, 60, 62, 63
 'An die Hoffnung' 54
 'Brot und Wein' 55
 'Der blinde Sänger' 53–4
 'Die Liebe' 54, 55–6
Homer 10
Hopf, Andreas 19
Horkheimer, Max 21
Humboldt, Alexander von 2
Huxley, T. H. 69

Johannisnacht 24, 43, 79, 83, 99, 100–8
Johnson, Uwe 35

Kafka, Franz 11
Kerbels Flucht 20–1, 22, 42, 45, 72
Kipphardt, Heinar 23, 33, 37
Kleist, Heinrich von 56, 60–1, 62, 63
Koeppen, Wolfgang 21, 29
Kopfjäger. Bericht aus dem inneren des Landes 9, 23, 43–5, 99
Kotzebue, Otto von 13
Kotzebue, August von 13
Kropotkin, Peter 29, 40, 68–72
 Gegenseitige Hilfe in der Entwicklung 40, 68–9

Landauer, Gustav 69
 'Aufruf zum Sozialismus' 69
La Perouse 12
Lenin, Vladimir Ilyich 57
Lévi-Strauss, Claude 39

Linse, Ulrich
 Ökopax und Anarchie 68–9

Malinowski, Bronislaw 38
Marcuse, Herbert 21, 50, 56
 Kultur und Gesellschaft 56
Mao Tse-Tung 57
Markovic, Mihailo 57
Marx, Karl 57
 Pariser Manuskripte 62
Mead, Margaret 38
Migge, Leberecht 68, 71
Morenga 2, 21, 22, 32–6, 39–42, 45, 66–72, 75, 79, 80, 82

Nadolny, Sten 17
Natural Born Killers 37
Norris, Ted 39, 43

Ohnesorg, Benno 50

Pausewang, Gudrun 66
'Peter Handke oder sicher in die 70er Jahre' 48
Picasso, Pablo 8
Plenzdorf, Ulrich 65

Rabinow, Paul 42, 45
Rennschwein Rudi Rüssel 24
Rimbaud, Arthur 61
Robien, Paul 68, 71
Roggeveen, Jacob 3
Rolling Stones 57

Said, Edward 3, 9
Schiller, Friedrich 52, 55
Schmidt, Arno 29
Schmitt, Carl 56
Schnabel, Johann Gottfried 61
Schneider, Peter 17, 28, 30, 45
Schnurre, Wolfdietrich 29
SED (Sozialistische Einheitspartei Deutschlands) 20
Simmel, Johannes 48, 52

SDS (Sozialistischer Deutscher Studentenbund) 17–18, 20, 29, 32, 50, 56
Springer, Axel 50
Strauß, Botho 30
Süskind, Patrick 37

Taschau, Hannelies 19

Vargas Llosa, Mario 10
Vogel, friß die Feige nicht. Römische Aufzeichnungen 22–3

Vogeler, Heinrich 68, 69, 71
Voß, Johann Heinrich 10

Walser, Martin 29
Widersprüche 18
Winckelmann, Johann 10
Wohmann, Gabriele 66
Wolf, Christa 65, 66

'Zwischen Unterhaltung und Aufklärung' 18, 48